Passionate Virtuosity:
The Fiction of John Barth

PASSIONATE VIRTUOSITY: The Fiction of JOHN BARTH

Charles B. Harris

UNIVERSITY OF ILLINOIS PRESS

Urbana and Chicago

Library of Congress Cataloging in Publication Data

Harris, Charles B.
  Passionate virtuosity.

  Bibliography: p.
  Includes index.
  1. Barth, John—Criticism and interpretation.
I. Title.
PS3552.A75Z68 1983   813'.54   83-4976
ISBN 0-252-01037-X

For Victoria

Contents

Preface

In a recent essay John Barth compares God to a novelist, the world to His novel-in-progress. We should be slow in judging the world, Barth cautions, since "the story's not done yet: who knows what plot reversals the Author may have up his/her sleeve for the denouement?"

Such warnings apply as well to critics temerarious enough to write books about living authors. If the author happens to be John Barth, whose story's far from done and whose work shifts in mode and manner from book to book, the warning becomes even more worth heeding. So it is with as much timidity as temerity that I offer this booklength study of Barth's fiction.

Passionate Virtuosity: The Fiction of John Barth is an examination of Barth's first seven books, *The Floating Opera* (1956) through *LETTERS* (1979). I have chosen to conclude this study with *LETTERS* because, in my view, the novel represents the end of a stage in Barth's development as an artist. The multifaceted, complex nature of this developmental stage resists concise summary; indeed, it is the burden of this entire study to describe it. But at its core lies the idea of unity. The problem, stated in simplest terms, is this: If language (specifically print, the writer's only medium) is by nature *irreal* since it does not refer except in the most arbitrary sense to an antecedent reality, then how can the writer become a writer-in-the-world? Can words and world resolve themselves into a unified harmony? From the first two novels (in which the theme of unity is submerged, even incipient) through the next four works (in which the idea of unity receives more explicit focus) Barth pursues this problematic notion. In

LETTERS the problem of unity, while not solved, is resolved — in ways which are too complicated to summarize here but which are treated in detail in the final chapter.

Barth pursues the idea of unity across a variety of intellectual terrains: the epistemological, the psychological, the ontological, the mythological, and of course the esthetic. I do not hesitate to draw ideas from thinkers in a variety of disciplines if those ideas help illuminate aspects of Barth's fiction. But in my sometimes detailed treatment of thinkers such as Heidegger and Nietzsche, Joseph Campbell and Mircea Eliade, Jung and Lacan and R. D. Laing, I am not suggesting influences on Barth's fiction; rather, I am following out certain intellectual currents in the *Zeitgeist*, attempting to clarify certain salient ideas common to a variety of thinkers and writers. As Barth has said of writers he admires, "They are not only alive to the ideas in the air, but responsible for those ideas being in the air." The same is true of John Barth.

While I frequently grapple with the theoretical notions of others and attempt an occasional theoretical flight of my own, *Passionate Virtuosity* is first and foremost an exercise in applied criticism. I must own up to the belief (hopelessly outmoded in some quarters) that a Maryland writer named John Barth writes books that, while not without certain antecedents and intertextual traces, are nonetheless uniquely *his.* A critic may at least potentially discern and partially delimit that uniqueness, although the critic's own uniqueness will color his response. (The term *intersubjectivity*, so recently de rigueur but now hors de combat, flickers at the edges of my consciousness.) So while I am not unfamiliar with structuralist and post-structuralist principles, even using them as they fit my purposes (particularly in my analyses of form and language in Barth's fiction), I am not above giving detailed treatment to such antiquated concerns as theme, character, and even plot. Such concerns remain important to Barth as well.

In writing this manuscript I have benefited from the excellent essays and books on Barth's fiction. Wherever appropriate, I have attempted to enter into dialogue with their authors, whose insights have prompted many of my own. For those essays read but not cited, I also owe a general debt of gratitude and wish to record it here. A specific debt is owed Joseph Weixlmann, who read an early draft of Chapter 6 and who has provided materials otherwise inaccessible to me. I also wish to thank the Graduate School of Illinois

State University for summer grants which provided some of the time and money this study required. Earlier drafts of Chapters 2, 5, and 6 appeared in *Critique, Studies in the Novel,* and *The Psychocultural Review;* I am grateful to their editors for permission to use some of that material here. To Ann Lowry Weir of the University of Illinois Press, whose careful editing resulted in a better book, I also owe a debt of gratitude. John Barth graciously answered questions about Chapter 5 and read a version of Chapter 2; his comments, while characteristically brief, are deeply appreciated.

As usual, my greatest debt is to my wife and colleague, Victoria, who read my manuscript far more than once and whose suggestions led to far more than one revision. Without her patience and constant encouragement this study would not have been possible.

1

Passionate Virtuosity: An Introduction

John Barth's seminal essay "The Literature of Exhaustion" first appeared in the August 1967 *Atlantic Monthly*. It has since become one of the more frequently reprinted, widely commented upon, and highly influential documents of the "postmodern" literary esthetic. Barth advances three major ideas: first, his contention that the dilemma faced by contemporary novelists is the "used-upness of certain [narrative] forms or . . . possibilities"; second, his perception that a writer like Jorge Luis Borges confronts this dilemma by paradoxically transforming "the felt ultimacies of our time into material and means for his work — *paradoxically* because by doing so he transcends what had appeared to be his refutation" of the possibility of accomplishing "new and original literature"; and, third, his affirmation that despite the considerable technical ingenuity required by the successful implementation of an "intellectual dead end . . . against itself," the writer must "manage nonetheless to speak eloquently and memorably to our still-human hearts and conditions, as the great artists have always done." Writers like Borges avoid the passionless sterility of the "intermedia" arts, even as they avoid the formal obsolescence of writers whose work, while it still moves us, remains "technically old-fashioned." That is, writers like Borges successfully combine moral seriousness *and* technical virtuosity.

While they have received the most attention, the first two ideas advanced in "The Literature of Exhaustion" are not altogether original with Barth; they echo not only the conception but at times the very language of an essay by José Ortega y Gasset published in

1925, "The Dehumanization of Art."[1] "In art," Ortega writes, "repetition is nothing. Each historical style can engender a certain number of different forms within a generic type. But there always comes a day when the magnificent mine is worked out." The "present infecundity" of the "romantico-naturalistic novel" and the drama, Ortega continues, derives not from a decline in artistic talent but from the fact "that the possible combinations within these literary forms are exhausted."[2] One response to such exhaustion is deviation from representationalism, mimesis giving way to style. And "to stylize means to deviate from reality, to derealize." A primary manifestation of stylization is self-reflexiveness, art's turning back upon itself comically: "Instead of deriding other persons or things—without a victim no comedy—the new art ridicules itself. . . . Thanks to this suicidal gesture art continues to be art, its self-negation miraculously bringing about its preservation and triumph."[3] For Ortega as for Barth, then, the exhaustion of artistic possibilities may be overcome by the self-conscious confrontation and parodic use of narrative ultimacy.

Yet Barth deviates from Ortega in one crucial respect. Whereas Barth insists upon the moral relevance of art to human conditions, Ortega argues that art can survive only by "dehumanizing" itself, by emphasizing its separateness from human life—not out of an arrogant "disgust for the human sphere," but out of a sense of modesty. Modern art, no longer taking itself seriously, has renounced its importance. "Art which . . . used to be very near the axis of enthusiasm, that backbone of our person, has moved toward the outer ring. It has lost none of its attributes, but it has become a minor issue." Through dehumanization and "derealization," art rids itself of "human pathos," becoming "a thing without consequence—just art with no other pretenses." Behind Ortega stands the unmistakable shade of T. E. Hulme, whose preference for "geometrical" as opposed to "vital" art derives from a similar desire to separate art from the "real." The *tendency to abstraction* that undergirds geometrical art, Hulme writes, proceeds from "a feeling of separation in the face of outside nature."[4] Like Ortega, Hulme sees modern art in terms of an abstract formalism which feels no romantic or Arnoldian responsibility to improve mankind. Such romanticism, in Hulme's famous phrase, is little more than "spilt religion."[5]

Barth nowhere makes the enormous claims for art that a Shelley or an Arnold or, more recently, a John Gardner might make.[6] But if literature contributes little to the salvation of man or culture, Barth seems to believe it can make at least some things happen. His "modesty" more closely resembles Frost's than Ortega's. Poetry, for Frost, "ends in a clarification of life — not necessarily a great clarification, such as sects and cults are founded on, but in a momentary stay against confusion."[7] Similarly, for Barth, "the treasure of art, which if it [can]not redeem the barbarities of history or spare us the horrors of living and dying," can at least sustain, refresh, expand, ennoble, and enrich "our spirits along the painful way."[8] Barth, then, is not — nor has he ever been — the strict formalist that both his supporters and detractors have sometimes portrayed him as being. He makes this point explicitly in an interview that appeared in the same year as "The Literature of Exhaustion":

> My feeling about technique in art is that it has about the same value as technique in love-making. That is to say, on the one hand, heartfelt ineptitude has its appeal and, on the other hand, so does heartless skill; but what you want is *passionate virtuosity*. By my personal standards . . . experiments must be moving and passionate and eloquent and not just tricksy. If my writing were no more than an intellectual fun and games that *Time* magazine makes it out to be, I wouldn't be interested in it myself.[9]

So important is this sentiment to Barth's esthetic that he includes it with only minor revision in *Chimera* (1972, p. 24), allowing the genie, his obvious surrogate in the novel, to speak the words.

Form for Barth is always a metaphor for other concerns, never an end in itself. "One must distinguish between meretricious or gratuitous experiment and genuine experimental writing. The writer who transforms his contrivance into a powerful, effective, and appropriate metaphor for his concerns has made a piece of art, whatever its imperfections." Nor is the writer always cognitively aware of what those concerns are:

> Never mind the spiritual or psychological reasons why one is interested in . . . any . . . particular narrative device. Anybody who sets out to be interested just for the sake of elaborateness would be a bloody idiot. Somewhere in your artistic sense, you intuit that this is a metaphor for other things you are concerned with. You don't explain why it's a metaphor — you're no bloody critic at this point. . . . You just know that

some concepts haunt you, speak to you, in electrical ways, and you learn to trust your intuition.[10]

If talk of intuition seems oddly inappropriate in a writer justly celebrated for his cerebration, Barth has nonetheless insisted upon its primacy from the beginning. When questioned in his first major interview about his conscious intentions in composing *The Sot-Weed Factor*, Barth answered:

I had some things in mind when I wrote it, and it is interesting and cheering to find out later that I had more in mind than I thought I had. I don't really say that facetiously — one works by hunch and guess and intuition, with some conscious patterns in mind, too, and one has a character do *this* instead of *that* because one feels this is appropriate. Maybe in the act of setting it down you say, "I know why he did that," but then you are looking at it as a college teacher. More often you read a piece years later by some bright fellow, interpreting your work, and you realize that . . . he's got your number . . . in a way you recognize for the first time yourself. This is a rather upsetting, but pleasantly upsetting, experience: to be told by somebody else what you were up to, and recognize that he's right.[11]

Such sentiments recall Melville's feeling that "the names of all fine authors are fictitious ones . . . — simply standing, as they do, for the mystical, ever-eluding Spirit of Beauty, which ubiquitously possesses men of genius,"[12] or "Borges and I," Borges's famous little parable which begins:

The other one, the one called Borges, is the one things happen to. . . . I live, let myself go on living, so that Borges may contrive his literature, and this literature justifies me. It is no effort for me to confess that he has achieved some valid pages, but those pages cannot save me, perhaps because what is good belongs to no one, not even to him, but rather to the language and to tradition. Besides, I am destined to perish, definitively, and only some instant of myself can survive in him. . . . Thus my life is a flight and I lose everything and everything belongs to oblivion, or to him.

And then the marvelous, profound closing sentence: "I do not know which of us has written this page."[13] Similar passages occur in Barth's own writings, particularly the more self-reflexive fictions of *Lost in the Funhouse* (1968). "In his heart of hearts," muses the self-recorded fiction of "Autobiography" about his father-creator, "he wonders whether I mayn't after all be the get of a nobler spirit, taken by beauty past his grasp." The narrator's realization that he *has* a "father-creator" is accompanied by the consequent realization that his own "first words weren't [his] first words," but the father-creator's, whose own voice, indeed, may be but the vehicle of what Samuel Beckett calls "this anonymous voice self-styled quaqua the voice of us all."[14] Similarly, the narrator of "Life-Story" suspects that he is a *character* in someone else's story, not the author of his own. The compulsion to utter words not perhaps one's own, particularly in the face of the perceived depletion of narrative resources, can lead to those weary fictions Beckett has described: "the expression that there is nothing to express, nothing with which to express, nothing from which to express, no power to express, no desire to express, together with the obligation to express."[15] Indeed, many of the early stories in *Funhouse* do embody this weariness. More characteristically, however, Barth's fiction reflects the grim if often comic — and at times noble — determination to find new ways to express the old (which is to say *fundamental, essential*) significances. When the nameless minstrel of "Anonymiad" arrives at the Melvillean conclusion that his "only valid point of view" is "first person anonymous," the tone of his resolution is anything but pessimistic. He, like Menelaus in the immediately preceding story, has come to realize that the source and inspiration of all fiction is "Beauty's spouse's odd Elysium: the absurd, unending possibility of love," and that his tales constitute "a continuing, strange love letter."

Part of the burden of this study will be to show that love in Barth's fiction is not the "facile thematic imperative"[16] that one critic has dismissed it as being. Rather, love refers to that "tremendous intuition striving for expression" that Jung calls the "primordial experience": contact with the realm of the archetype.[17] Barth has approvingly quoted one of Borges's editors to the effect that "For [Borges] no one has claim to originality in literature; all writers are more or less faithful amanuenses of the spirit, translators and annotators of pre-existing archetypes."[18] But since archetypes are purely *formative*, possessing no form of their own, the forms they stimulate, the esthetic constructs, may — indeed, must — be unique. To use Borges's metaphor, the archetypal fire remains constant and unchanging from generation to generation; the algebra — the artifact itself — varies, not only from generation to generation but also from artist to artist. To allow the artist's "algebra," his form and technique, to harden into stale, exhausted formulae is to risk extinguishing the "fire." Thus Barth's constant drive for unique and original expression. Yet this drive also involves risk: the writer may become so concerned with formal means that calculation totally replaces intuition — a danger, we shall see, which Bellerophon fails to avoid. Neither algebra nor fire can achieve poetic power without the other, although "algebra is easier to talk about than fire."[19] Passionate virtuosity: algebra and fire — such is Barth's formula for all truly mythopoeic fiction.

Of course, Barth did not arrive at this formula first and then construct his fictions from it. Rather, the esthetic grew out of the fictions which it informs. Or, to phrase it differently, Barth arrived at his esthetic statements inductively, by studying the esthetic pattern in his works *after* their composition. "You shouldn't pay very much attention to anything writers say," a still young Barth somewhat brashly told John Enck,

> They don't know why they do what they do. They're like good tennis players or good painters, who are just full of nonsense, pompous and embarrassing, or merely mistaken, when they open their mouths. All sports, for example, all knacks and skills, become close to second nature with experts. When writers speak of things like inspiration and characters taking over and space-time grids, it's usually because they don't know why they do the things they do. . . . At least I have never heard much that any writer has said about writing that didn't embarrass me, including the things I say about it.[20]

Seven years later, Barth offered a more reflective comment on how a writer becomes aware of the esthetic informing his own work:

> Particularly since I've been in my thirties and forties, I really do try to see what it is I've been up to. Especially when I'm thinking of what I want to do next, I like to look back. . . . I try to seek out patterns — the thematic and structural directions, the personality of the voices, other such things — in the books leading up to where I am at that moment. Sometimes, ten years after you've finished a piece, you can see the patterns and suggestions more clearly; perhaps you were not

very aware of them at the time or were only half-intuitively groping for their formulation.[21]

Structure as well as theme, then, emerges in part from the mythopoeic process, from unconscious wellsprings as well as from conscious intentions and knowledge.[22] The tale, not the teller, should be trusted — even by the teller himself.

This volume traces the pattern of Barth's structural and thematic concerns as it develops through his first seven books. The developmental nature of that pattern is of crucial importance to Barth. "If a writer's not simply going to repeat himself," he told his audience at a Library of Congress reading in 1967, "he has to keep changing, reinventing himself. Hopefully, the changes are development; hopefully his stages are all pushing the same joyload towards its orbit, in their different ways; and hopefully, since some stretches of the trip are bound to be tougher than others, his audience will stay with him across the troll-bridges and they'll reach the cabbage-fields together."[23] Indeed, Barth's fictions do become increasingly difficult, although each is informed by a similar vision, a vision I believe to be genuinely mythopoeic. The central idea of the mythic, as Joseph Campbell and others have demonstrated, is cosmic harmony, unity in multeity, and this idea recurs implicitly or explicitly in each book. Barth's first two protagonists, terrified by the unity they glimpse, retreat behind a shield of words. In *The Sot-Weed Factor*, on the other hand, Henry Burlingame deliberately seeks cosmic harmony, and in *Giles Goat-Boy* George, transcending categories, achieves it. But each of Barth's protagonists, like Barth himself, is a writer in the world, not a mystic. The problem of the mythopoeic writer is how to translate mythic intimations, which are finally ineffable, into words capable of evoking that which may not be articulated. Barth's next two books, *Lost in the Funhouse* (1968) and *Chimera* (1972), address this difficulty, the former focusing primarily on the relationship between sex, language, and myth; the latter, by far the most "socially conscious" of Barth's first six books, showing how myth may inform life as well as art. *LETTERS*, Barth's seventh book, completes this return to the world while affirming that it is a *worded* world after all. Language, properly employed, is the mythic though perhaps not mystic ligature connecting man, time, and world in a dynamic unity.

Each of Barth's books, as well as his major concerns — ontological insecurity, the nature of "reality," cyclology and cosmogeny, ethics, epistemology, esthetics, love, sex, and language — may most profitably be understood in the context of his constantly expanding mythopoeic imagination. That imagination is rooted not only in the suspected unity of all things, but in the concomitant realization that "reality" is nothing more than our conceptions about "reality" hypostatized. As a brief glance at intellectual history indicates, such hypostatizations last briefly, as one age, one *Weltanschauung*, one coordinating myth inevitably gives way to its successor. As a metaphor for this ineluctable process, Barth works out certain intellectual positions in one book, only to "contradict them" in the next. "My writing has finally nothing to do with polemics or the propagandizing of some philosophical position of my own," he has said. "To the extent that [my books] are novels of ideas — and that's a very limited extent — they are that because they *dramatize alternatives to philosophical positions.*"[24] Each book offers positions that refute, or at least qualify, the positions offered in the work preceding; taken collectively, they achieve the effect of a constant grasping for meaning, on the one hand, balanced by the realization that all meaning is *projected* — invented, rather than discovered, and therefore relative and contingent — on the other. Yet Barth's dramatization of the desire to imagine alternative philosophical positions, which is really the desire to invent alternatives to "reality," affirms the value of such imaginings. Their value remains constant from age to age, although the "realities" imagined are themselves ephemeral. In Barth's fictions *the passionate desire to construct meaning* — not meaning itself — assumes the status of a universal value. If anything is sacred, it is not a particular form of human "reality" but *that which forms* human "reality." The best art gives the clearest evidence of this mythopoeic passion working through men of genius. I shall now turn to a close examination of the developing mythopoeic consciousness in the fiction of one such artist.

NOTES

1. Reprinted in Ortega y Gasset, *Dehumanization of Art,* pp. 3–54.

2. Ibid., pp. 13–14. Ortega develops his ideas about the exhausted possibilities of the novel more specifically in "Notes on the Novel," pp. 57–103.

3. Ibid., p. 48. I discuss at some length the function of self-reflexive parody and burlesque in the recent novel in my *Contemporary American Novelists of the Absurd*.

4. T. E. Hulme, "Modern Art" [1914], reprinted in Bate, ed., *Criticism*, pp. 562–64.

5. T. E. Hulme, "Romanticism and Classicism" [1924], reprinted ibid., pp. 564–73.

6. Gardner, *On Moral Fiction*. The "preservation of the world of gods and man," affirms Gardner, is "what true art is about" (p. 16). Barth is among those novelists whom Gardner lists as writers of "immoral" literature.

7. "The Figure a Poem Makes," in Frost, *Complete Poems*, p. vi.

8. Barth, *Chimera*, p. 17.

9. Prince, "Interview," p. 62.

10. Gado, ed., *First Person*, p. 133.

11. Enck, "Interview," reprinted in Dembo and Pondrom, eds., *Contemporary Writer*, p. 29.

12. "Hawthorne and His Mosses" [1850], reprinted in Melville, *Moby-Dick*, p. 536.

13. Borges, *Labyrinths*, pp. 246–47. Cf. also Heidegger's statement that "in great art . . . the artist remains inconsequential as compared with the work, almost like a passageway that destroys itself in the creative process for the work to emerge" ("The Origin of the Work of Art," in *Poetry, Language, and Thought*, p. 40).

14. Beckett, *How It Is*, p. 139.

15. Beckett and Dothuit, "Three Dialogues," *Transition Forty-nine* no. 5 (1949), reprinted in Sears and Lord, eds., *Discontinuous Universe*, p. 18.

16. Klinkowitz, *Literary Disruptions*, p. 8.

17. Jung, "Psychology and Literature," in *The Spirit in Man*, p. 97.

18. Barth, "Literature of Exhaustion," p. 33.

19. Ibid., p. 32.

20. Enck, "Interview," p. 24.

21. Gado, ed., *First Person*, p. 128. In another interview Barth says, "You . . . work to a large degree by hunch and intuition, and inspiration, as they say. Then retrospectively you may understand a great deal more in the theoretical way about what it was that you in fact did, than you did at the time. When we talk about it, we're talking retrospectively, so I think sometimes we give the impression that we're all terribly theoretical when we sit down at the desk, which of course we aren't" (Bellamy, " 'Algebra and Fire,' " pp. 14–15).

22. Cf. Bly's "Looking for Dragon Smoke," in *Naked Poetry*, ed. Berg and Mezey, pp. 161–64. "In the true poem," writes Bly, "both the form

and the content rise from the same place; they have the same swiftness and darkness. Both are expressions of a certain rebellious energy rising in the psyche: they are what Boehme calls 'the shooting up of life from nature to spirit.' What is important is this rebellious energy, not technique" (p. 164). Barth does not share Bly's alleged scorn for technique, nor are the two writers similar in temperament or artistic sensibility; but I evoke the name of Bly, who perhaps more than any other living writer is associated with the function of the unconscious in literature, to emphasize more strongly my point that Barth, too, despite the evident cerebration and erudition in his work, may be seen as "intuitive" in the best sense of that much-abused term.

23. This statement, from Barth's introduction to his reading of "Title" and "Autobiography" at the Library of Congress on 1 May 1967, is on file in the Library of Congress manuscript room. See description in Weixlmann, *Barth: Bibliography*, E62, p. 58.

24. Prince, "Interview," p. 57, italics mine.

2

Todd Andrews, Ontological Insecurity, and *The Floating Opera*

Early critics of *The Floating Opera* (1956, 1967) tended to read the novel as distinctive but conventionally realistic, a false start which, along with *The End of the Road* (1958, 1967), represented the young Barth's apprenticeship before he turned to more avant garde and therefore more important later novels.[1] More recently, however, Thomas LeClair has demonstrated that despite its realistic surface the *Opera* includes many "aesthetic qualities" (complicated formal design, parodied literary conventions, "outrageous artifices," technical virtuosity and idiosyncrasy) that recur in the later fictions.[2] Todd Andrews, narrator of the *Opera*, employs these techniques as a means of falsifying a reality that "stinks of finality." He denies the "integrity of fact" in order to avoid the one fact with which he cannot, yet must somehow, live: his own possibly imminent death. LeClair adequately demonstrates Todd's fear of death and ably examines some of the novel's technical complexities, but more remains to be said about the cause-and-effect relationship between death and novelistic form. And while LeClair also records Todd's attempts to mislead the reader about the novel's real intentions, further explanation of *why* Todd wishes to trick his audience is necessary.

Having said that, let me quickly disclaim any intention of reading *The Floating Opera* as a purely "psychological" novel. As John Hawkes points out, "Barth and I are not concerned with realism, not even with psychological realism." Yet, Hawkes adds, "we are both working with psychic substance or substance of the mind, are both starting with the materials of psychic or cerebral derangement in our efforts to arrive at 'aesthetic bliss.'"[3] The particular nature of the psychic derangement plaguing Todd Andrews is schizophrenia and should be analyzed as such. Ultimately, however, Barth is concerned not with literal schizophrenia, but with the esthetic and metaphysical implications of schizophrenia. As such, the tools of Freudian analysis offer little aid in understanding the Opera's teller. More pertinent is the humanistic and existential approach of R. D. Laing.[4]

Andrews is the first of several Barthian protagonists whose world suddenly ceases to make sense. While the resulting anxiety closely approximates Camus's "feeling of the absurd,"[5] it also resembles the schizophrenic experience that Laing calls "ontological insecurity," a pervasive anxiety about the vulnerability of the self. In discussing this schizophrenic terror of the other, Laing employs the term "implosion":

> This is the strongest word I can find for the extreme form of what Winnicott terms the *impingement* of reality. Impingement does not convey, however, the full terror of the experience of the world as liable at any moment to crash in and obliterate all identity. . . . "Contact" with reality is . . . experienced by [the schizophrenic] as a dreadful threat because reality, as experienced from this position, is necessarily *implosive* and thus . . . *in itself* a threat to what identity the individual is able to suppose himself to have.[6]

Todd uses terms similar to Laing's in his explanation of the false selves or "masks" he assumes in attempting to cope with his own feelings of ontological insecurity: "I know for certain that all the major mind changes in my life have been the result not of deliberate, creative thinking on my part, but rather of pure accidents — events outside myself *impinging* forcibly upon my attention — which I afterwards rationalized into new masks."[7] In every case, these events remind Todd of his mortality. He learns of his bad heart and becomes a rake. He is almost killed by Betty June Gunter in a Baltimore whorehouse and becomes a saint. He finds his father hanging from a rafter in his basement and becomes a cynic. Jane Mack calls attention to his clubbed fingers, thus reminding him of his heart, which symbolizes the death each successive mask had been half-consciously cultivated to evade, and he falls into despair and plans his suicide. The masks are calculated to shield Todd from his bad heart, from the physical symptom of his mortality. Physicality and death — flesh and death — become obsessively linked in Todd's imagination.

Images of decaying flesh fill the novel. When Todd discovers his father hanged in the basement, his father's physical condition obsesses him. He notes almost compulsively the "black and ruptured flesh" and the popped eyes, "the very veins of which are burst" (183–84). His father's ravaged flesh recalls one of Todd's earliest memories, the "cold, hard, dirty, stringy, scaly, dead yellow feet" of a chicken his father had killed when Todd was five. Again Todd focuses intently on the feel of the dead flesh, the string of adjectives used to describe that flesh reflecting the compulsive nature of a memory that, fifty years later, still makes him ill. Similarly, the experience in the Argonne Forest that continues to haunt Todd is the "tiny, horrible puncturing sound" of his bayonet sliding into the flesh of the German soldier. No mere abstraction, death to Todd Andrews is a palpable physical fact, and he concentrates on its sight, feel, and sound.

Even the "perfect" body of Jane Mack is not immune, a circumstance upon which Todd speculates as he imagines the aftermath of his planned showboat explosion: "Calmly I thought of Harrison and Jane: of perfect breasts and thighs scorched and charred; of certain soft, sun-smelling hair crisped to ash. Calmly too I heard somewhere the squeal of an overexcited child . . . not impossibly Jeannine. I considered a small body, formed perhaps from my own and flawless Jane's, black, cracked, smoking" (243). Missing from this passage is the sense of anxiety conveyed in his earlier descriptions; the tone is calm, almost exultant. Such ambivalence is significant. On the one hand, the vulnerability of human flesh either terrifies Todd or, as when Jane calls attention to his fingers, fills him with an irrational disgust for his "whole skinny body" (225). On the other hand, the very fragility of human flesh can prove a source of security. As Laing points out, ontologically insecure persons often "come to experience themselves as primarily split into a mind and a body." Since the body, perceived as a thing in the world, seems vulnerable, "usually they feel most closely identified with the mind."[8] Thus divided, Todd can calmly consider the physical devastation the steamboat explosion will cause, since at this moment the body seems to Todd a mere object in the world, fully dissociated from the "real" inner self.

The most striking example of Todd's mind-body dualism occurs during the Argonne battle. Face down in a mudhole, his bodily functions out of control, he suffers the "purest and strongest emotion" of his life. A part of him, however, manages to transcend his condition: "I could actually, for a part of the time it lasted, regard myself objectively" (63). His body, then, is dispassionately observed as an object in the world by an entirely separate part of Todd's self. Such dualistic splitting may seem less than abnormal because of the severity of Todd's circumstances, but the scene is important as a model with which we can compare other times when Todd reacts similarly, even though no real physical danger exists.

While copulating with Betty June Gunter, for example, the seventeen-year-old Andrews suddenly spies himself in the mirror—again viewing himself objectively, as others see him—and is convulsed with unmanning laughter. Alone in the bedroom with the willing Betty June, Todd faces no physical danger, yet the similarity of his reactions here and in the Argonne Forest is unmistakable. Indeed, Todd himself makes the association, calling the bedroom experience the "second of two unforgettable demonstrations of my animality" (124). In both instances Todd is momentarily overwhelmed by the demands of his body. In both he forces essentially spontaneous emotions, fear and passion, into purely intellectual frames of reference: dispassionate objectivity on the one hand, and high humor on the other.[9] While authentic danger exists only in the battle scene, the similar responses in both scenes indicate that Todd feels threatened in the bedroom as well. From his ontologically insecure perspective, flesh means death; thus submission to the body's sexual urges risks vulnerability.

The sex-death analogy becomes one of the novel's controlling metaphors. To give it added emphasis Barth even changed a scene: in the novel's first edition (1956), Chapter 11 begins when a pregnant cat obstructs the path of some pallbearers.[10] In the revised edition Barth changed the cat to a pair of copulating dogs. Although Todd responds identically in both versions, chiding nature for its "clumsy 'life-in-the-face-of-death' scenario," the change is nonetheless instructive. In the later version Todd associates death not with life so much as with flesh and its demands, an association better pointed up by copulating dogs than by pregnant cats. In the next chapter the figure is repeated with a slight variation, as the still-joined dogs wander by the loafer's bench where sits Todd's "chorus of oysters," a group of old men. Little more than living corpses who, as Captain Osborn laments, are dying "a piece at a time" (13), the old men serve as apt correlatives to the coffin of Chapter 11. The figure is given yet another turn when Todd, on what is to be his final day, offers Jane to the octogenarian Osborn. As Jac Tharpe observes, this gesture "shows the mordant view that [Todd] has acquired. . . . Both [Jane and Osborne] are merely flesh"[11] — and therefore vulnerable to the hostilely implosive universe. In each scene fleshly pleasures, represented by copulating dogs and the mistress with whom Todd copulates, are associated with and canceled by decaying flesh, represented by the dying or the already dead.

Todd's response to sex remains generally consistent throughout the novel. "Nothing to me," he reveals, "is so consistently, profoundly, earth-shakingly funny as we animals in the act of mating" (124). Copulation — between dogs, crabs, people — makes him smile. His stance is of course defensive, a means of enclosing that which is physical and emotional in a humorous, therefore rational, frame. By emphasizing the rational at the expense of the emotional, Todd tries to sever himself from the dying animal to which he is fastened — in Laing's terms, seeking "by being unembodied to transcend the world and hence be safe."[12] The radical nature of Todd's reliance on rational control is suggested by the paucity of his emotional experience. He has had only five emotions in his life, each of which he has carefully counted and classified, as though simple enumeration can convert the affective and spontaneous into the cognitive and controlled. In his rage for quantification he has also counted the number of times his heart has beat since 1919, when Dr. Frisbee informed him of his myocardial infarction, and he has even tallied each of the 673 times he has copulated with the luscious Jane Mack.

While his affair with Jane suggests a surrender to the flesh, Todd never completely loses rational command of this situation. Not only does he carefully count each copulation, but he makes rational conjectures about the future course of their affair, listing these in the form of propositions in his *Inquiry*. Moreover, his general attitude toward the Macks throughout the affair betrays his characteristic dualism. "I scarcely regarded myself as involved in [the affair] at all," he writes. "My curiosity lay entirely in the character of Harrison and, to a lesser degree, of Jane" (36). The Macks, then, become mere objects to Todd, specimens that he can dispassionately observe and manipulate. After his first experience with Jane on the Mack's boat, Todd lies so convincingly about the "loss" of his virginity that the Macks never doubt him, thus falling prey to his machinations. Later he temporarily terminates the affair with another lie, telling the racist Harrison that he and Dorothy Miner, a black client, enjoy sexual relations. In both situations Todd maintains control by hiding his own motives while accurately predicting the Mack's expectations and responses. He exploits their good-natured gullibility by concealing a part of himself behind a shield of duplicity.[13] He is able to submit to his body's desires on the one hand, while simultaneously controlling and "transcending" them on the other.

Todd's excessive reliance on rational control, like his masks and his mind-body split, may be seen as a schizophrenic reaction to a deep-seated ontological insecurity most obviously shown in his irrational fear of the human body. Each reaction represents what Laing calls a "false self," the external complement "of an 'inner' self which is occupied in maintaining its identity and freedom by being transcendent, unembodied, and thus never to be grasped, pinpointed, trapped, possessed. Its aim is to be pure subject, without any objective existence."[14] When Jane calls attention to Todd's clubbed fingers, however, Todd realizes that his various poses — rake, saint, cynic — had not been stages in his intellectual development but *masks*, false selves calculated to conceal his heart from his mind and his mind from his heart (223). He realizes that the masks will no longer work, that "where cynicism had failed, no future mask could succeed" (226). Gripped by a near-paralyzing sense of futility, Todd considers prayer; realizing that the heavens are void, he joins Jane in bed, buries his head in her lap, and, assuming a fetal position, fights despair the night through "as one fights appendicitis" (227). The next morning he decides to kill himself and 699 fellow townspeople by blowing up the showboat.

Or does he? Barth has made it clear that, because of "practical physics," Todd's plan to blow up the steamboat could not work.[15] Todd probably realizes this himself, since Captain Adam, in response to Todd's query about the danger of acetylene footlights, carefully explains the boat's safety features (202–3). Indeed, Adam's explanation seems to provide the primary reason for including Chapter 22 ("A Tour of the Opera") in the novel.

If Todd knows that his plan has little chance to succeed, why does he go through with it? As we have seen, all of Todd's defenses against a hostile reality have failed by now, and he has fallen into a state of desperate anxiety. His condition closely resembles Laing's description of the schizophrenic teetering on the verge of psychosis. Terrified of the engulfment it is helpless to avoid, the self adopts "the most extreme defensive posture that can be adopted."[16] It attempts to murder itself. Seldom is this attempt literal; rather, it often takes the form of a simple declaration that the self is dead. At any rate, the posture remains defensive; therefore it is not destructive, but ultimately protective. Todd sees suicide as "the end of masks" (227) because it represents the "ultimate and most paradoxically absurd possible defense, *beyond which magic defenses can go no further.*"[17] Fully aware that his plan cannot work, Todd never intends to kill himself. Rather, his actions represent an *existential* suicide, a *symbolic* denial of being that is paradoxically intended to preserve being. If the self is dead, it cannot be destroyed.

Todd's suicide "attempt" is another evasion, another mask. The fact that he justifies suicide on philosophical grounds indicates that he has forced despair, as he has previously forced fear and lust, into a cognitive frame. Again he has taken rational command of the situation. "There was no mastering the fact with which I lived," he reasons the morning after his night of despair, "but I could master the fact of my living with it by destroying myself, and the result was the same — I was the Master" (227). The realization that suicide represents mastery seems sufficient; actual suicide becomes unnecessary, although a pretense at its attempt is required. After returning from that "attempt" intact, Todd saves Mr. Haecker's life, in an action consistent with his desire to preserve life. Then he adds to his *Inquiry* the final, logical link in his chain of rationalizations: "*There's no final reason for living (or for suicide)*" (250).

Todd continues to live — but not without masks. His last mask is *The Floating Opera* itself.[18] Todd's methods of storytelling, like his actions, derive from his sense of ontological insecurity. The reader must contend with "two" Todds: Todd the *character*, the "pre-1937" Todd,[19] whose various masks and activities are directed "inward" toward the other characters and incidents in the novel; and Todd the *author*, the post-1937 Todd whose activities as narrator are directed "outward" toward his audience. Todd-the-character lies to the Macks to protect his "real" inner self. Todd-the-author lies to his audience for the same reason.

As author, Todd conceals his real meanings behind a series of formal quirks and discontinuities that parallel the "formal peculiarities" Laing describes as characteristic of schizophrenic deception. While pretending to be solicitous of his reader—Todd promises that if the reader is an "average fellow" he will be able to "keep track of the plot as it sails in and out of view" (8)—Todd really wants to throw him off the track. He diverts the reader's attention from the novel's real significance by constant references to its *expository* dimension, particularly its so-called digressions. No incident, however, is ever really beside the point; each reflects Todd's concern with mortality and his attempts to evade it. Every character is a projection of this concern; some are actual or partial *doppelgängers*. In other words, not only does Todd fragment his identity into the various masks he wears as *character*, but as *author* further fractures his personality and concerns into the various characters he creates and scenes he relates.

Among Todd's more obvious doubles is Harrison Mack, Sr. The only clearly insane character in the novel, he allows Todd to introduce into his fiction the idea of madness. Moreover, the most dramatic symptom of the pickle magnate's mental illness—the hoarding of his feces in 129 pickle jars—not only suggests the schizophrenic's fascination with bodily waste but also reflects what Laing calls the schizophrenic's fear of "letting anything of himself go," a fear that is a corollary to the schizophrenic's need to be always in control.[20] The Freudian association of feces and control is a familiar one. The will to power, Norman O. Brown explains, is an attribute of human reason "first developed in the symbolic manipulation of excrement and perpetuated in the symbolic manipulation of symbolic substitutes for excrement." The primary substitute for feces is money. Indeed, Brown argues, "Money *is* feces, because the anal eroticism continues in the unconscious. The anal eroticism has not been renounced or abandoned but repressed."[21] In the later stages of his mental illness the elder Mack evidently regresses to the anal stage, confusing feces with money and power. Thus Barth provides a solid psychological basis for the pickle tycoon's antics, as Mack uses his stored feces along with the estate to exert control over his heirs, threatening to disinherit his wife and son if they fail to obey his wishes.

Most critics have read this episode as a satiric commentary on the irrationality of the law[22] (which, in part, it is), and they have not concentrated at all on Mack's schizophrenic behavior. So it is not surprising that no one has noticed the similarities between Todd Andrews and Harrison Mack, Sr. Although Todd never actually confuses feces and money, his courtroom victory in the three-million-dollar inheritance case is associated in various ways with excrement. His secretary's indecorous fart, for example, suggests the method Todd employs in winning the case, and Mrs. Mack's disposal of her late husband's waste provides the grounds for that victory. Moreover, like the schizophrenic tycoon, Todd uses money and feces as a means of exerting control over Harrison, threatening to "disinherit" him unless he behaves in a manner of which Todd approves. "I believed Harrison was undeserving of the money," Todd explains, "unless he overcame his former weakness. It was my opinion that in order for him to be worthy of the inheritance, he had to demonstrate a strength of character that would make the loss of it unimportant" (146).

As it turns out, Harrison's behavior has little to do with Todd's decision to seek the injunction necessary for winning the settlement. Trying to make that decision, Todd flips a coin; the outcome indicates that he should drop Eustacia Callader's crucial letter into the creek. Determined to be always in control, however, Todd will not allow himself "to be dictated to by a miserable nickel" (216). He files the letter instead of discarding it and eventually secures the necessary injunction. Todd's desire for control, along with his indirect manipulation of feces and money, associates him with the schizophrenic Mack and provides an important clue toward a fuller understanding of the *Opera*'s elusive narrator.

Though in a much less obvious way, Harrison Mack, Jr., also functions as a partial projection of Todd's schizophrenia. The younger Mack is one of several characters who, while not themselves schizophrenic, exhibit characteristics that reflect and therefore help isolate certain schizophrenic symptoms in Todd himself. Since these characteristics seldom have direct bearing on the novel's plot, and since they frequently contribute little to our understanding of the character displaying them, the reader is likely to dismiss them as more of the novel's "irrelevant" digressions. One such symptom is Harrison's tendency to emulate Todd's various masks, a personality quirk that Todd notices when he first meets Harrison. While this tendency reveals little about Harrison's character, it has significance to Todd's, since it alerts the reader to the idea of "impersonation," a schizophrenic symptom used implicitly in Todd's discussion of his childhood.

Of that childhood Todd writes: "I was almost never an ill-behaved child . . . there were few restrictions on my behavior, nor were many needed. I was (and am) temperamentally disposed to observing rules—my desires seldom fall without their pale. And because I so rarely gave him cause for concern, my father was incurious about my activities" (117). Todd's reminiscence parallels Laing's description of the well-behaved childhood of "David," a schizophrenic patient: "his actions seem from the beginning of his life to have been in almost total compliance and conformity with his parents' actual wishes and expectations, i.e., he was a perfect model child who was never a trouble."[23] Characteristically, Todd attempts to mislead the reader about the significance of his early behavior by dismissing his model childhood as part of a general tendency to obey rules. But he seldom obeys rules—even as a child he violates the rules of boatbuilding. As an adult his transgressions are numerous: he commits adultery with his best friend's wife; he lies to Jane and Harrison on several occasions; he is willing "to bribe someone heavily" (105) to destroy the feces-filled pickle jars if his plan involving Eustacia Callader fails: he murders—in cold blood—a German sergeant; he drinks during Prohibition; he consorts with prostitutes; and of course he self-consciously violates many "rules" of fiction writing. Todd's deliberate falsification serves to conceal the real reason for his model childhood as well as his reason for relating the "irrelevant" material about his childhood in the first place: he is revealing to the reader, obscurely and indirectly, his schizophrenic desire to *emulate* his father as part of his false-self system.

While such a tendency (which Laing calls "impersonation") is often inconsistently followed, Todd emulates his father in a number of ways. Concerning his career, for example, Todd writes, "It had been assumed from earliest memory that I was to study for the Maryland Bar and enter Dad's firm, and I never protested" (73).

Compliant as usual to his father's wishes, Todd does both, even studying at Johns Hopkins, his father's preference.

The extent to which Todd pushes compliance is illustrated in his obsessive devotion to his *Inquiry*. The announced intent of the *Inquiry* is to discover why the elder Andrews hanged himself. The discovery of that answer, Todd realizes, involves coming as close as possible to his father, learning how his father's mind worked, reading the books his father read — in short, merging with, *becoming*, his father insofar as possible. The extremeness of this desire suggests Laing's point that the eventual result of impersonation often borders on caricature, as the "most hated aspects of the person who is the object of the identification come to the fore by being exposed to ridicule, scorn, or hatred through the medium of the impersonation."[24] For Todd, the "most hated aspects" of his father seem to involve a propensity toward order, a compulsive need to be in rational control of all events that Todd carries to absurd extremes.

We have already seen Todd's desire for rational control exhibited in a number of ways, but at least one crucial example remains to be mentioned. Todd, like his father, frequently does manual labor in his good clothes. Devoting an entire brief chapter to the fact, he cautions the reader not to impute too much significance to the parallel between the two Andrews: "Perhaps I shouldn't even have mentioned working on my boat in my good clothes" (72). The statement, unlike any Todd makes elsewhere, resembles rationalization; he simply protests too much. He has let the reader get too close to his "inner" self. The information imparted is too relevant to his real concerns, so Todd warns the reader against reaching what would be the correct conclusion — another example of the diversionary tactics Todd employs throughout the novel.

Todd pushes his father's need for order to caricature because secretly he knows that rational control must finally fail in the face of irrational death. When Todd finds his father hanging in the basement, he focuses almost obsessively on his physical aspect, but he also notices the order of the room and of his father's person: "there was not a smudge of dirt anywhere on him. . . . His clothes were perfectly creased and free of wrinkles, and although his face was black and his eyes were popped, his hair was neatly and correctly combed. Except that the chair upon which Dad had stood was kicked over, everything in the cellar was in order" (182). Death has intruded in the midst of all this order. Todd's father's control was simply useless in the face of death, a fact that Todd never forgets — or only half-forgets — although he himself adopts his father's stance in facing it.

A third character who helps isolate Todd's schizophrenic symptoms is Colonel Henry Morton. The richest man in Cambridge, Morton is surprised to receive a no-strings-attached gift of $5,000 from Todd Andrews, whom he barely knows. Boasting that he has "never been obligated to any man" (186) yet reluctant to return the cash, Morton makes various attempts to cancel his obligation. He finally succeeds when, during a wild New Year's Eve party, he discovers his nude wife and Todd in the shower enjoying a drunken dance. Though it is one of the funniest scenes in the novel, little in the chapter-length episode seems of immediate structural or thematic relevance, and critics have generally ignored it. Yet the Colonel's vigorous efforts to avoid indebtedness to any man serve as a comic projection of Todd's own schizophrenic desire to avoid obligations.

Because Todd views others as part of an objective and therefore potentially implosive reality, he fears any meaningful I-Thou relationships, substituting instead what Laing terms "a quasi-it-it interaction."[25] Any authentic emotional response to another must be checked, since such responses demand a degree of openness that invites impingement by the other. Todd prefers giving to receiving, since receiving may evoke in him feelings of obligation. For similar reasons he confesses early in the novel that he has never felt love, even hinting that he doubts its existence (36). As Laing explains, schizophrenics fear the "other's love . . . more than his hatred, or rather all love is sensed as a version of hatred. By being loved one is placed under an unsolicited obligation."[26] Todd, then, fears relationships involving anything more than feigned love or obligation. The resulting isolation is "a corollary . . . of the need to be in control."[27] As a projection of this need, Colonel Henry Morton plays an important role in Todd's seriocomic psychodrama.

One of the more significant doubles in *The Floating Opera* is Mr. Haecker. Nearing eighty, Haecker, like Todd, fears death. Like Todd, he erects a rationalistic facade as a shield against death's finality. When the facade fails, Haecker, like Todd, attempts to murder himself with a theatrical flourish. Todd nowhere

comments explicitly on these obvious parallels because his characteristically evasive method forbids such directness, but in the relatively brief Chapter 18 ("A Matter of Life and Death") Haecker
may be seen in many ways as an older version of Todd Andrews.
For example, Todd describes Haecker as "tuning his piano" (163), a
phrase Todd applies to himself in Chapter 1; he also acknowledges
the similarity between Haecker's sick smile and his own, refers to
Haecker's false stances as "masks," and observes Haecker "watching himself be strong" (166), employing the same protective divi-
sion-of-self that Todd uses several times. Before the chapter ends
Haecker has even adopted Todd's rationale for suicide. When
Haecker finally kills himself, he has acted out a role that Todd had
created for himself and then abandoned.

In the novel's plot Haecker is Todd's victim. In a larger psychological context, however, Haecker provides Todd the author with
a method for imaginatively killing himself. Haecker becomes a
symbolic substitute, an imaginary scapegoat. Todd the *author* first
creates Haecker in his own image and then kills him, an action
that is as much a symbolic and existential suicide as are the actions
of Todd the *character* aboard the showboat on his "final" day.
Thus the novel is defensive in yet another sense. Whereas Haecker
derives justification for living and ultimately for dying from books
he has read, Todd keeps himself alive by *writing* a book. His reper-
tory of masks and evasions having failed, Todd turns to fiction as
a last resort. By submitting "reality" to the reordering powers of his
imagination, he is able to exert an artistic control over the painful
facts of his existence. He keeps at bay an implosive reality by
imaginatively transforming that reality according to his own artistic whim.[28]

The Floating Opera is largely lies posing as autobiography.
Many of these lies are not even very original. The plot is laden
with clichés, a fact that Todd entices the reader to dismiss by paradoxically calling attention to it. For example, regarding his Fitz-
gerald-like activities as a student at Hopkins, he defends their
authenticity with an appeal to the reader's common sense: "remember that the lampoons didn't appear out of the air: they were written mostly by men who lived through just this sort of life" (130).
Similarly, when he and the Macks are reunited over the crib of the
sleeping Jeannine, Todd anticipates the reader's possibly offended
sensibilities by acknowledging that "it was like a scene arranged by

a heavy-handed director" (159). He then criticizes Jane's bad taste for arranging the sentimental "tableau." Todd also calls the reader's attention to the many implausible coincidences in his narrative, first by cautioning him to ignore the coincidences as one ignores similar incidents provided by Nature, that "heavy-handed symbolizer" (109), then by flattering his reader, "whose perceptions are not so rudimentary" (110) as to impute significance to such similarities. We are both too sophisticated, Todd implies, to see meaning where none exists.

Flattery and feigned solicitude are narrative devices calculated to soften the reader's normal objections to such implausibilities so that he will later accept without question the most implausible fabrication of all: Adam's Original and Unparalleled Floating Opera. The correspondence between this chapter-length scene and the novel as a whole is too complete to be disposed of as merely a "natural" coincidence; it could only occur in a work of fiction, and it reflects the ordering consciousness responsible for that fiction. Beginning with allusions to suicide (Whittaker's rendition of Hamlet's soliloquy) and role-playing (Whittaker's recitation of Jaques's speech from As You Like It) and concluding with Burley Joe's imitation of the great steamboat explosion, Adam's "Opera" parallels as it parodies Todd's Opera. Like Todd's narrative, Adam's "Opera" displays spectacle, virtuosity, and, as a conventional minstrel show, cliché. Like Todd, Captain Adam plays many roles, serving as director, master of ceremonies (narrator), and performer. Like Todd, Adam controls his audience's responses, at one point eliciting from his enthralled spectators cheers, sympathy, raucous laughter, resentful disappointment, and appreciative applause, all in rapid succession.

This pivotal scene serves as a paradigm for the novel as a whole and clearly presents the esthetic implications of Todd's ontological insecurity. Art provides Todd a means for manipulating his audience's responses in order to evade their understanding. In this sense, he "invents" his audience as surely as he invents his fiction.[29] That fiction, in its sheer inventiveness, proclaims the "mastery" of Todd's imagination over the materials of his existence. Language becomes the alchemy by which Todd transmutes, and therefore controls at least for a time, an otherwise menacing reality.

But what is the source of Todd's ontological insecurity? What caused his pervasive sense of dread? Todd associates his fear of death with his bad heart, but he learns of his heart condition in 1919, *after* he begins exhibiting symptoms of ontological insecurity. His myocardial infarction, while it may aggravate his neurotic fear of death and forms a convenient symbol for it, does not constitute its cause. Neither does the Argonne Forest experience, the Betty June Gunter episodes, or the death of his father, since each is preceded by schizophrenic displays. Indeed, Todd's earliest memory involves his compulsive reaction to a dead chicken, and his "model" childhood itself suggests the beginnings of mental illness. Despite a number of apparent causes — each of which may be another red herring — no single incident in the novel is itself the cause of Todd's illness. While we can generally categorize Todd's behavior as "schizophrenic," the exact source of such behavior remains a mystery. Our relationship to the facts concerning Todd's schizophrenia resembles Todd's relationship to the facts concerning his father's suicide: it is one thing to pore over the many documents that survive his father, but "it is another thing to examine this information and see in it, so clearly that to question is out of the question, the *cause* of a human act" (218). Following Hume, Todd concludes that "causation is never more than an inference; and any inference involves at some point the leap from what we see to what we can't see" (218).[30]

Be that as it may, certain passages in the novel provide clues, if not to the specific cause of Todd's ontological insecurity, then at least to the general nature of that cause. On what he believes will be his final day, for example, Todd makes two notes for later inclusion in his *Inquiry*. The first refers to the copulating crabs that sailors consider a "doubler," a single crab, just as Plato "imagined the human prototype to be male and female joined into one being" (54). Elaborating upon a similar idea, Joseph Campbell observes that, "according to the mysticism of sexual love," this lost union is symbolically restored in the act of sexual intercourse. "The ultimate experience of love is a realization that beneath the illusion of twoness dwells identity: 'each is both.' This realization can expand into a discovery that beneath the multitudinous individualities of the whole universe . . . dwells identity."[31] Such concepts, while perfectly at home in *Giles Goat-Boy*, seem oddly out of place in *The Floating Opera*, particularly when entertained by Todd Andrews, who forces distinctions and thrives on dualisms. Equally uncharacteristic is the attitude implied in Todd's second note, which concerns that "seeker of wisdom" who, having picked his toenails, sniffs his fingers in secret glee (206). While typical of a Whitman or a Ginsberg — or of *The Sot-Weed Factor's* Henry Burlingame, who literally makes love to the world — this sentiment seems inconsistent with the general attitudes of Todd Andrews, who feels disgust with his body and distrust of the physical. Both notes seemingly allude to that mystical realm where opposites merge and traditional dualisms — male/female, mind/body — dissolve, suggesting an integrated unity that seems inconsistent with Todd's schizophrenic commitment to separate and discrete details.

Yet Todd's muddy embrace with the German sergeant results in the same union of opposites that his *Inquiry* notes suggest, and it adumbrates the epiphanic embrace George and Anastasia share during their climactic descent into WESCAC's belly in *Giles Goat-Boy.* "Never in my life," Todd recalls, "have I enjoyed such intense intimacy, such clear communication with a fellow human being, male or female, as I enjoyed with that German sergeant. . . . For the space of some hours *we had been one man*, had understood each other beyond friendship, beyond love" (66). Todd should have added "beyond articulation," since the two soldiers speak different languages yet share perfect communication. The truth Todd glimpses in the Argonne transcends not only ego boundaries but, in its ineffable inclusiveness, linguistic categories as well. That Todd intuitively sought a similar transcension of categories as a boy of twelve is suggested by his first attempt at boatbuilding, "a deed almost holy in its utter desirability" (58). He wished to "provision" his boat "and some early morning to slip quietly from [his] mooring, to run down to the river, sparkling in the sun, out into the broad reaches of the Bay, and down to the endless ocean" (58). The image clearly suggests escape from finite boundaries ("my mooring") to the unbound infinite ("endless ocean"). Such passages imply, however obliquely, a metaphysical dimension to Todd's schizophrenia.

In examining the metaphysical implications of schizophrenia in general, John Vernon argues that "map consciousness," the propensity to see "reality" in terms of opposites (inner/outer, fantasy/reality, being/nonbeing, good/evil) is gradually giving way to "garden consciousness," the ability to perceive reality as integrated and whole.[32] Schizophrenic vision catapults one into the realm of the garden, where the various categories human reason invents to harness a fluid reality dissolve and man and his universe become one. Laing, too, discusses the schizophrenic experience as a potentially transcendental one, not breakdown but breakthrough.[33] At the height of this experience (which resembles traditional mystical vision) the human ego, itself another invented category, also dissolves, as Todd's does when he merges with the German. Because social reality is ego oriented, the schizophrenic fears the dissolution of what he has been conditioned to consider his real self. Filled with anxiety (ontological insecurity), he struggles against his vision, projecting emotion from his "inner" self to the outer world, introjecting elements from the outer world to the inner. Thus distorted, the holistic reality he perceives, as well as the everyday world to which he is accustomed, becomes frenzied and frightening. His autonomous ego threatened, he adopts evasive strategies and "fictive" shields against what now seems a destructively chaotic universe. Not only schizophrenic behavior, then, but also what might be called the schizophrenic esthetic — both the impulse to create alternative "realities" and the nature of those creations — grow out of a desperate need to preserve the threatened ego. The behavioral and esthetic implications of schizophrenia can best be understood in terms of its *metaphysical* implications.

Todd's behavior as character and the esthetic theory implicit in his narrative reflect his ambivalent fear of and longing for that unity he has evidently glimpsed and to which he obliquely refers. His longing for physical union with the other draws him to the German sergeant, to Betty June, to Jane; his fear of that unity drives him to murder, to cruel laughter, to psychosomatic impotence. Because he longs to be at one with the world, he relishes the stench of the crabhouse and revels in the odors of his secretary's embarrassment and his own picked toenails. Yet he fears that world, so he retreats behind false selves and a mind-body dualism. He longs for communication with the other and wishes to be understood, so he begins the *Inquiry*, a major part of which is *The Floating Opera*. But any form of understanding threatens his whole defensive system, so he conceals his true meaning behind equivocation and evasions. In composing the *Inquiry* he realizes that total understanding of his father — or, for that matter, of anything — "requires the understanding of every other thing in the world" (7). He has hit upon the key to all mystical thinking: in the "garden" one thing contains all things. But Todd, fearing the very unity he seeks, retreats into the labyrinthian discreteness of the map and tries to grasp the whole one item at a time. Union with the other frightens him; withdrawal from the other leaves him empty and ultimately despondent. As Laing points out, "The polarity is between complete isolation or complete merging of identity rather than between separateness and relatedness. The individual oscillates perpetually, between two extremes, each equally unfeasible."[34]

Todd's motives and methods as both character and narrator derive from ontological insecurity. But, as previously suggested, Barth's ultimate concern is not with literal schizophrenia. Born in 1900, Todd is this century's child; his schizophrenia provides Barth with a metaphor for the condition of the artist in modern times. Like so many writers of this century, Barth finds himself wandering between two great coordinating mythologies, one dead, the other, if not powerless to be born, at least not fully formulated. The resulting confusion may be transitional; it may also be permanent, for the realization that great truths of the past were really fictions makes it difficult to maintain faith in contemporary truths. As Gerald L. Bruns succinctly puts it, "Fictions, after all, tend to assuage but not to survive disbelief."[35] Not that we need new truths (which is to say, new lies) any less. The dilemma of modern man, in Kurt Vonnegut's famous phrase, is "the heartbreaking necessity of lying about reality, and the heartbreaking impossibility of lying about it."[36] Art may always have framed "the human universe," as Albert Hofstadter argues, ordering and arranging an otherwise undifferentiated flow of sensations.[37] But in the past man could mistake his words for things, his invented realities for Reality itself. It is one thing to construct fictions while under the delusion that they are truths, quite another *knowingly* to construct fictions that must nonetheless satisfy the need for belief. Within the tensions of this paradox Barth's (and Todd's) fiction lies.

Such fiction necessarily becomes not only defensive but also desperate. Some fiction, perhaps, always has been. "Scheherazade's my *avant-gardiste*," Barth once declared, referring to that ancient teller whose tales literally stood between her and death.[38] Fiction in the hands of a Scheherazade or a Todd Andrews does not imitate reality; it evades it. Yet the apocalypse it seeks to avoid trembles between the lines of its artifice. Regarding that artifice, Barth describes Scheherazade's tales as "artfully . . . involuted, compounded, and complicated,"[39] a description that applies to *The*

Floating Opera as well. Desperation, it seems, begets the baroque. Todd Andrews, like so many artists of this and past centuries, has confronted a world suddenly grown threatening in its inscrutability. His dilemma recapitulates that primal dilemma when ancient man, confronted with the primordial void, called a world out of nothingness.[40] Like an aboriginal poet-magus, Todd confronts chaos with art — the lies that order. If the narrator of *The Floating Opera* is a liar and his tale is comprised of lies, those lies, like Stevens's angel, are necessary.

NOTES

1. Not all critics greeted Barth's shift to the fabulative mode with praise. Robert Garis's vituperative "What Happened to John Barth?" provides the most celebrated dissent, but see also Earl Rovit's dismissal of *The Sot-Weed Factor* as "a bewildering plaything" in "The Novel as Parody."

2. LeClair, "Barth's *Floating Opera*." Representative of those critics who dismiss the earlier novels as conventional is John Stark. While he finds *The Floating Opera* and *The End of the Road* "two reasonably impressive novels," Stark omits both from the main concerns of his study because they are "quite conventional and realistic" (*Literature of Exhaustion*, p. 118).

3. Hawkes, "*The Floating Opera* and *Second Skin*," p. 20. "Aesthetic bliss" is, of course, Nabokov's phrase. For an arresting perception of Todd's possible psychological problem, see Martin, "Desire and Disease."

4. The two books by Laing with which I will be concerned are *The Divided Self* and *The Politics of Experience*. I am not suggesting a Laingian influence on Barth. Indeed, *The Floating Opera* appeared *before* Laing's books. Rather, we seem to have here another case of "cultural convergence," when two men of genius express similar ideas at roughly the same time but through different media. On the general phenomenon of "cultural convergence," see Peckham, *Man's Rage for Chaos*, pp. 6–21.

5. A fact not lost on early critics; see especially Lehan, *Dangerous Crossing*, pp. 172–75, and Kennard, *Number and Nightmare*, pp. 57–82.

6. Laing, *Divided Self*, pp. 45–46.

7. Barth, *The Floating Opera*, rev. ed. (Garden City, N.Y.: Doubleday, 1967), p. 22. Subsequent references to this edition are noted in parentheses in the text.

8. Laing, *Divided Self*, p. 66.

9. An excellent analysis of how man orders his responses by organizing his experience into various frames is provided by Goffman in *Frame Analysis*.

10. Barth, *The Floating Opera* (New York: Appleton-Century-Crofts, 1956), p. 116.

11. Tharpe, *Barth*, p. 19.

12. Laing, *Divided Self*, p. 80.

13. At the same time, a part of Todd is physically and emotionally committed to Jane. So powerful is this commitment, in fact, that Todd's reliance on mere reason cannot control it. Instead, subconscious defenses take over, one symptom of which is an increasing sexual impotency that is probably psychosomatic and that would have made continuation of the affair impossible even if Jane had not ended it when she did.

14. Laing, *Divided Self*, pp. 94–95.

15. Gado, ed., *First Person*. In the interview Barth paraphrases Captain Adam's explanation: "Given that much cubic space and the fact that the windows would have been open to provide ventilation in the muggy southern Chesapeake Bay summertime, it was near impossible for it [the steamboat] to blow up" (p. 119).

16. Laing, *Divided Self*, p. 176.

17. Ibid., p. 149, italics mine.

18. A point LeClair also makes: "Barth's *Floating Opera,*" p. 721.

19. Joseph, *Barth*, p. 11.

20. Laing, *Divided Self*, p. 83.

21. Brown, *Life against Death*, pp. 191–92. Cf. Korkowski, "Excremental Vision."

22. See, e.g., Schickel, "The Floating Opera," p. 61.

23. Laing, *Divided Self*, p. 101.

24. Ibid, p. 102.

25. Ibid., p. 82.

26. Ibid., p. 45.

27. Ibid., p. 83.

28. Cf. LeClair, "Barth's *Floating Opera,*" p. 719.

29. As do all writers, according to Walter J. Ong. See Ong's provocative argument in *Interfaces of the Word*, pp. 53–81.

30. It is probably passages such as this that Barth has in mind when he says of Todd's decision to kill himself, "It's more a Humean than a Camusian thing, actually" (Gado, ed., *First Person*, p. 117).

31. Campbell, *Hero with a Thousand Faces*, p. 280.

32. Vernon, *Garden and the Map*, pp. 3–28.

33. Laing, *Politics of Experience*, especially Ch. 7. It is instructive to compare Laing's account of a schizophrenic "journey" in this chapter to Campbell's general account of the archetypal heroic journey in *Hero with a Thousand Faces*.

34. Laing, *Divided Self*, p. 53.

35. Bruns, *Modern Poetry*, p. 222.

36. Vonnegut, *Cat's Cradle*, p. 189.

37. Hofstadter, *Truth and Art*, p. 12.

38. Enck, "Interview," p. 21.

39. Barth, "Muse, Spare Me," p. 28.

40. Cf. Northrop Frye's analysis of the relationship between imagination and reality in "Literature and Myth," in *Relations of Literary Study*, ed. Thorpe, pp. 27–56. Myth, Frye argues, expresses not so much the world man lives in but the world man builds. "Literature is only a part, though a central part, of the total mythopoeic structure of concern which extends into religion, philosophy, political theory, and many aspects of history, the vision a society has of its situation, destiny, and ideals, and of reality in terms of those human factors" (p. 41). In other words, literature is just one of the various fictions that constitute the coordinating mythology of a given age. Todd's case stands as a metaphor for that situation faced by the artist when a coordinating myth begins to crumble.

3

Articulation and Absolutes:
The End of the Road

On the general phenomenon of multiple personalities, Barth has written,

> I've always been impressed by the multiplicity of people that one has in one. It seems to me that the plurality of selves that Thomas Browne, and others speak of, is a simple psychological fact. I've never been impressed by any unity of identity in myself. . . . And so, one of the images that . . . recur through my novels, is . . . the pair of opposites — the two men in the triangle are usually contraries. Well, you know, unless you're [an] awfully single-minded and simple-minded person, as you go along you get more and more impressed by the contrarities in yourself.[1]

The various characters in *The Floating Opera* serve as clues to and projections of the multiple selves of Todd Andrews, narrator of the novel and single artificer of his world. Written in the same year, though not published until two years later, *The End of the Road* (1958, 1967) also reflects Barth's interest in schismatic selfhood.[2] It, too, may be read as a psychodrama whose major characters embody and help isolate various personality traits of Jake Horner, the novel's protagonist and narrator. Moreover, just as Todd Andrews adopts an "approach and avoid" narrative stance, employing language that protects him from while it links him to a world he simultaneously fears and desires, in *The End of the Road* language also becomes an important emblem of Barth's larger concerns.

The most obvious of Jake's doubles is Joe Morgan. Whereas Joe limits his vision of life to a single, coherent view, thus remaining certain of everything, Jake is able "to maintain with perfectly equal unenthusiasm contradictory, or at least polarized, opinions at once on a given subject,"[3] and thus is certain of nothing. Despite this apparent opposition, Rennie perceives a similarity in the two men: "You work from a lot of the same premises" (59), she tells Jake. Rather than representing Unreason to Joe's Reason, as Herbert Smith argues,[4] Jake also works from rational premises, though their conclusions vary widely. Both resemble Todd Andrews. Like Todd before his suicide attempt, Jake rationally deduces his nihilistic position; like Todd after that attempt, Joe rationally concludes that one "shouldn't consider a value less real just because it isn't absolute, since less-than-absolutes are all we've got" (247).[5] As David Morrell observes, "Todd Andrews is thus still alive, thought not very well—extreme, miserable, fragmented in *The End of the Road*."[6]

Though less obvious than Joe's, Jake's rationality is evident throughout the novel. He pretends to recoil from systematic analysis (41), but he is pleased when he scores logical points in his debates with Joe. His reliance on logic is even more apparent in his various discussions with Rennie, particularly when she attempts to represent her husband's position. When she phones to invite Jake to dinner, he cruelly adopts Joe's line of reasoning to catch her in a logical contradiction, a maneuver Joe later approves as "sensible" (40). Both Jake and Joe exhibit the close attention to minute details that reflects Todd Andrews's need to be in rational control. Like Todd, who tallies the times he copulates with Jane Mack, Joe keeps close account of Jake and Rennie's affair: who was on top the first time, on which shoulder Rennie bit Jake, even the brand of condoms Jake uses and the number of times he had to use them. In a similar fashion, Jake scrupulously records the various possible positions his arms and legs might take in the Progress and Advice Room, describes the precise details of a "suppositive gesture" (5), and even parses a portion of one of his sentences for us (2–3). Such examples suggest that for Jake and Joe, as for Todd, reason may serve as a psychological defense.

Robert Rogers advances this very argument in his useful study of the double in literature. He finds "transparent" Joe's use of "reason as a massive dyke [sic] to hold back whole seas of perverse sexual and aggressive impulses which threaten to engulf him." Indeed, Rogers maintains that Joe is "literally insane"; his "'reasoned' facade about taking marriage seriously . . . masks sadistic, masochistic, voyeuristic, and homosexual proclivities, as his fanatical probing of the intimate 'facts' of Jake's sexual relationship with Rennie reveals plainly enough."[7] Rogers's diagnosis seems fundamentally sound, but he curiously overlooks the fact that each of Joe's "proclivities" is present in Jake's character as well. Jake may perceive the homosexual implications of the triangle himself. "Perhaps," he muses, "it was Joe Morgan, after all, that I loved" (140). His voyeurism is clearly displayed when he encourages Rennie to join him in spying on Joe. "You mean you never spy on people when they're alone?" he urges. "It's wonderful! Come on, be a sneak! It's the most unfair thing you can do to a person" (65). Masochism supplies at least a plausible explanation for Jake's embroilment in the Morgan affair despite his doctor's warning to avoid complications and the obvious fact that Joe has deliberately thrown Jake and Rennie together. It may also explain why Jake is "thrilled" when Joe threatens to shoot him (140). But what in Jake's character suggests sadism? Joe's sadistic tendencies are clear enough: not only does he torment Rennie psychologically, but on two occasions he knocks her unconscious, a circumstance which understandably appalls Jake. Yet Jake also hits Peggy Rankin twice (once to woo her, once because she will not help him find an abortionist) and he deliberately and repeatedly exploits her sexually despite the evident mental anguish it causes her. Indeed, it is his skillful imitation of Joe Morgan that helps Jake seduce Peggy a second time, and at one point she whips her head "in a manner quite like Rennie's" (166). Their relationship, then, clearly mirrors Joe and Rennie's, thus helping to isolate Jake's sadistic tendencies.

More importantly, Jake's relationship with Rennie frequently parallels Joe's. Joe treats Rennie "as if she were a patient" (41); similarly, as he begins his riding lessons Jake regards himself "as the examiner and her as the subject" (47). During a subsequent conversation with Rennie, he attacks Joe's philosophy, "not to make a point, but to observe Rennie" (51). Even his affair with Rennie, which he initially dismisses as "insignificant, unimportant, and, as far as I was concerned, inconsequential" (95), is regarded simply as an act of "masculine curiosity: in other words, first I wanted to copulate, then I wanted to copulate with Rennie and in addition to learn not only 'what she was like in bed,' but also what the intimate relationship (I do not mean sexual relationship) would be like which I presumed would be established by our intercourse" (95). What sympathy he does feel for Rennie is held firmly in check, "observed impersonally and with some amusement from another part of [himself]" (52). Like those bloodless scientists of Hawthorne's fiction, Jake and Joe are capable of regarding other people as specimens rather than as human beings (though Jake, as we shall see, does eventually close the gap between himself and others). Such similarities tend to outweigh the apparent differences between the men, whose actions, in Rogers's words, dramatize "some of the problematic aspects of the synergistic relationship between man's intelligence and his emotions."[8] Both men, that is, employ reason as a shield against emotional involvement.

Jake's cosmopsis is particularly symptomatic of his fear of emotional involvement. In Rogers's words, it "serves as a perfect rationalization for avoiding commitment, especially any kind of emotional commitment," and indicates "inhibitions in the sphere of the emotions as much as the will."[9] Rogers's diagnosis is rooted firmly in Freudian psychology, particularly Freud's early studies of obsessional neurosis. The "inconsistent and vacillating behaviour" of obsessional neurotics, Freud suggests, is a protective measure which grows out of the need for uncertainty and doubt in their lives. "The creation of uncertainty is one of the methods employed by the neurosis for drawing the patient away from *reality* and isolating him from the world—which is among the objects of every psychoneurotic disorder."[10] As uncertainty intensifies, what Freud terms a "regression" from acting to thinking occurs until action ceases altogether. Cultivated doubt leads to a paralysis of the decisionmaking powers which "gradually extends itself over the entire field of the patient's behaviour."[11] Jake's cosmopsis, then, is not so much a paralysis of the will as a willed paralysis, a strategic withdrawal from the world of action. "Not to choose at all is unthinkable," he says. "What I had done . . . was simply choose not to act" (70).

The Doctor's treatment of Jake's condition, which includes Informational Therapy—Jake is to read the *World Almanac* regularly—and the principles of Sinistrality, Antecedence, and Alphabetical Priority—which force Jake to make arbitrary decisions—is intended to reacquaint Jake with the physical, factual world from which he has withdrawn and to help resolve doubt by restricting possibilities.

More behavioristic than Freudian ("Forget about causes; I'm no psychoanalyst" [72]), the Doctor remains unconcerned about the
source of Jake's affliction. Freud, however, locates the source of
obsessional neurosis in "the chronic coexistence of love and hatred,
both directed towards the same person and both of the highest degree of intensity."[12] Interestingly, Rennie describes her feeling
toward Jake in similar terms. "For Christ's sake try to remember
one thing, anyhow," she tells him; "if I love you at all, I don't *just*
love you. I swear, along with it I honestly and truly hate your
God-damned guts!" (134). Typically, Jake converts Rennie's authentic confusion into an abstraction, generalizing about her
"pseudo-ambivalence whose source was in the language, not in the
concepts symbolized by the language" (135) — an arresting enough
notion, to be sure, but one hardly responsive to Rennie's present
anguish. In fact, Jake's speculations may be a diversionary tactic
calculated to call our attention away from Rennie's painful ambivalence, since that ambivalence may offer a clue to Jake's own personality. Jake seems to be up to Todd Andrews's tricks, for it is he,
not Rennie, who is neurotically obsessed. Having said that, we are
no closer to having isolated the precise cause of Jake's condition,
for if Rennie's love-hate confusion alludes (whether deliberately or
coincidentally) to Freud's diagnosis of the cause of obsessional
neurosis, thus supplying a basis for our speculation about the
nature of Jake's malady, little evidence in the novel allows us to
posit love-hate ambivalence as the *cause* of his malady.

Be that as it may, general ambivalence is clearly an aspect of
Jake's pathology. The rational control he exerts over his emotions,
for example, begins to flag during the events surrounding Rennie's
pregnancy. At one point he confesses to experiencing "relief, ridic-
ulousness, embarrassment, anger, injured pride, maudlin affection
for the Morgans, disgust with them and myself, and a host of other
things, including indifference to the whole business" (176). The initial items in Jake's list describe emotions and feelings; the final
item — indifference — suggests a conscious holding back of involvement, a rational distancing from the situation and the people in it.
What is conveyed is neither a dominance of reason over emotion
nor emotion over reason, but a mounting ambivalence between
the two. This ambivalence becomes sharper a few pages later,
when a terrified Rennie is led to the Treatment Room. "My eyes
watered," Jake writes. "I didn't know how to go about distinguish-

ing compassion from love: perhaps it was only compassion I felt for her" (178). Again Jake attempts to submit felt emotions to the ordering processes of the intellect, just as earlier he had converted Rennie's confusion into an abstraction. But the emotion this time is Jake's, not Rennie's, and it is powerful enough to bring tears to his eyes. Clearly, emotion is beginning to strain against reason's barricade. This tension continues throughout Rennie's abortion, until, after her horrible death, emotion completely breaks through Jake's defenses. During the early stages of the abortion Jake's tear-filled eyes prevent him from seeing Rennie clearly. When she begins bleeding he is barely able to swallow the vomit that rushes to his mouth; he begins to "catch Rennie's fear" (180). Upon her death he is "stunned past weeping" (182), as shock immediately sets in. Fighting "nausea and faintness" (182), he is unable to speak. Finally, totally in the grip of emotions unmediated by reason, he falls into a dead faint.

Only once before has Jake experienced anything resembling this powerful overflow of emotions. Driving to the Morgans' shortly after his first adulterous meeting with Rennie, Jake is suddenly gripped by guilt which "poured in with a violent shock that slacked my jaw, dizzied me at the wheel, brought sweat to my forehead and palms, and slightly sickened me" (96). In both instances emotion triggers intense physical reactions. "What is more," Jake adds to his description of the first incident, "my anguish was pretty much unself-conscious. I was not aware of watching Jacob Horner suffer anguish" (96). The causal relationship between lack of self-consciousness and emotional trauma, though not directly mentioned, seems clear enough, for as soon as self-consciousness returns Jake is once again safely distanced from his emotions: "And now I was self-conscious again; I watched myself refuse to recognize that beside my bed was a telephone by means of which one could call Joe Morgan; that parked out front was a Chevrolet by means of which one could drive out there. . . . My curiosity returned with my self-consciousness. I placed my hand on the telephone and for some time studied with interest the blushing, uncomfortable fellow who would not pick it up" (100). Jake's mind-body split, repeated several times in the novel, clearly resembles Todd's schizophrenic response to ontological insecurity and suggests that Jake, like Todd, may fear his physical as well as his emotional self.

After the fatal abortion Jake's efforts to gain a rational perspective on his trauma are not so successful. Seeing Rennie's corpse curled on the back seat where the Doctor and Mrs. Dockey have placed it, he says of his situation, "It was too big a thing to know what to think about it, to know how to feel" (183). At first Jake's statement seems to equate his thinking and feeling faculties, and to suggest that both have been stunned. This is not the case, however. Jake says he does not know *how* to feel, not that he does not know *what* he feels. Again thinking, not feeling, is first in his cosmos. Jake is casting around in his mind for an appropriate term with which to label and thereby contain the riotous emotions which have so recently felled him. He eventually seizes on *responsibility:* "Unless [Joe] requested differently, I intended to answer everybody's questions truthfully, and I hoped the Doctor had been mistaken: I hoped with all my heart that there was some way in which I could be held legally responsible. I craved responsibility" (184). This seems an admirable sentiment, suggesting that Jake has finally overcome his careless indifference toward others. Yet Jake does not say he *feels* responsible for Rennie's death; rather, he desires — his word is "craves" — responsibility. By assuming full responsibility, Jake will gain credit for having been in control of a situation that in reality overwhelmed him. Even the disgrace and criminal liability such credit entails seems a small price for Jake to pay for the chance to successfully reinvent his past. As he says in another context, "What had been done had been done, but the past, after all, exists only in the minds of those who are thinking about it in the present, and therefore in the interpretations which are put on it. In that sense it is never too late to *do* something about the past" (105). When Joe refuses to implicate Jake, however, Jake is deprived of even the retrospective control he seeks. Felt experience, in all its "raggedness" and "incompleteness," has resisted Jake's efforts to order it rationally. He thus relapses into his earlier dilemma. "I could not even decide what I should *feel:* all I found in me was anguish, abstract and without focus" (187). Torn between a desire to feel and a fear of feeling, his taut ambivalence once again approaches paralysis.

Jake's emotional condition has passed through several distinct stages. Early in the novel he is safely distanced from all emotional involvement. During Rennie's abortion, however, protective self-consciousness begins to crumble until he is totally engulfed by emotions. Afterward he struggles to regain rational detachment from his emotional and physical self. Commenting on this final stage, Campbell Tatham writes, "[Jake] continues to detach himself from himself . . . instead of existing in what-he-is. . . . Thus, he expects to *decide* what he should *feel:* thus, the anguish he pretends to experience is what he *finds* in his self-conceptions, as if he were somehow situated outside his own body, observing 'its' response. It is indeed abstract and without focus, for that is the way Jake . . . prefers to take his 'reality.'"[13] But Jake's anguish, the result not primarily of Rennie's death but of his own engulfment, is authentic enough. And the "reality" he prefers, though an abstraction, is hardly without focus; on the contrary, when it loses its focus—when Jake is unable to impose upon it a clear and rational definition—"reality" becomes frightening. Jake requires as clearly defined a perception of "reality" as Joe, although he is able to entertain simultaneously different versions of "reality" or to move adroitly from one version to another. As Rennie says, "Whenever [Joe's] arguments were ready to catch you, you weren't there any more, and worse than that, even when he destroyed a position of yours it seemed to me that he hadn't really touched you—there wasn't that much of you in any of your positions" (62). But Jake's strategic refusal to believe in his various formulations should not detract from his desperate need to formulate. After all, articulation is his absolute, and an unarticulated "reality" cannot "be dealt with at all" (112). Precisely because he cannot *decide* what to feel, because he cannot verbally restrict inchoate anguish, he abandons job, car, and the bust of Laocoon and commits himself to the protective therapy of the Doctor at the Immobilization Farm. "Terminal," the word with which Barth's novel concludes, does not prophesy Jake's suicide, as one critic has intimated,[14] but implies that language itself has been taken to the end of the road.

Jake's muteness is only temporary, as the existence of his narrative testifies. Composed at the Immobilization Farm, presumably under the Doctor's supervision as an exercise in "Scriptotherapy," Jake's story is written two years after the events it relates. In the interim he has apparently regained enough detachment from those events to simplify them so that they may be articulated. For "to turn experience into speech," as Jake says, "is always a betrayal of experience, a falsification of it; but only so betrayed can it be dealt with at all" (112). Characterization accounts for much of this falsification, since "role-assigning is at best an arbitrary distortion of

the actors' personalities." Yet it, too, is necessary — and "probably
inevitable" (26) — if one is "to get on with the plot" (25).

 The End of the Road, like *The Floating Opera*, is lies posing as
autobiography. But unlike Todd Andrews, who tries to fool his
reader, Jake candidly admits his story's basis in artificiality. After
relating one of Joe's speeches, for example, Jake explains: "Now it
may well be that Joe made no such long coherent speech as this all
at once . . . I put it down here in the form of one uninterrupted
whiz-bang for convenience's sake, both to illustrate the nature of
his preoccupations and to add a stroke or two to *my picture* of the
man himself" (44, italics mine). Later he admits to the same
authorial shorthand in his account of a speech by Rennie (60).
Todd Andrews also calls attention to the artificial nature of his
narrative, but he pretends that it is the result of authorial inepti-
tude and inexperience. A narrative smoke-screen, Todd's feigned
sincerity is calculated to convince us that in his bumbling way he is
telling the truth. Jake has no such pretense. His formulation is a
self-proclaimed falsification; moreover, the reader has no way of
testing the degree to which it falsifies experience. Ultimately, however, the factual authenticity of Jake's narrative is irrelevant. His
story is not history but psychodrama. According to the Doctor, so
is "all fiction and biography, and most historiography" (83). Not
objective representations of life as it exists "out there," each is a
psychological projection onto life of its author's concerns, fears,
moods, values, and general sensibility. To perceive life is to
change it. "So in this sense," the Doctor concludes, "fiction isn't a
lie at all, but a true representation of the distortion that everyone
makes of life." Not only "the heroes of our own life stories — we're
the ones who conceive the story, and give other people the essences of minor characters" (83). Those essences reveal less about
the character to whom they are assigned than about the narrator
who assigns them.

 Both Joe and Jake-as-character represent reason and the diverse
conclusions to which it may lead; thus they serve as projections of
Jake-as-narrator's reliance on rationality. What role does Rennie
play in Jake's mytho-therapeutic psychodrama? Clearly, she represents the body. Though Jake presents himself as "never highly
sexed" and generally "as unarousable as a gelding" (92), immediately upon meeting Rennie he appraises her "in sexual terms" (28). As
surely as Todd is attracted to the smell of the crabhouse, to the

German sergeant, and to Jane, Jake is irresistibly attracted to the powerful "force" of Rennie's physicality (47). Despite that attraction (or *because* of it) he describes Rennie's physicality in denigrating terms. She is a "clumsy animal" (37); she lurches and blurts (47), flops and fidgets; her body is "heavy," "simply without style or grace"; her face, "chunky enough to begin with," grows "red and puffy" when she cries (50). Only when engaged in activities such as horseback riding, for which there exist "traditional and even reasonable rules for one's posture every minute of the time," does Rennie achieve grace and beauty. "But she could not handle her body in situations where there were no rules" (50). In other words, only when Rennie submits her unwieldy physicality to the restraints of reason does she become something more in Jake's eyes than a clumsy animal. Coupled with Jake's revulsion towards the emotional, such observations reveal less about Rennie's clumsiness than about Jake's distrust of the physical.

This distrust is everywhere apparent in the novel. Human flesh, when dwelled upon at all, is portrayed as fragile, distasteful, even grotesque. This unsettling synecdoche is used to describe women on the beach at Ocean City: "a forest of legs ruined by childbirth; fallen breasts, potbellies, haggard faces, and strident voices; a rats' nest of horrid children, as unlovely as they were obnoxious" (21). Peggy Rankin, Rennie's double, is described in similarly unflattering terms: "She was slender, not very full-breasted, well tanned, and in no way extraordinary" (22). Like Rennie, when she cries "little of loveliness" (26) is left in her face. In general, however, Jake's physical descriptions are circumspect to the point of curtness. The Doctor's physical appearance, for example, is dispensed with in a single sentence: "He was bald, dark-eyed, and dignified, a Negro, and wore a graying mustache and trim tweed suit to match" (69). Joe is drawn in three words: "tall, bespectacled, athletic" (14).

Such reticence extends to descriptions of the physical environment. Except for three rooms (the Doctor's Progress and Advice Room, the Morgans' living room, and Jake's apartment) which function less as settings than as rhetorical devices, the external world receives scant notice in *The End of the Road*. This has led Tony Tanner to complain of "an absence or attenuation of environment"[15] in Barth's early fiction, and Daniel Majdiak to observe that "Horner's tendency is to ignore the physical world and concentrate on the mental."[16] If the very fact of Jake's narrative removes him at least once from the experiences he has turned into speech, the abstract nature of that speech removes him even further. Jake's frequently grandiloquent style also contributes to this detachment. While Barth has done much to help dispel the myth that a naturalistic style is somehow less artificial and therefore more mimetic of "reality" than are highly rhetorical styles, naturalistic style nonetheless preserves the *illusion* of intimacy with the physical world. The more grandly "inflated" a style becomes, the less secure becomes the illusion of mimesis. Jake's style, particularly its syntax, frequently strains toward the sublime: "A turning down of dinner damped, in ways subtle past knowing, manic keys on the thin flute of me, least pressed of all, which for a moment had shrilled me rarely" (19). Such locutions are self-consciously crafted, their ornamental artificiality proclaimed. Confronting them, the reader "is never allowed to forget . . . the tenuous relationship between the artifact he is encountering and the dimensions of 'reality' in which he is himself immersed."[17] The exiguity of the physical in Jake's narrative is reinforced by the self-conscious artificiality of its style. Jake is removed, at least metaphorically, from the world of physical and emotional involvement, thereby displaying his fear of such involvement.

In Chapter 12, however, these narrative devices are suddenly abandoned. Style becomes straightforward and unadorned, presentation starkly dramatic. The physical realm is confronted directly and the physical details of Rennie's abortion are recorded in graphic, "naturalistic" terms. This seemingly precipitous shift in modes has prompted Jac Tharpe's speculation that the account of Rennie's death may once have formed a separate short story.[18] But the sudden use of excessive naturalistic details assumes an integral function in Barth's narrative. We are subtly prepared for this shift in the previous chapter. Jake's zany efforts to secure erogate for Rennie having failed, he desperately seeks aid from the Doctor. Before making his plea, he glances at the surrounding landscape: "It was cool outside, even chilly, but the sun shone brightly, and out over a marshy creek behind the farmhouse a big gray fish hawk hung motionless against the wind" (170). Despite the offhand manner of its presentation, the description arrests our attention, for it is one of the few instances when Jake has noticed the natural realm at all and is easily his most extended description of it thus far. Moreover, we realize that the description is not entirely "objective." The fish hawk hanging "motionless" in the wind evokes Jake's earlier immobility. Indeed, the description may be seen as a figure of Jake's ambivalence. On the one hand, it points to the realm of physical (and, by analogy, emotional) involvement in which his "play for responsibility" has indubitably embroiled him. On the other, its hint of paralysis recalls his instinctive aversion to that realm. The passage thus represents a pause, a cautious hesitation between two alternatives, before Jake makes his fatal commitment to Rennie and the physical and emotional world.

Chapter 12 dramatizes the result of that commitment. Jake's choice having been made, he refuses to flinch from the sight, sound, and feel of Rennie's torment.

> The Doctor washed his hands and drew up the sheet from Rennie's abdomen. . . . A minute or so later, when the Doctor slipped his hands into rubber gloves, greased the fingers, and began the internal examination, she started sobbing. . . . The surgical instruments clinked in the sterilizer, and Rennie's sobbing became looser and louder. She twisted a little on the examination table and even began to raise herself. . . . A wide leather strap was secured across Rennie's diaphragm. . . . [Her] legs were drawn up and spread wide in the lithotomy position. Mrs. Dockey gripped one, pressing the calf against the thigh, and I, very reluctantly, held the other. . . . A few moments later — I would guess that the Doctor had applied his curette . . . — she began screaming, and tried to kick free. . . . Mrs. Dockey pushed Rennie's head down and clamped a hand over her mouth. Rennie kicked wildly with her free leg; the Doctor jumped clear, upsetting his stool, and cursed. I inadvertently glanced away and saw blood on the sheet under Rennie's abdomen, blood on her upper thighs, blood on the Doctor's glove. [179–80]

This, Jake seems to insist, indicates the ravages to which all flesh is heir. For if Rennie is Jake and Joe's victim, as some have argued,[19] the context of the novel makes clear that she is also the victim of her own physicality. Despite the calculated efforts of Jake and Joe, Rennie conceives. Frightened and in pain, Rennie wants to "hold still" during surgery but cannot. Given gas to constrain her, she seems "anxious to lose consciousness" (181), but again her body betrays her and she chokes on her own vomit. Like Hemingway's Catherine Barkley, Rennie has succumbed to "the biological trap."

Not surprisingly, it is the physical aftermath of her strangulation
with which Jake is obsessed and that he compulsively records:

> And so this is the picture I have to carry with me: the Treat-
> ment Room dark except for the one ceiling floodlight that il-
> luminated the table; Rennie dead there now, face mottled,
> eyes wide, mouth agape, the vomitus running from a pool in
> her mouth to a pool under her head; the great black belt lying
> finally unbuckled across the sheet over her chest and stomach;
> the lower part of her body nude and bloody, her legs trailing
> limply and clumsily off the end of the examination table. [182]

An echo of Todd's description of his hanged father's swollen face,
the passage makes clear that Chapter 12 serves as a rationalization
for Jake's abandonment of the world of sensory involvement. He
has gotten involved, and this is the result. The devastation of Rennie, symbol of the body, functions in Jake's narrative as explanation of and justification for his exchange of the "lived" world for a
verbalized one.

The ethical implications of Jake's retreat into language have
troubled some critics. Campbell Tatham, after complaining that
"the act of turning an experience into speech does not so much fal-
sify as *nihilate* . . . it, necessarily removes it from the experiential
realm altogether,"[20] hints that Barth may share Jake's love of abstraction. Similarly, Tony Tanner, disturbed by the "very nominal
sense of concrete reality" in *The End of the Road*, writes,

> those things which usually circumscribe consciousness and
> with the direct pressure of their presence help to condition
> thought have receded or been excluded and in the resultant
> cleared ground the mind runs free. This is why it is of some
> importance whether we take that mind to be only Horner's —
> or Barth's as well. Not because one is interested in knowing
> whether there is anything autobiographical in the book, but
> because it influences our assessment of Barth's own attitude to
> that ambiguous license enjoyed by a mind for which words
> are no longer answerable to things.[21]

Yet the very absence of the world from Jake's narrative validates
the presence of the world in his consciousness. When Jake turns at
last to face that world in Chapter 12 and it comes crashing through
his defenses, we should realize that he takes no solace in the fact
that "words are no longer answerable to things." His retreat into

articulation represents his efforts to regain verbal superiority over an implosive universe. In this respect his effort may be a paradigmatic esthetic act. Like most great artists of our age, Jake has peered beneath the mask that hides nature's flux, only to discover what Rennie finds within herself: nothingness. His response to his horror is not the madness of a Kurtz or an Ahab, though the symptoms of madness inform portions of Barth's metaphor; rather, he chooses the solution of a Marlowe, or of the Ishmael faintly echoed in the first words of his narrative, or, for that matter, of a Todd Andrews. He chooses the lies-that-order: art.

Articulation is his absolute, for "reality" only exists in a manner of speaking. While it may be true, as Tatham argues, that talk about the world necessitates a turning away from the world, it is equally (if paradoxically) true that such talk also restores the world to man. Language may be a hermetic system of purely self-referential signs, but *articulation* — the conversion of language into speech (or writing) — opens language's closed system to the world. To talk about the world is to *intend* the world, to imbue it with intelligibility and thus to make it accessible. (Recall the Doctor's words about fiction as a true representation of the way people perceive "reality.") "It is language," writes Mikel Dufrenne, "which introduces the requisite distance between the signifying and the signified. It is by the mediation of language that the interval is created where thought can come into play. Nevertheless . . . the mediation is one that separates and unites at the same time. If language digs a trench between the world and me, it also throws a bridge across it."[22] We become *human* beings-in-the-world, "alive and kicking" (112–13), only when that world has been made intelligible by language. An unarticulated "reality" is a contradiction in terms. Since Jake's retreat is into articulation, not into the silence of cosmopsis, it represents a bid for intelligibility and thus for life. His narrative is ethical as well as orphic.[23]

Yet the ethical concerns of Barth's novel remain implicit. Indeed, the only fully formulated value system in the novel (Joe's) is clearly rejected by Barth. Barth's point seems to be that although language defines the boundaries of our world, it by no means circumscribes everything of human value. Joe's error lies in his belief that it does. His insistence that "a man can act coherently" and "in ways that he can explain, if he wants to" (43) opens him to the same charge of romantic rationalism that Iris Murdoch levels against Sartre;[24]

moreover, it edges his position in the direction of logical positivism. "Have I got to agree with Rennie that you don't even exist?"
(111) he exclaims when Jake is unable to supply a motivation for
his adultery with Rennie. Like the logical positivists who derive
their philosophy from a misinterpretation of Wittgenstein's *Tractatus*, Joe maintains that if something exists it can be talked about,
and, conversely, if it cannot be talked about it does not exist. But
Wittgenstein, whom the Doctor quotes, believes that while language sets the *logical* limits of what "the case" is, much exists that
cannot be logically deduced and therefore cannot be spoken
about. Values, for example, lie outside the province of rational discourse and therefore must be "consigned to silence." Logical
"propositions can express nothing of what is higher," Wittgenstein
writes; therefore "it is clear that ethics cannot be put into words."[25]
Like all values Wittgenstein found authentic, ethics belong to the
ineffable realm of the "mystical." Perhaps Barth has sentiments
such as these in mind when, in comparing his first two novels, he
says, "I deliberately had [Todd Andrews] end up with that brave
ethical subjectivism in order that Jacob Horner might undo that
position in #2 and carry all *non-mystical* value-thinking to the end
of the road."[26]

As a *codified* body of values, ethical systems are rooted firmly in
language and are definitely nonmystical. Like all generalizations,
they often float disembodied above the particular situations they
are powerless to inform. Jake complains after reading Sartre, "I
. . . had difficulty deciding how to apply him to specific situations
(How did existentialism help one to decide whether to carry one's
lunch to work or buy it in the factory cafeteria?)" (81). More to the
point, what ethical system could possibly clarify the human complexities surrounding Rennie's pregnancy? Should Jake follow the
example of Joe, who out of a specious sense of "love" is willing to
let Rennie shoot herself? Or should he violate the law and his own
inhibitions, not to mention risking Rennie's health, and secure for
her an abortion? Do his feelings of responsibility for getting Rennie that abortion excuse his cruel manipulation of Peggy Rankin?
Like Abraham's famous dilemma, Jake is caught in an ethical double bind, and much fear and trembling accompanies it.

But if ethical values transcend language, the *revelation* of those
values through human action[27] depends paradoxically on the principle of falsification intrinsic in language. For ethics are predicated

not only on the belief that human beings matter but also on the belief that each human being possesses some kind of autonomous essence. Jake, however, has reached the conclusion that "Existence not only precedes essence; in the case of human beings it rather defies essence" (122). If this is true, to relate effectively and meaningfully to a human being one must be able to *simplify* that human being, at least to a degree, in order to ignore his or her fundamental *in*essentiality. This, too, proves problematic. Excessive simplification leads to caricature, a denial of another's relative worth as a human being. Insofar as Jake engages in such caricature in his first affair with Peggy, his behavior is reprehensible. But an unqualified assent to the full complexity of a human being also denies "essential" humanity, for it involves the realization that human essence is not intrinsic but ascribed. Human beings partake of the same flux they occupy. Our perceptions of others must find some middle ground between what, in another context, Tony Tanner describes as "stasis" on the one hand and a "fluid jelly" on the other.[28] Language, when used responsibly, supplies the necessary mediation. Two phrases recur like refrains throughout *The End of the Road:* "I don't give a damn" and, in counterpoint, variations on the phrase "You're oversimplifying." The former recurs nine times; the latter, eleven.[29] In order to give a damn, the motif suggests, a degree of simplification short of oversimplification is necessary. Because people matter, articulation matters — and vice versa.

Ralph Ellison has written, "We cannot live . . . in the contemplation of chaos, but neither can we live without an awareness of chaos, and the means through which we achieve that awareness, and through which we assert our humanity most significantly against it, is great art."[30] Insofar as *The End of the Road* acknowledges while it asserts itself against chaos, one is tempted to consider Ellison's noble words as a coda to Barth's novel. But these words, as the Doctor might say, are based on "good existential premises" (82), and Barth, as his treatment of Joe's philosophy indicates, is no more an existentialist than the Doctor is. A "super pragmatist," the Doctor is interested in the efficacy, not the truth or falsity, of our formulations. Indeed, falsity must be taken for granted, at least in any ultimate sense. In Jean Kennard's astute observation, "What the Doctor does in fact is to apply the Existentialist premise that there are no absolutes to Existentialist premises themselves. . . ."[31] When the Doctor scolds Jake near the end of the novel, he tells him, "If you'd studied your *World Almanac* every day, and thought of nothing but your grammar students, and practiced Sinistrality, Antecedence, and Alphabetical Priority—*particularly if you thought them absurd but practiced them anyway*—nothing that happened would have been a problem for you" (171, italics mine). The trick is to be aware that our lies about "reality" are indeed lies, yet to remain simultaneously convinced by them. Fruitful paradox, this principle maintains a delicate balance between the destructive positivism of a Joe Morgan and the immobilizing nihilism of a Jake Horner. As embodiment of this paradox, the Doctor—mysterious, protean, tricksterlike; half-charlatan, half-sage—adumbrates his various avatars: Henry Burlingame III, Harold Bray, Proteus, Polyeidus, and, with the exception of Lady Amherst, comes as close to a normative character as one is likely to find in Barth's fiction.

But Barth is not an existentialist for yet another reason. Predicated on a belief in a Cartesian split between consciousness and world, existentialism, particularly Sartrean existentialism, is at base dualistic.[32] Indeed, the quotation from Ellison betrays an identical disjunction, pitting man in Camusian revolt against the chaos which contains him. Despite Jake's neurotic tendency to perpetuate a similar split, the hint of mystical unity found in *The Floating Opera* recurs in *The End of the Road*. Jake's remarks on "the Janusian ambivalence of the universe . . . the world's charming equipoise, its ubiquitous polarity" (130) imply a nondualistic conjunction of opposites and resemble Todd's equally uncharacteristic musings on the Platonic implications of the "doubler" crab. Indeed, as Jac Tharpe observes, Jake's cosmopsis is "a transcendentalism," a mystical "view of the whole."[33] Contained in the "absurdist" context of Barth's early novels, such holistic inklings disclose the suspicion that chaos, if viewed from a more visionary perspective, might resolve itself into that "order complex unto madness" visualized by Bellerophon four books later. Not mystics, Todd and Jake interpret their intimations of immortality as threats of utter annihilation; thus they erect mytho-therapeutic shields against their vision. These shields, their respective fictions, are emblematic of each protagonist/narrator's ambivalent fear of and desire for the world of physical reality.

Yet a progression in the two novels may be discerned. Todd's linguistic reappropriation of "reality" remains tenuous, cautious;

ontologically insecure, he trusts no one, least of all his reader. Moreover, his protective use of language seems instinctive, less a planned strategy than a diagnostic symptom of his paranoia. In *The End of the Road*, however, what for Todd is a psychological reflex action becomes for Jake a conscious therapeutic program. Rather than concealing the fictive nature of his narrative, he uses the Doctor's words about mythotherapy to justify his artifice. He still fears the threat of a potentially implosive physical world; nevertheless, his return to that world through language seems less hesitant than Todd's. This progression continues in Barth's next novel, which examines physicality—both the world of things and man's carnal nature—with rare comic relish. Moreover, the vision of unity glimpsed in the first two novels is faced more squarely in *The Sot-Weed Factor*, as mythotherapy begins to give way to mythopoesis.

NOTES

1. Prince, "Interview," pp. 56–57. Recently Barth attributed his preoccupation with doubles and doubling to the fact that he is an opposite-sex fraternal twin. "My books tend to come in pairs," he writes, "my sentences"—referring to his love of the semicolon—"in twin members." Barth also relates his concern with schizophrenia as well as his general theory of language to the fact of his twinship. See "Some Reasons Why I Tell the Stories I Tell."

2. Barth calls it the "companion piece" to his first novel; Prince, "Interview," p. 47.

3. Barth, *The End of the Road*, rev. ed. (Garden City, N.Y.: Doubleday, 1967), p. 114. Subsequent references to this edition appear in parentheses in the text.

4. Smith, "Barth's Endless Road," p. 72.

5. Cf. Todd's statement near the end of *The Floating Opera:* "I considered too whether, in the real absence of absolutes, values less than absolute mightn't be regarded as in no way inferior and even be lived by" (pp. 251–52).

6. Morrell, *Barth*, p. 19.

7. Rogers, *Psychoanalytic Study of the Double*, pp. 170–71.

8. Ibid., p. 171.

9. Ibid., p. 170.

10. Freud, "Notes upon a Case of Obsessional Neurosis," in *Collected Papers*, III, 368.

11. Ibid., p. 376.

12. Ibid., p. 374.

13. Tatham, "Message," p. 280.

14. McConnell, *Four Postwar American Novelists*, p. 130.

15. Tanner, *City of Words*, p. 240.

16. Majdiak, "Barth and the Representation of Life," p. 62.

17. Tatham, "Message," p. 274.

18. Tharpe, *Barth*, p. 32.

19. E.g., Nolland, "Barth and the Novel of Comic Nihilism," p. 247; Stubbs, "Barth as a Novelist of Ideas," p. 107.

20. Tatham, "Message," p. 274.

21. Tanner, *City of Words*, p. 240.

22. Dufrenne, *Language and Philosophy*, p. 73.

23. An excellent analysis of the orphic use of language is found in Bruns, *Modern Poetry*, especially Ch. 8. My own thinking about the significance of language and articulation in Barth's work has been greatly influenced by Bruns's insightful study.

24. Murdoch, *Sartre, Romantic Rationalist*.

25. Wittgenstein, *Tractatus Logico-philosophicus*, p. 145.

26. Bluestone, "Wain and Barth," p. 586.

27. As Justin Hartnack points out, Wittgenstein believed that values are "associated with *feeling*" and "can be revealed but not put into words" (*Wittgenstein and Modern Philosophy*, p. 40).

28. Tanner, *City of Words*, pp. 18–19.

29. The first phrase occurs on pp. 20, 39, 45, 56, 104, 126, 138, and 146 (twice); the second on pp. 18, 21, 35 (twice), 36, 63, 106, 115, 144 (twice), and 147.

30. Ralph Ellison, "Society, Morality, and the Novel."

31. Kennard, *Number and Nightmare*, p. 66. See also Jac Tharpe's brief but penetrating discussion of the denial of existentialist principles in *The End of the Road* (*Barth*, pp. 27, 30).

32. Barrett, *Irrational Man*, pp. 256–57.

33. Tharpe, *Barth*, p. 27. See also McConnell, *Four Postwar American Novelists*, pp. 132–33, which discusses cosmopsis as an inversion of the romantic epiphany.

4
The Language of Experience: "Reality" in
The Sot-Weed Factor

"The discrepancy between the idea of the rational life and the kinds of facts of our nonrational or counter-rational nature with which we indeed live interests me," Barth has said.[1] This is an understatement, for the discrepancy to which Barth refers is of central focus in his fiction. Four characters in Barth's first three novels involuntarily beshit themselves, and another is mortified by her inadvertent fart. In his relationship with Jane, Todd is chagrined first by a premature ejaculation, then by intermittent impotency (a condition that similarly embarrasses Perseus). The wayward male genital also troubles George Giles, who, having embraced Anastasia, makes the following observation: "My penis rose, unbid by *George*; was it a George of its own? A quarter-billion beasties were set to swarm therefrom and thrash like salmon up the mucous of her womb; were they little Georges all?"[2] Driven by similar "counter-rational" urges, that arch-rationalist Joe Morgan masturbates while picking his nose; Ebenezer Cook, pledged to a life of virginity, twice almost rapes the woman who inspired his oath; George, fired by the compulsion to "be," nearly ravishes his mother. Barth's vision can be marvelously carnal, and he takes a Swiftian delight in the instinctive side of man's nature.

But even if human excrement can be wildly funny in certain contexts, there is nothing humorous about the blood which stains Rennie Morgan's thighs or the vomit she fatally aspirates. Sex's dark double is death. Sex begets protoplasm; protoplasm decays.[3] Death is the reality against which Barth's first two protagonists erect their shields of words. If a retreat into language constitutes a symbolic act of annihilation, as some critics have charged, the failure to retreat may result in literal annihilation, as the final chapter of *The End of the Road* powerfully dramatizes. Yet Jake's withdrawal from experience in order to articulate experience paradoxically constitutes a return to experience, or at least makes that return possible. Jake's narration is a verbal reappropriation of a "reality" whose implosive destructiveness has driven him from it. In reconceptualizing the world Jake regains the world — and it regains him. Just as those "reflective intervals," those pensive rests "before returning to the swim," keep the literate spermatozoon of "Night-Sea Journey" afloat, so mankind is kept afloat by "the conceptual network through which [we] view the world."[4]

This conceptual network, what Thomas S. Kuhn terms a "paradigm," does not describe "reality" so much as it constitutes it. Indeed, without paradigms it becomes questionable whether perception is even possible. "What a man sees," Kuhn explains, "depends both upon what he looks at and also upon what his previous visual-conceptual experience has taught him to see. In the absence of such training there can only be, in William James's phrase, 'a bloomin' buzzin' confusion.'"[5] Henry Burlingame III expresses a similar idea during one of his debates with Ebenezer: "'Tis but a grossness of perception, is't not, that lets us speak of *Thames* and *Tigris*, or even *France* and *England*, but especially *me* and *thee*, as though what went by those names or others in time past hath some connection with the present object? I'faith, for that matter how is't we speak of *objects* if not that our coarse vision fails to note their change? The world's indeed a flux, as Heraclitus declared: the very universe is naught but change and motion."[6]

It should be emphasized that Henry's formulation stops short of solipsism. Barth never doubts the existence of the external world; rather, he questions our ability to perceive it "objectively." Indeed, it is the arbitrary *thereness* of phenomenal reality that Barth describes as "a driving impulse for writers." A "certain kind of sensibility," he theorizes, "can be made very uncomfortable by the recognition of the *arbitrariness* of physical facts and the inability to accept their *finality*. Take France, for example: France is shaped like a tea pot, and Italy is shaped like a boot. Well, okay. But the idea that that's the only way it's ever going to be, that they'll never be shaped like anything else—that can get to you after a while."[7] Barth does not add what is implicit in Burlingame's words—that if we see France as a teapot and Italy as a boot, it is because "France" and "Italy," "teapots" and "boots" exist in our minds. *They* are our ideas. What actually *exists* is a configuration of mass and energy manifested as an undifferentiated flow of sensations impinging upon our perceptual apparatus. Our conceptual paradigm, really a theory about the world, then filters and differentiates the flow of sensations, arresting its Heraclitean flux, perceptually and conceptually subdividing the world in a certain way. As Colin Murray Turbayne observes, "We cannot say what reality is, only what it seems like to us, imprisoned in Plato's cave, because we cannot get outside to look. The consequence is that we never know exactly what the facts are. We are always victims of adding some interpretation. We cannot help but allocate, sort, or bundle the facts in some way or another."[8] What this activity reduces to finally is metaphor, figures of speech. Call this "France," that a "teapot"; I, in a sense, am "Jacob Horner." The search, then, is not for truth, but "for the best possible metaphor."[9]

The major theme of Barth's first two novels is the way man invents himself through metaphors. Todd Andrews and Jake Horner undergo what might be termed gestalt switches. The old familiar world suddenly grows threatening in its inscrutability; ontological insecurity results; both protagonists erect metaphorical constructs, their respective narratives, to regain psychic equilibrium. At some point between the completion of those first two novels and the composition of the third, Barth must have realized that what happens to individuals happens as well to entire cultures. If the world, though "real" in its ontological thereness, is also fictive in that our consciousness of it is always intentional, it stands to reason that as our perceptions of the world change, the world itself changes—not figuratively, but literally.

Scientific revolutions are precipitated by just such perceptual changes. An anomaly is proposed that resists assimilation into existing scientific paradigms. If accommodation between the competing paradigms fails, full-scale revolution breaks out. Sometimes these revolutions are restricted to fields so narrowly specialized that outsiders view them as simple progress, as normal developments in human knowledge—for example, the impact of the discovery of

X-rays on radiation therapy and cathode-ray tube research. Sometimes they are Copernican in scope, issuing in totally new *Weltansichts*. The shift from a geocentric to a heliocentric universe changed the world so drastically that men were actually able to perceive things they had been incapable of seeing before. "Can it conceivably be an accident," Kuhn asks rhetorically, "that Western astronomers first saw change in the previously immutable heavens during the half-century after Copernicus' new paradigm was first proposed"[10] — changes that Chinese astronomers, with far less sophisticated instruments but a cosmological paradigm that did not preclude heavenly change, had been recording for centuries? More significantly, what might be termed the Copernican succession invalidated the sixteenth-century conception of an uninterrupted correspondence between macrocosm, geocosm, and microcosm — the universe, man, and the terrestrial globe. Ptolemy and Plato gave way to Bacon, Galileo, Descartes, and finally Newton, whose *Principia* completed the transformation of animate universe to clockwork machine. In Marjorie Hope Nicolson's elegant phrase, the sixteenth-century "Circle of Perfection" was broken.[11]

Against this historical backdrop Barth sets the events of *The Sot-Weed Factor*. In doing research for that novel he must have been struck by the congenial spirit linking that age to his own. Caught between the ebb of an old *Weltanschauung* and the incipient flood of the new, we also occupy a time of paradigmatic shift. Early in this century the Newtonian model of the universe began to yield to new metaphoric formulations of the universe. Non-Euclidean curved space, relativity and discontinuity, the interpenetration of space and time, the interchangeability of mass and energy — such notions may not yet have become part of our consciously felt realities ("As individuals we still live in calendar and clock time," Barth observes, "and no matter how that time may be discredited by physicists, it's nevertheless the kind of time we live in during most of our waking experiences."[12]), but their effect on our unconscious lives may be considerable. Our celebrated sense of *Angst*, a seemingly endless succession of wars and crises, religious and political upheavals, an intense intellectual fermentation in which truths previously held self-evident are radically called into question — each of these, if not the effect of a paradigmatic shift, may be among its more prominent manifestations.

That Ebenezer Cooke's seventeenth century was an age of similar confusion and desperation is epitomized in Donne's somber threnody, "The First Anniversary" (written in 1611), characterized by Marjorie Hope Nicolson as "a dirge upon the decay and death of man, of the world, of the universe."[13] Such eschatological sentiments should ring familiar to readers of modern and postmodern literature, with its similar themes of entropy and spiritual anomie. Indeed, as Frank J. Warnke observes, the apocalyptic imagination forms as integral a part of the Baroque period in literature (1580–1680) as of the postmodern. The "theme of disenchantment, *desengano*, the refusal to entertain either a facile sense of order or a facile faith in progress, gives the writers [of this age] an obvious modern relevance, as does their feeling for the absurd, issuing as a preoccupation with paradox and complex irony." Other features of the literature of this era — a self-reflexive and irrealistic quality ("Baroque poetry, whether as the vivid distortion of the senses or as the witty subversion of the intellect, is a kind of art at the farthest remove from the naive imitation of observed reality"); a love of paradox and contradiction; a conception of the world as essentially fictive ("Reality is merely something played, but at the same time the something played is reality, in the only terms in which we can understand it"); and a blackly humorous combination of levity and seriousness, playfulness and sobriety — reveal further resemblances to the literature of our own age.[14]

But while Barth sets *The Sot-Weed Factor* in these turbulent times, and while his novel incorporates certain themes and techniques reminiscent of the literature of the seventeenth century, the form he most clearly imitates is the eighteenth-century novel. He is thus able to evoke simultaneously the origin of the novel as a genre and the development of the worldview out of which that genre grew. Like its Baroque antecedents, the eighteenth-century novel reflects many of the assumptions of the "New Science"; unlike those predecessors, however, it does not resist but affirms and indeed embodies these assumptions. In one sense, the novel may be seen as our first "anti-Aristotelian" genre in its rejection of the notion of universals which undergirds world views from classicism through the late Renaissance.[15] According to the "New Science," truth was discoverable through the senses, as individual scientist objectively observed the *particulars* of experience. Implicit in the empirical model is the freedom of the investigator from past models and traditions in his disinterested pursuit of truth. The new focus, then, was on particular, not general, truth; on innovative, not traditional, methods. The novel, in Ian Watt's words, "is the form of literature which most fully reflects this individualist and innovating reorientation."[16]

Particularly in the novels of Defoe and Richardson, the primacy of individual experience is asserted over the previous domination of plot (which for Aristotle is the "soul" of tragedy). Moreover, plots were not derived from previous literature, in the manner of Chaucer and Shakespeare, but were *original* in the new sense of the term. (As Watt points out, a semantic reversal in the eighteenth century changed the meaning of *original* from its earlier definition — "having existed from the first" — to its modern meaning — "underived, independent, first-hand").[17] Emphasis on the particular also affected characterization. Particular individuals in particular settings at particular times replaced the general human types who had been placed "against a background primarily determined by the appropriate literary convention" (e.g., the pastoral, tragedy). Language, too, became plainer, more referential to empirical experience, less reliant on rhetorical flourish or generic decorum. Style in the new genre aimed for an air of authenticity. The narrative conventions constituting formal realism, then, grew out of or at least concomitantly to philosophical and scientific realism. "The premise, or primary convention" of the eighteenth-century novel was that it "is a full and authentic report of human experience, and is therefore under obligation to satisfy its reader with such details of the story as the individuality of the actors concerned, the particulars of the times and places of their actions, details which are presented through a more largely referential use of language than is common in other literary forms."[18] This premise, with important modifications, persists to the present day.

The fact that *The Sot-Weed Factor* departs radically from the conventions of the realistic novel is obvious. By burlesquing many of the eighteenth-century novel's conventions and totally upending others (through the use of an elaborate plot, for example, or of language that calls attention to itself, or of characters that in their protean transformations lack particularity), Barth rejects the conventions of realism in general and the assumptions that gives those conventions validity. In this respect, at least, *The Sot-Weed Factor* may be seen as a metanovel; it comments on the origins and, by implication, the history of the novel. Moreover, just as the novels of Defoe, Richardson, and to a lesser extent Fielding[19] represent a drastic movement away from the literature of the past, so *The Sot-Weed Factor* represents Barth's declaration of independence from the conventions of the no-longer-so-novel genre in which he works. "*The Sot-Weed Factor* was composed," he told an interviewer, "with certain things in mind about the history of the novel, including the history of my own novels. By the time I began to compose *The Sot-Weed Factor* . . . I was more acquainted with the history of literature than I'd been when I began to write fiction. And so I set about to untie my hands; I presumptuously felt them tied by the history of the genre and, less presumptuously, by the kinds of things that I myself had been writing before."[20] Finally, just as the innovations of the early novelists grew out of as they reflected a new worldview, Barth's innovations similarly signal the advent of a new *Weltanschauung*.

Barth properly insists that *The Sot-Weed Factor*'s "final relevance is strictly contemporary,"[21] a relevance partially conveyed by the novel's submerged analogy between two ages suffering the throes of paradigmatic conversion and the forms of fiction those throes produced. This may explain Barth's decision to widen the scope of the novel and to abandon the realistic mode of his first two novels (although the assumptions of those novels are not realistic). Whereas his interest in the earlier novels had been in the artist's response to the psychological trauma that results when one's bearings in "reality" are suddenly lost, that interest turns in *The Sot-Weed Factor* to the fictive nature of "reality." To phrase it differently, because his first two novels may be seen as metaphors for the condition of the artist in a postmodern world, Barth restricts his focus to the respective consciousness of single individuals and the extension of those consciousnesses into narrative form. *The Sot-Weed Factor*, on the other hand, stands as a metaphor for the nature of postmodern "reality" itself.

Perhaps the distinguishing characteristic of postmodern "reality" is not its fictiveness (all eras are similarly fictive) but its self-conscious awareness of that fictiveness. Barth's task was to create a form that accomplished at least the following: (1) As a new novel growing out of and reflecting the incipient postmodern *Weltanschauung*, it should evoke the history of the novel, which had its inception in and was a reflection of an earlier, entirely different *Weltanschauung*. That is, as an imitation of an eighteenth-century novel it should mock both the assumptions of realism and the novelistic conventions based on those assumptions. (2) As an embodiment of the particular postmodern view of "reality" Barth finds most compelling, his novel should suggest the essentially fictive (which is to say, linguistic) basis of all reality constructions without at the same time denying the existence of the corporeal world. All the while it should reflect our postmodern self-consciousness about this fictiveness through a style and form that is itself self-consciously artificial. (3) As the putative final installment of a trilogy the first two novels of which had already been published, it should maintain the theme of those early novels, that of an individual's attempt to gain psychic balance through a reliance on metaphor, but extend that theme to include the similar teetering between paradigms of an entire culture. Altogether, this was an ambitious undertaking, but one that Barth accomplishes with consummate artistry.

Metonymy and *metaphor* are the terms Roman Jakobson uses to designate his formulation of the bipolar structure of language. *Metonymy* refers to the syntagmatic or "horizontal" axis of discourse, whereby "any linguistic unit at one and the same time serves as a context for simpler units and/or finds its own context in a more complex linguistic unit."[22] *Metaphor*, on the other hand, refers to the "vertical" or paradigmatic axis of discourse, and involves the selection, from a large but finite number of possibilities, of the single word ultimately used. Discourse involves the art of selecting items from a range of similar items and the act of combining in a certain way those items selected. In narrative, particularly realistic prose narrative, the reader is aware almost exclusively of metonymic processes. That is, no matter how great the author's struggle for *le mot juste* in his act of composing a work, no matter how many possible words he has considered and rejected, we see only the words actually chosen. Moreover, unless we are deliberately concentrating on style, we tend to "read through" the words themselves to the narrative events—the metonymic dimension—that claim our interest. Quoting Jakobson, Gerald Bruns describes the method of realistic narration as follows: " 'following the path of contiguous relationships, the realistic author metonymically digresses from the plot to the atmosphere and from the characters to the setting in place and time,' and by this means he builds up a system of details whose coherence is comparable to that of ordinary experience, in the sense that . . . our world is organized as a horizon within which things and events, persons and activities, present themselves to us on a contiguous basis."[23] In a novel such as *Finnegans Wake,* on the other hand, language veers sharply from the metonymic to the metaphoric pole of discourse. The absence of a contiguous narrative line, as well as the Joycean locutions, the tendency to collapse separate words, often from different languages, into a single word ("he sternely struxk his tete in a tub for to watsch the future of his fates but ere he swiftly stook it out again"), almost completely displaces the predicative, syntagmatic context, emphasizing solely the substitutive or metaphorical. This is hermetic language with a vengeance, a virtually unmitigated displacement of world by word.

Despite some Joycean influence, language in *The Sot-Weed Factor* purposely stops short of such radical displacement, maintaining, rather, an exuberant equilibrium between metaphor and metonomy. The metonymic dimension is evident enough in the novel's marvelously architectonic plot. One of Barth's intentions in writing the book was to "make up a plot that was fancier than *Tom Jones.*"[24] Although more than one critic has been tripped up in his attempt to summarize that plot, John Stark's contention that it is "haphazard," "oblivious to consistency," and "nearly impossible for anyone to understand"[25] is simply incorrect. As David Morrell points out, when the editors at Doubleday requested that Barth omit several scenes, "they discovered that, unlike the usual picaresque novel, *The Sot-Weed Factor* was so carefully and integrally plotted that no part could be eliminated without damage to the whole."[26] Not only its meandering path of contiguous relationships, but also the memorable and often hilarious qualities of the separate incidents which compose those relationships emphasize the element of narrative, compelling us to "read through" Barth's language to the event it conveys. Moreover, Barth's use of historical personages and events, his quotations from actual documents of the times and implicit and explicit allusions to others, and his deliberate evocation of the intellectual and cultural milieu of seventeenth-century England and America provide a rich contextual dimension that is similarly metonymic.

The novel's metaphoric dimension is equally conspicuous, however, particularly its mimicry of eighteenth-century locutions and syntax. Yet "foregrounding," Tony Tanner's term for Barth's mode of discourse, may be inappropriate except for certain isolated passages. In the formulation of Jan Mukarovský, the Prague structuralist from whom Tanner indirectly borrowed the term, foregrounding pushes "communication into the background as the objective of expression and of being used for its own sake; it is not used in the service of communication but in order to place in the foreground the act of expression, the act of speech itself."[27] As I have been suggesting, however, language in *The Sot-Weed Factor*, while certainly obtrusive, remains for the most part a transitive act; it does not push communication "into the background" so much as share center stage with it. A better description of Barth's use of language (one which he himself has applied to his fiction) is *irrealistic*. Barth attributes the term to Borges, but it probably originates with the French critic Maurice Blanchot.[28] "Irrealism," in Blanchot's usage, applies to *all* works of fiction, even those rich in descriptive "realistic" details, since all narratives are fabrications of language—an obvious enough observation, but one constantly forgotten. "It seems incredible," William H. Gass wryly muses, "the ease with which we sink through books quite out of sight, pass clamorous pages into soundless dreams. That novels should be made of words, and merely words, is shocking, really. It's as though you had discovered that your wife were made of rubber: the bliss of all those years, the fears . . . from sponge."[29]

Yet novels are words nonetheless. That being the case, Blanchot concludes, fiction's essence lies not in its image of reality but in the *absence* of reality, *le monde de l'irréalité*. "The more a writer moves us, by the several devices of his language, to acknowledge the artificial character of his writing," says Bruns paraphrasing Blanchot's argument, "the more securely does he situate his work in an 'irreal' world."[30] Unlike foregrounding, irrealism does not necessarily displace content with language, but insists that content *is* in fact language, that the fictional world, no matter how familiar, is artificial, irreal.[31] This is what Barth seems to have had in mind when he made his now famous statement about *The Sot-Weed Factor*: "A different way to come to terms with the discrepancy between art and the Real Thing is to affirm the artificial element in art (you can't get rid of it anyhow), and make the artifice part of your point."[32] The other part of his point is that the Real Thing is also "irreal," at least to the extent that its disclosure, its presence, depends on language. Perception thus resides in paradox. The presence of imaginary worlds in works of fiction depends upon the literal absence of those worlds, since they are words, not worlds, after all. Similarly, the presence of the world we occupy depends in part upon its absence, since our consciousness of it is always filtered through "terministic screens," the conceptual and perceptual paradigms which are at base linguistic.[33] In *The Sot-Weed Factor* the relationship between language and "reality" outside the novel is paralleled inside the novel by the relationship between metaphoric and metonymic activities of discourse. This latter relationship never quite achieves the balance of a status quo, instead maintaining a shifting, constantly adjusting rapprochement.

One might say that *The Sot-Weed Factor* "occurs" at that borderline between the purely expressive use of language and the transitive language of narrative. This counterpoise is appropriate, since the novel is concerned with borders of various kinds. Its temporal setting is an era of paradigmatic shift, as one worldview edges out another. Its physical setting similarly evokes the notion of borderlines. Explaining his choice of Maryland as a setting, Barth remarks, "Something like a border state (that's what Maryland is called, it's historically one of the border states, as well as being a tidewater area where the boundary between the land and the water, between one physical state and another, is negotiable and somewhat in doubt) can be a kind of emblem for other sorts of border states, ontological states, of personality, and the rest."[34] Indeed, characters in the novel do exist "in a kind of ongoing border state of existence."[35] Barth's use of historical events and personages in an obviously fabulative work produces yet another kind of borderline, what Raymond M. Olderman refers to as the "blurred distinction between fact and fiction."[36] In its self-conscious vacillation between two axes of discourse, language in *The Sot-Weed Factor* becomes emblematic of a concern with borderlines in general.

The celebrated seven-page kitchen debate between two scullery maids who exchange various epithets for "whore" in two languages provides a good illustration of how language occasionally shifts from one axis of discourse to another. Having just insulted Susan Warren (Joan Toast), Eben is pursuing the weeping prostitute through the house when he happens upon three women (also whores) playing cards in the kitchen. He asks if they are servants of the house, and one responds by identifying another as a "hooker," thus igniting the swearing contest. We are only a few lines into this bilingual tussle before the sheer virtuosity of Barth's language totally displaces narrative context. What had begun as a verbal contest modulates into a verbal *catalog,* veering from the metonymic axis of discourse horizontally undergirding the scene toward a vertical axis of absolute language. Another, perhaps less radical example is the rhyming duel between Burlingame and Eben on the road to Cambridge. The ebullient wit of the double and triple rhymes — and, in one exuberant burst of ingenuity, a sextuple rhyme: *"Piccadilly bombast"* with "sick-o'-filly-bum-blast" — also momentarily displaces the language of narrative. So does the inventory of foods to be consumed during the Ahatchwhoop eating contest:

> Of *keskowghnoughmass,* the yellowe-belly'd sunne-fish, tenne apiece.
> Of *copatone,* the sturgeon, one apiece.
> Of *pummahumpoughmass,* fry'd star-fish, three apiece.
> Of *pawpeconoughmass,* pype-fishes, four apiece, dry'd. [563]

And so on, for almost a full page. But how many of us read carefully every item in these catalogs? And need we? Is it not, rather, the *idea* that Barth has matched 114 English synonyms for *whore* with an equal number of French synonyms that interests and delights us? Indeed, the catalog itself, the actual piling up of words on the page, tends to overwhelm communication, liberating language from its narrative context. Passages such as these do deserve Tanner's designation as examples of foregrounding.

Yet Tanner's concern that they reflect as well "a major mood of the book, namely the dominance of words over things, the potency and independence of sheer language"[37] is only partially valid. These vertical flights of pure language are invariably retarded by the centripetal pull of the novel's narrative force. The whores' harangue ceases; Ebenezer is off again, locates Susan Warren, is coerced into marrying her; the contiguous horizontal relationships of Barth's byzantine plot flow on. Similarly, the culinary catalog is surrounded on both sides by carnality. Anticipating the feast, Burlingame and Attonce slap their bellies, bump their bums on the ground, blubber their lips, snap their fingers, open and shut their jaws "with great rapidite"; the "wondrous feast" commenced, they "pound and stryke" their backs and bellies, thrust fingers down their throats to induce vomiting; then Attonce lets "flie a tooling fart" and dies "upon the instant where he sat" (564). *The Sot-Weed Factor* abounds with flatulence, fornication, and feces, with pox, perversion, and plain old death — the blight man is born to. To be sure, the pure language of art and the language which constructs and transmits a fictional "reality" generally referential to the corporeal world as it is conventionally perceived compete in *The Sot-Weed Factor*, but the competition ends in a deliberate draw. Neither finally assumes a subordinate relationship to the other. The self-consciously bipolar nature of Barth's medium becomes his message: the world is both real and irreal, both physical and fictive.

One other element of the metaphoric axis of discourse is conveyed by the examples of purely expressive language we have been discussing. Any word contains an implicit vertical or paradigmatic dimension, for "it makes us think of the other words with which we associate it . . . and any other words formed on the same stem . . . and any other words rhyming with it or having a similar internal organization; and hosts of other associations as innumerable, indeed, as are the types of sentence or syntagma that might be formed around the [word] taken as a horizontal entity."[38] In the rhyming and swearing contests, this substitutive dimension implicit in all words is explicitly rendered. Both contests not only are exercises in but also may be seen as emblems of the substitutive dimension of discourse. They may point as well to a similar quality in "reality." Things are things, words words, but in the act of perception things and words spring together in ways already discussed. To change the way we talk about the world is to change the way we apprehend the world. Hence the world — or at least its linguistically constituent part, perhaps the only part we perceive — shares the same syndrome of substitutability that characterizes discourse.

As a metaphor for "reality" conceived in these terms, *The Sot-Weed Factor* conveys the idea of substitutability in a variety of ways — even, indeed, by what Barth calls *"the fact of the artifact itself."*[39] Implicit in the physical existence of the 1967 authorized edition of *The Sot-Weed Factor* are all other versions of the novel, not only the actual — such as the 1960 edition which Barth later revised, and all the early drafts of the book available in the manuscript room of the Library of Congress — but the *potential*, since one can extrapolate from the whores' catalog the fact that for every word in the authorized version several other words could have been substituted. The possibilities inherent in this notion are realized with hilarious results in Barth's "modernized" version of *Oedipus Rex* in *Giles Goat-Boy*, and recently we have had alternative versions of *Macbeth* (Ionesco's *Macbett*), *Hamlet (Rosencrantz and Guildenstern Are Dead)*, and *Beowulf* (Gardner's *Grendel*). Indeed, portions of *The Sot-Weed Factor* represent John Barth's substitute version of John Smith's version of the Pocahontas story. Actually, Barth gives us two versions, Smith's and Sir Henry Burlingame's; the historical John Smith gave us four, all variant and none (as Philip Young points out) any more authentic than Barth's.[40] *The Sot-Weed Factor* also constitutes Barth's substitute version of early Maryland history, the materials for which he gleaned from the versions contained in *The Archives of Maryland;* and his version of the life of Ebenezer Cooke, the materials for which he borrowed from yet another version, Lawrence Wroth's biography.[41]

Barth's use of narrative viewpoint and perspective contributes further to the substitutive context of *The Sot-Weed Factor*. For the first and only time, he departs from the first-person narrative point of view. Unlike the first two novels, which may generally be seen as "closed structures" in Sharon Spencer's definition, *The Sot-Weed Factor* has an open structure: "Whereas novels with closed structures are erected upon a deliberate restriction of perspective to one point of view . . . open-structured novels embody multiple perspectives, some of which are actually contradictory." Because such openness often constitutes "an intellectual exploration undertaken by a novelist who actually is not certain what he believes about the nature of reality," borderline states ("fact versus fictions, imagination versus observation, feeling versus thought, creation versus reportage, and so on") are not uncommon in these novels. Creators of open-structured works aspire toward the "approximation of diffusion; of flux; of constantly forming, dissolving, and re-forming relationships among the elements of the work"[42] — an approximation that closely resembles the worldview implicit in *The Sot-Weed Factor*.

One of the ways in which Barth achieves this openness is through his use of interpolated narratives. The novel contains at least twenty-five of them related by no less than seventeen different narrators. Despite the third-person narrative point of view, then, the omniscient authorial voice contributes very little pertinent information. The "marvelous plot . . . afoot" in the novel is in reality many different plots, each contained in one or more of the separate stories told at various times by various people. For example, we learn of Henry's early life — his childhood with Captain and Melissa Salmon, his sojourn among the gypsies, his stay at Cambridge — through the "diverting tale" he relates to Eben. When the two are reunited after a seven-year interval, Henry resumes his history, but with the added news that he is now actively searching for clues to his identity. His quest consists of piecing together fragments from various sources, chief among these the journals of Smith and Burlingame. Others also tell stories containing important elements of Henry's past; among them is Father Thomas Smith, who relates the history of Henry's maternal grandfather, Father Fitzmaurice the "martyr," a portion of which Smith surmises from a tale told him by Charley Mattassin, Henry's brother; and Chicamec, Henry's father, whose story, told to Eben who in turn relates it to Henry, supplies the final clues to Henry's identity. The story of Henry's life, therefore, is actually several stories — or, more accurately, several *versions.* For Sir Henry Burlingame and John Smith supply different perspectives on similar events, and Father Smith's version of Father Fitzmaurice's fate, like Herbert Stencil's portrait of V. in Pynchon's novel of that name, is a pastiche of information assembled from diverse sources: the Vatican's mission records, inquiries made among the Indians, and pure "rumor and conjecture" (350). Moreover, the tale is self-consciously fictionalized: "I shall speak henceforth," Smith tells his audience, "from the martyr's point of view, as't were, adding what I can surmise to the things Charley Mattassin told me. 'Twill make a better tale than otherwise, and do no violence to what scanty facts we have" (358). Henry's identity is as much invented as discovered. The chain of causes of which he is the apparent effect must, in true Humean fashion, be inferred; Henry must make what Barbara C. Ewell terms a "leap of faith" from scanty fact to opinion.[43]

While his identity is more secure, Eben similarly learns much about his own past through stories. Andrew tells him certain facts of his birth and early childhood; Henrietta — who, like Father Smith, invents "colloquies for the sake of interest" (671) — relates the story of the Invulnerable Castle, from which Eben deduces his

relationship to Roxanna; and Roxanna, mistress to Andrew, wet-
nurse to Eben and Anna, and mother of Henrietta, the twin's half-
sister, confirms Eben's suspicion and fills in the remaining blanks of
his life story. (Henry's tale of having sported on the beach with
Roxanna and Henrietta after their escape from pirates adds yet a
further chapter to the history of Eben's family.) Moreover, Eben
learns of Anna's activities in the colonies through stories told successively by Mary Mungummory, Harvey Russecks (who loves a
story, the more tangled its plot the better), and Anna herself. Both
as "Susan Warren" and as herself, Joan Toast twice relates the circumstances which brought her to America, with each version con-
tradicting the other. And so on. Barth's "open" novel embodies a
vast multiplication of perspectives and narrative viewpoints. The
fact that "every single one" of them is, as Barth promises, "wrapped
up absolutely and securely"[44] at the end of his carefully structured
plot does not detract from the fact that *The Sot-Weed Factor* is not
a single fabrication but several, each told from a different point of
view. The implicit analogy between the "world" of Barth's novel
and the world we occupy suggests that the reader, like Eben and
Henry, is also adrift among versions or fictions, some of his own
making, some the constructions of others, any one of which could
be replaced by others equally authentic, equally false.

Characterization, too, functions in the novel's substitutive context. The title Adaline Glasheen gives her table of cross-references
in *Finnegans Wake* — "Who Is Who When Everybody Is Somebody
Else" — applies almost as aptly to *The Sot-Weed Factor*.[45] Characters constantly exfoliate into multiple identities: Henry assumes at
least eight disguises, is replicated by his two brothers (the dark
double Charles Mattassin and the light Billy Rumbly), and is
linked by what Barth claims are inadvertent allusions to numerous
wandering heroes from myth and legend. Or they meld suddenly
into a single personality: Dreppecca, Dick Parker, and Drake-
pecker turn out to be the same African king. Indeed, all the novel's
major characters — Joan Toast, Anna Cooke, Ebenezer, Bertrand,
John McEvoy, Henrietta, Roxy — either pretend to be or are mistaken for somebody else at least once. Each of these characters possesses sufficient autonomy so that he or she is not quite the "nexus of
character equivalents" that Bruns describes Joyce's Earwicker as being; yet Henry, the most protean of the group, does exist in what
Bruns calls "something like a state of transformation."[46]

In an early debate Henry insists upon this fact. "The world can alter a man entirely, Eben," Henry says, "or he can alter himself, down to his very essence. . . . Nay, a man *must* alter willy-nilly in's flight to the grave; he is a river running seawards, that is ne'er the same from hour to hour" (125). Eben, who has just determined his "absolute" identity as Poet and Virgin, resists Henry's contention, citing memory as the thread that "marks [his] path through the labyrinth of life" and connects him with his "starting place" — a postulate Henry promptly dismantles logically. This debate, despite its obvious contemporary relevance, evokes the seventeenth-century intellectual context as well. Eben's position parallels Locke's argument in *An Essay Concerning Human Understanding* (1690) that memory is the single necessary and sufficient criterion of personal identity.[47] Henry's rebuttal resembles Hume's argument in a *Treatise of Human Nature* (1739) that change destroys identity, and that conceptions of "self" and "substance" are merely inventions which allow us to overlook the fact that people are "nothing but a bundle or collection of different perceptions in a perpetual flux and movement."[48] "Your true and constant Burlingame," Henry similarly tells Eben, "lives only in your fancy, as doth the pointed order of the world. In fact you see a Heraclitean flux: whether 'tis we who shift and alter and dissolve; or you whose lens changes color, field, and focus; or both together. The upshot is the same" (330). But Henry extends Hume's argument another step. The locus of man's mutable identity, he insists, is language (for Hume it is the association of ideas). "The man is whate'er he chooses to *call* himself," he says to Cooke, but his sentiment applies equally to himself and, by implication, to everyone. "One must needs make and seize his soul, and then cleave fast to't, or go babbling in the corner; one must choose his gods and devils on the run, quill his own name upon the universe, and declare, ' 'Tis I, and the world stands such-a-way!' One must *assert, assert, assert,* or go screaming mad" (345). As for Jake, so for Henry: articulation is his absolute. My point is not only that *The Sot-Weed Factor* symbolizes a "metaphysical reality that suggests . . . unbounded multiplicity," as Max F. Schulz says; or that it mocks the written history we often naively accept as fact, as Phillip E. Diser concludes; or that it participates in the "supramodernist" consensus which finds "all interpretations of 'reality' arbitrary and therefore at the same time both accurate and absurd," as Mas'ud Zavarzadeh suggests,

although each of these points seems essentially valid and collectively they are analogous to my earlier comments about the fictive
nature of "reality."[49] My point, rather, is that *The Sot-Weed Factor*
not only proclaims the contingent, multiple nature of postmodern
"reality," but that it locates the *source* of that multiplicity, the fundamental substitutive nature of "reality," in language, which is the
primary constituent of "reality" as we know it.

Harold Kaplan has perceived a quality of passiveness in much
modern fiction. Quoting Camus's contention that for "the absurd
man . . . everything begins with a lucid indifference," Kaplan
maintains that in the fiction of most great moderns action is decidedly subordinate to "a particularly passive and unpragmatic intelligence. The writing of Flaubert and Joyce made the artist the
only hero of his own work; he becomes the hero by his power to
acknowledge chaos, or to translate into the artifice of form a life
reality which resists every success except that of contemplation."[50]
What Kaplan calls "contemplation" (or, elsewhere, "consciousness") we have been discussing as a particular use of language
which tends to displace the "real" world. To a degree, this retreat
from "reality" into the language of intelligence or abstraction
characterizes Barth's first two protagonist/narrators as well as
Ebenezer Cooke. For Henry, however, despite the implicit Car-
tesianism in his tribute to assertion ("'Tis I, and the world stands
such-a-way!'"), language never becomes a passive substitute for
active engagement in the world. This fact becomes clearer if he is
compared to Hemingway's Jake Barnes, one of the passive heroes
Kaplan examines. Both men share similar physical deficiencies;
what nature has robbed from Henry, Jake has lost in the war.
Their different responses to this debility are instructive. "Jake
Barnes," Kaplan writes, "represents the man interrupted in life and
spoiled by his wound; his striking dimension in the novel is actually his passivity." Only certain kinds of action are sought, those
which fall into Barnes's capacity to control. Generally, however,
Barnes shares the "general essence of Hemingway's protagonists
. . . who act either by indirect, private motives or exist simply as
observers."[51] Even as narrator Barnes practices the art of evasion.
His taciturn, emotionless concentration on objects in the physical
world (the contents of his mail, the balance in his bank account,
the tables at the Rotonde, the Dome, the Closerie des Lilas) delib-

erately diverts his attention from the inner consciousness of psychic pain. That is, style itself, as Chaman Nahal and others have observed, constitutes an evasion of painful experience and is emblematic of a general willed withdrawal into passivity.[52]

Henry's response, on the other hand, is "bold resolve," a program for action that he twice exhorts Eben to follow. Not only a "glutton for adventure," as Eben describes him, but "a glutton for the great world, of which I ne'er can see and learn enough" (145), Henry evades nothing intentionally. In considering Henry's success at practicing what he preaches, two matters of some significance should be kept in mind. First, Henry has suffered "since childhood" (14) the same unrestrained capacity for imagining alternatives and possibilities that immobilizes Jake Horner and Ebenezer. Second, he is functionally if not technically impotent. His "cosmophily," his itch to unite carnally with the world, is impeded by the same physical defect that prevents Jake Barnes from enjoying sexual relations with Brett Ashley. Unlike Barnes, who bitterly accepts his forced celibacy, usually rejecting the "perverted sexual satisfaction"[53] Brett offers, Henry cultivates, indeed *justifies*, perversion. "Ah, sir," he tells Eben while impersonating Timothy Mitchell, "no amorous practice is itself a vice — can ye be in sooth a poet and not see that? Adultery, rape, deceit, unfair seduction — 'tis *these* are vicious, not the coupling of parts: the sin is not in the act, but in the circumstances" (325–26). Given his congenital shortcoming, what path can Henry pursue but the erotopathic? He has thus taken one defect, a profligate "cosmopsic" imagination, harnessed it, and used it as compensation for his second defect. Like all the Burlingame brothers, Henry serves passion with virtuosity. As Mary Mungummory tells Eben, Charley Mattassin, though "less blest by half than most boys in their cradles," had "learnt strange and wondrous means to reach his end! Thus had good Mother Nature cleared her debt to him, after the fashion of the proverb: what she had robbed from Peter, she bestowed on Paul" (414). Anna, too, though technically a virgin, enjoys the "bold resolve" with which Henry and Billy Rumbly overcome their physical deficiency. In matters of sex, as "Timothy Mitchell" tells Eben, *"There are more ways to the woods than one"* (326).

Not only imagination serves virtuosity; erudition, too, plays its part. If lovers "read as well, they have the amorous researches of the race at their disposal: the pleasures of Cathay, of Moors and

Turks and Africans, and the cleverest folk of Europe" (326). Thus passion, imagination, intellect, and experience of the physical world combine to form Henry's sexual agendum. Obviously this combination constitutes his general modus operandi as well. Henry has come a step beyond Jake Horner, who had progressed a step beyond Todd Andrews. Whereas the latter's contact with the world is covert, and Horner's less so, Henry's relationship to "reality" is *engagé*, boldly assertive in every sense of the word. He embodies the dialectical relationship we have been examining between word and world. Assertion, on the one hand, he declares his absolute; the physical world, on the other, he not only vigorously occupies but literally makes love to. "I love the world, sir," he tells Eben, "and so make love to it! I have sown my seed in men and women, in a dozen sorts of beasts, in the barky boles of trees and the honeyed wombs of flowers; I have dallied on the black breast of the earth, and clipped her fast; I have wooed the waves of the sea, impregnated the four winds, and flung my passion skywards to the stars!" (328). That passage, with its strong iambic rhythms, alliteration, and poetic imagery, combined with its contextual significance (that is, its thematic relevance and its contribution to plot) is a perfect example of the equilibrium Barth generally maintains between the metaphoric and metonymic activities of discourse. Thus the passage serves as an emblem of sorts for the similar state of equipoise that Henry maintains between assertion and action, words and world.

Ebenezer, on the other hand, resembles at least initially the passive hero of Kaplan's study. Like Jake Barnes, he is more an observer than an actor. Like Todd Andrews, he avoids sexual intimacy, first through sheer awkwardness, then by choice, claiming virginity as his essence. Like Jake Horner, he interposes a language of abstraction between himself and the world of physical experience. He begins his ode to Maryland, for instance, before his journey there has even commenced; thus its words are purified of referentiality to anything but his own idealistic conceptions. Similarly, he proffers an imagined love to a woman who exists solely in his fancy. "There's naught o' the divine in Joan [Toast], my friend," an exasperated John McEvoy tells him. "She's mortal clay and hath her share o' failings like the rest of us. As for this vision ye speak of, 'tis the vision ye love, not the woman. 'Twere impossible it could be otherwise, for none o' ye save I e'en knows the woman" (62). Indeed, the language of the love song Eben composes to Joan—that poem's style—reflects Eben's habitual response to life as clearly as Henry's prose style mirrors his lifestyle. As Barbara C. Ewell observes, the single revision Eben makes of that song, "the deletion of the poem's only concrete reference, 'Joan,' does indeed make the poem 'perfect,' as he says—not a perfect reality, however, but a perfect abstraction, and as such, without relevance in the finite and imperfect world."[54]

Eben's idealistic approach to experience is reflected in his hermetic use of language. That Ebenezer himself may be partially aware of this relationship is suggested in an early colloquy with Henry. Eben distinguishes between two categories of virtue, the "plain" and the "significant." Virtues in the first category (honesty, charity, fidelity) are referential in that they stand for prudence; virtues in the second category, on the other hand, are nothing "but signs," thus "refer to naught beyond themselves" (156). Their independence from the world of things renders them "*purer*, after a fashion," than virtues of the first sort (157). Moreover, such signs are wholly arbitrary, their meaning entirely dependent upon their use in a particular context. All virtues, Eben maintains, "mean naught when taken by themselves, like the strokes and scribbles we call *writing*—their virtue lies in what they stand for" (156). The parallels between the theory of language implicit in Eben's defense of virtue and the theories of Ferdinand de Saussure are strikingly evident, if probably coincidental.[55] Nonetheless, this view diverges markedly from the view of language implicit in Burlingame's words and deeds, a view which more nearly coincides with the orphic theory of, say, Heidegger.[56] Henry values language even more than does Eben, but he refuses to divorce it from the world of experience. Ebenezer, on the other hand, wishes to remove significance from the world of physical experience altogether. For him, *to write* is, in Roland Barthes's famous phrase, an "intransitive verb."[57] The less relevance a virtue has to anything outside itself (to prudence, say), the less *instrumental* or practical it is, the purer that virtue becomes for Eben, thus the greater its value. As Henry reminds him, the "cant" term describing such virtues is *terminal*, the word with which Barth's second novel ends and which, in the context of that novel, signifies the temporary closing off of experience in the world.

Eben's retreat from actual into purely verbal experience so resembles the similar retreats of Jake Horner and Todd Andrews that one suspects a similarity of motive: the fear of death. Some evidence in the novel supports this suspicion. The final stanza of his song to Joan, for instance, reads:

Preserv'd, my Innocence preserveth Me
    From Life, from Time, from Death, from History;
Without it I must breathe Man's mortal Breath:
    Commence a Life — and thus commence my Death! [59]

Later, after having been forced by Tom Pound to walk the plank and finding himself awash in the "mid-Atlantic" (actually he is just off Maryland's shore), Eben reflects: "That lives are stories, he assumed; that stories end he allowed — how else could one begin another? But that the teller himself must live a particular tale and die — Unthinkable! Unthinkable!" (271). Despite such passages, Eben's fear of death seldom seems compulsive, as in the cases of Todd Andrews and, to a lesser extent, Jake Horner. Nor does his love of abstractions seem to indicate a neurotic aversion toward involvement with the physical. Rather, his attraction to the abstract recalls Todd's account of his youthful yearning for the sea. "Never have I regarded my boyhood as anything but pleasant," Todd explains, "but the intensity of this longing to escape [to the sea] must be accounted for by the attractiveness of the thing itself, not by any unattractiveness of my surroundings. In short, I was running *to*, not running *from*, or so I believe."[58] Such statements by Todd are probably diversionary and should thus be regarded with suspicion, but when applied to Eben the general sentiment fits. Ebenezer remains virtually innocent of the world for almost thirty years because he *is* in fact an innocent, a bona fide *naïf*. When he elevates his innocence to the level of an ideal, it is because, in the absence of any experience to the contrary, he sincerely believes in ideals. He is running not *from* the phenomenal but *toward* the noumenal. Indeed, the earnestness with which he upholds these ideals provokes consternation in the worldly John McEvoy and Henry Burlingame. "Your senses fail ye," McEvoy tells him, "your busy fancy plays ye false and fills your head with foolish pictures" (62). To be sure, Eben backslides occasionally, as when he twice attempts to rape Joan or on several occasions denies his identity; but these deviations derive less from hypocrisy than from circumstances (Bertrand's skillful imposture aboard the *Po-*

seidon, for instance, forces Eben temporarily to renounce his identity) or from innocence of his own inherently carnal nature (his
sudden attack of concupiscence aboard the *Cyprian* is utterly "incomprehensible to him" [264]). Such "apostasies" are followed by
intense feelings of authentic guilt. Eben's retreat into abstraction is
neither neurotic nor paranoiac, as in the cases of Todd and Jake,
but platonic. He does not deliberately or instinctively use metaphors as a shield against an implosive universe. On the contrary,
metaphors use him.

A recurring term throughout this chapter, *metaphor* has been
used in at least two senses: in what might be called an epistemological sense insofar as the paradigms that undergird our construction
of reality are metaphors, and in a linguistic sense insofar as the
paradigmatic or substitutive axis of language is concerned.
Though contextually different, both uses are related. Language in
general, not just its metaphorical axis, may be seen as fundamentally substitutive. Referring to "the incommensurability of language, the fact that language can never really express any *thing:*
only relationships . . . or sheer absence," Fredric Jameson concludes: "Thus language has of necessity recourse to indirection, to
substitution: itself a substitute, it must replace that empty center of
content with something else, and it does so either by saying what
the content is *like* (metaphor), or describing its context and the
contours of its absence, listing the things that border around it
(metonymy)."[59] As we shall see in Chapters 6 and 8, the empty
center that structuralists find at the heart of language may also be
seen as the ground of being in the Heideggerian sense. Yet even if
words allow things to appear by calling them forth from the eternal
flux, words are not the *Ding an sich.* Regardless of the particular
linguistic theory one favors, language may be seen as metaphoric,
substitutive, in that it connects us with the world (wherever that
world is "located") by *standing for* the world. As Colin Murray
Turbayne observes, "It begins to seem as though the world may be
illustrated just as well, if not better, by *making believe* that it is a
universal language instead of a mighty machine."[60]

Turbayne chooses his words carefully, as I have indicated by
italicizing "making believe" in the above statement. All metaphors
involve *sort-crossing* — in Gilbert Ryle's words, "the presentation of
the facts belonging to one category in the idioms appropriate to
another."[61] That is, they involve pretense: one acts *as if* something

is the case when it is not.[62] "When the pretense is dropped either by the original pretenders or their followers," Turbayne warns, "what was before . . . a *screen* or *filter* is now more appropriately called a *disguise* or *mask*. There is a difference between using a metaphor and being used by it, between using a model and mistaking the model for the thing modeled. The one is to make believe that something is the case; the other is to believe it." Errors of the latter case Turbayne terms *sort-trespassing*. In a brilliant discussion he describes the processes by which Descartes and Newton began their investigations into the nature of "reality" by developing useful new metaphors, only to become eventually victimized by those metaphors. Newton, for instance, became so intrigued by the deductive chain of reasoning he employed in his procedures that he "exported the necessary connection invented between premise and conclusion to the realm of process in nature." Similarly, Descartes, after beginning with the following proposition: "I have hitherto described this earth, and generally the whole visible world, *as if it were* merely a machine," soon pushed his hypothesis beyond the boundaries of metaphor into the realm of accepted fact. "In short, enthralled by his own metaphor, he mistook the mask for the face, and consequently bequeathed to posterity more than a worldview. He bequeathed a world."[63]

Such notions complement Kuhn's discussion of paradigms and seem to be what Henry has in mind when he tells Eben, "I fear me thou'rt seduced by metaphors, as was Descartes of old" (126). Later, after his position on memory has been thoroughly dismantled by Henry, Eben cries, "Marry, your discourse hath robbed me of similes: I know of naught immutable and sure!" To which Henry responds: "'Tis the first step on the road to Heaven" (128). Henry is chiding Eben not for using metaphors (Who realizes the efficacy of apt metaphor more than Henry Burlingame!) but for allowing metaphors to use him and for misconstruing those metaphors for truth. The trick is to employ fictions knowingly, strategically, *as if* they are truths. Moreover, as Henry's activities make clear, while these fictions can seldom be derived from experience (they are, after all, the primary constituents of experience), paradoxically they must be tested in the crucible of experience. Henry would no doubt agree with the conclusion Eben sadly offers after his own considerable if belated experience, "that naught can be inferred to guide our conduct from the fact of our mortality"

(536). But if nothing of final value is deducible from life, values must nonetheless be asserted, then applied to and *from within* the world of experience. Metaphor, though unavoidable if one is to live in the world at all, must neither be mistaken for facts nor conceived in an experiential vacuum.

Eben begins to learn this lesson soon after accepting Joan's money for passage on the *Pilgrim* and then abandoning her. He justifies his desertion in terms of the metaphor by which he has been defining his essence. "What business hath a poet with the business of the world . . . and the nets of love?" he asks rhetorically, his rationalizations gradually assuming "the tone of a manifesto"; "I shall feel conscience only for my art, and there's an end on't! . . . For . . . I'm more a poet now than ever in my life (and thus obliged to no soul save my muse nor any institution save my craft)" (474–75). Only a page later, however, doubts arise about the legitimacy of his actions and the metaphors by which he justifies them. Arriving at Cambridge, he notices the morning star; "it pleased Ebenezer to imagine that it hung over the meridian of London like the star of old over Bethlehem, guiding him to the cradle of his destiny." The trope is followed immediately by this reflection: "There's a figure Henry Burlingame would make mince-meat of" (479). Henceforth, the pertinacity with which Eben had defended his metaphoric formulations begins to dwindle. At one point he actually plays Henry Burlingame to John McEvoy's Ebenezer Cooke, advising McEvoy to change his attitude toward a situation by changing his metaphorical conception of it (581–82). On another occasion he seems to accept the inevitability of the discrepancy between ideal and actual justice. (His earlier refusal to recognize this discrepancy led to his loss of Malden.) Almost simultaneously he realizes the immutable fact of vicissitude. Even the most noble and idealistic of human endeavors, those "meant to live in the public heart till the end of time," wither and fade from memory.

> Not long since, he would have gnashed his spiritual teeth at the futility of endeavor in such a world. Not improbably he would have railed at human fickleness in allegorical couplets: the Heart, he would have declared, is a faithless Widow: at the deathbed of her noble Spouse (whether Triumph or Tragedy) she pledges herself forever to his memory, but scarcely has she donned her Weeds before some importuning Problem has his way with her; and in the years that follow, for all her

ceremonious visits to the tomb, she shares her bed with a parade of mean Vicissitudes, not one of them worthy even of her notice. Now, however, though such fickleness still stung his sensibilities . . . he was not sure but what it had about it a double rightness: "Time *passes* for the living," it seemed to say, "and alters things. Only for the dead do circumstances never change." [606]

The tone of self-deprecation in this lengthy quotation should be evident. To a degree, Eben is mocking his earlier tendency to disassociate himself from "reality" through metaphoric barbs and irony. Moreover, his grudging acceptance of the realities of time and death seems to qualify, if not actually to undermine, the opposing sentiment contained in the fourth stanza of his song to Joan Toast. Most importantly, his late encounters with the world seem to have muted his willingness to pontificate authoritatively on most subjects, particularly matters of virtue. When McEvoy asserts that the inevitable loss of innocence makes it more "precious" and Mary Mungummory counters that that inevitability merely "proves its vanity," Eben's answer is Burlingame-like: " 'Tis beyond me what it proves. . . . I know only that the case is so" (608). The Wittgensteinian echo in those words seems to imply Eben's gradual acceptance of and assent to the world of physical experience ("everything that is the case") and a concomitant disillusionment with the metaphors by which he had initially defined his essence.

Eben's adventures in the New World strip him of both innocence and idealism, a fact widely commented upon by critics. But what one critic calls Eben's "demythologization"[64] results not in Eben's abandonment of metaphor, but in his exchange of an inferior metaphor for a better one. Earlier he had defined himself as a kind of prelapsarian poet, now as postlapsarian man. The first metaphor was conceived in innocence, the second in the pain of experience. That pain exceeds the pain of lost innocence, involving as well "the pain of responsibility. The fallen suffer from Adam's fall . . . but in that knowledge — which the Fall itself vouchsafed him — how more must Adam have suffered!" (695). Eben has moved from formulations about the world that separate him from it to a metaphorical conception of himself which links him to the world. In Howell's term, he has learned a sense of *complicity* with others, and an accompanying sense of responsibility for the pain his innocence has caused them. "That is the crime I stand indicted for," he concludes: "the crime of innocence, whereof the knowledged must bear the burthen. There's the true Original Sin our souls are born in: not that Adam *learned*, but that he *had* to learn—in short that he was innocent" (739). Significantly, Eben's assertion of his responsibility takes the form of a metaphor. He has moved from words to world and back to words. But in the process he has learned that world and words are inextricably linked. In his innocence Eben thinks himself a poet; in the loss of that innocence he becomes one. *The Sot-Weed Factor* is less a *Bildungsroman* than a *Künstlerroman*—as, indeed, are all of Barth's books.

Significance or value remains important to Ebenezer, yet he has gained the realization that any significance transcendent to the world of experience is but "a hollow madness," a "mere castle in the air." Significance, rather, is what man brings *to* the world: "what the world lacks we must ourselves supply" (629). Man must act *as if* his values have significance, then use them to structure his actions in the world. Though "right weary of innocence," virtue remains for Eben "a banner still," and thus it has earned at least this right: its loss must not "be devoid of a right *significance*" (629). That significance, as suggested, is the value of complicity. Eben's decision to consummate his marriage to the pox-plagued Joan Toast is motivated not by the desire to gain his legacy, but by a fervent desire for atonement. By "atonement" Eben apparently means redemption, but perhaps he also remembers Henry's earlier definition of *atonement* as "The making of two into one" (493). Thus significance, itself metaphoric—meaning supplied to an otherwise valueless world—is achieved by Eben through an appropriately metaphorical act: he gains at-one-ment with Joan, "no woman, but Womankind," whose gestures contain "the history of the race" (533), and with the world, for which Joan serves as the "very sign and emblem" (468).

Metaphor, Barth insists, is inescapable—except, of course, through death. Not only Eben's words and actions but the entire final scene contains metaphors suggesting redemption. On the one hand, it evokes metaphorically the Roman Catholic Eucharist: Eben craves redemption, Andrew Cooke calls for "Grace," wine is associated with Christ's blood (" 'Sblood, Grace, fetch us a rundlet!"). On the other hand, it parodies (indeed, inverts) what Leslie Fiedler calls the "sentimental love religion," essentially Protestant in origin, in which "the Pure Young Girl replaces Christ as the saviour" and "marriage becomes the equivalent of bliss eternal."[65]

The predominance of parody in this final scene completely under-
mines any affirmation in what is finally a mock happy ending, a
burlesque of the "closed" endings of traditional eighteenth- and nineteenth-century novels.[66] Lest we miss this point, Barth appends an
"Apology" to the novel proper, "opening" it again. "The *story* of
Ebenezer Cooke is told," the "Author" of *The Sot-Weed Factor*
states. "All the rest is anticlimax: the stairs that take him up to the
bridal-chamber take him down the steep incline of *denouement*.
To the *history*, on the other hand, there is so much more . . . that
the Author must risk those rude *cornadas* to resume it, and trust
that the Reader is interested enough in the fate of the twins . . .
and the rest, to indulge some pandering to Curiosity at Form's expense" (743–44). Barth's apology for his "Apology" recalls
Melville's justification for the disjunctive "sequel" chapters of *Billy
Budd*. "The symmetry of form attainable in pure fiction," Melville
writes, "cannot so readily be achieved in a narration essentially
having less to do with fable than with fact. Truth uncompromis-
ingly told will always have its ragged edges; hence the conclusion
of such a narration is apt to be less finished than an architectural
finial." As Edgar Dryden suggests, the concluding three chapters of
Billy Budd imply "the formless forces of barbarism and irrationality" that lurk beneath mankind's measured forms.[67] Like Melville,
Barth practices "the great Art of Telling the Truth." Stories end
symmetrically. Life, as Jake Horner learns, remains ragged and incomplete. Accordingly, his "sequel" is less an Apology than an
obituary. The "bliss eternal" of Eben's marriage ends abruptly as
Joan dies bearing a stillborn infant. The marriage of Henrietta and
John McEvoy is similarly abbreviated, as they, along with Roxy,
are lost at sea. Henry, after a brief reunion with Anna, disappears
forever into the Maryland marshes. Bertrand dies of exposure, Ben
Spurdance and Colonel Robotham of ague, Tom Tayloe of a beat-
ing by one of his "investments." The message is clear: metaphor
may palliate but it can never eradicate Death, the final fact of our
ineluctable carnality. Death is the silence at the heart of language.
Whether that silence represents total annihilation (as Todd fears)
or ineffable unity (as George Giles learns), it constitutes the end of
experience – the cancelling out of words and world.

For this reason alone, experience in the world attains value. Since
through language we actively participate in the constitution of the
intelligible world, the deliberate use of a language that would dis-

place that world becomes an act of annihilation. The language of silence is the language of death. Paradoxically, the abstractions that Jake and Eben employ as shields against death actually edge them nearer to the ultimate silence they would avoid. In any event, attempts to avoid the physical are fruitless. The hermetic language into which Jake withdraws cracks up like a frigate on the shoals of physical reality in the terminal chapter of *The End of the Road*. Thus *The Sot-Weed Factor* affirms not only experience in the physical world but also what might be termed the "language of experience"—not a language derived from and mimetic of the world, but a language that mediates between man and the "reality" he inhabits and in large part creates. What Roland Barthes calls the "mythical 'alibi' dominating the idea of literature"[68] is not, in *The Sot-Weed Factor*, the referent, the "real"; on the contrary, that "alibi" is the orphic conception of language by which the "real" is disclosed.

According to the orphic formulation, language discloses the world's discrete entities, its sticks and stones, by calling them forth from the primordial flux. Implicit in orphic theory is a vision of unity that exceeds the union of word and thing occurring in the act of discourse. Implied, rather, is a larger, all-encompassing unity, not transcendent to the world of things like some platonic Ideal, but immanent. This is the Heideggerian "ground of Being" that exists before utterance and out of which utterance emanates. Or, to change the figure, it is the primordial silence out of which all myth flows, the ineffable *Urword* of which all other words are but imperfect refractions. The source of language, it cannot be contained by language. An amalgam of all things, it cannot be located in any single thing or any collocation of things. It is this unity that Todd Andrews and Jake Horner have briefly and indeterminately glimpsed and from which they recoil into protective fictions. It is this unity that Henry Burlingame seeks. Driven by "a prime and massy urge to *coalescence*" (489), Henry loves "no part of the world . . . but the entire parti-colored whole, with all her poles and contradictories" (490). Yet he is fated to know his "great Bride part by part" only, to make "love to her *disjecta membra*, her sundry brilliant pieces" (497). Instructing Eben in geminology, he says of twins: "Yet whether their bond be love or hate or death . . . almost always their union is brilliance, totality, apocalypse—a thing to yearn and tremble for! . . . And 'tis this I yearn for too, and

naught besides: I am Suitor of Totality, Embracer of Contradictories, Husband to all Creation, the Cosmic Lover!" (497). As
token of "the seamless universe," twins *in coito* fascinate Henry.
He craves neither Eben nor Anna separately, "but the twain as
one," and longs for the time when, their "secret lust" having overcome their reason, he may "come upon [them] *sack a sack* as did
Catullus on the lovers, and like that nimble poet . . . skewer
[them] both like twin squabs on a spit!" (491).[69] Yet, as Henry must
realize, even that eventuality would be but a further token of the
Unity he seeks. Craving unity, but adrift (like all men) among categories of his own making, Henry — like Barth — must remain content with metaphors, substitutes.[70]

Emblems of the coalescence Henry seeks fill *The Sot-Weed Factor*. Its multiple coincidences, while parodic of the conventional
use of coincidence in eighteenth-century novels,[71] may possess a
metaphysical dimension as well. What Jung calls "synchronicity"
and the Austrian biologist Paul Kammerer "seriality" refers to a particular kind of coincidence that, inexplicable in terms of the laws
of causality, seems to point to a mysterious cosmic order linking
all things, what Schopenhauer in a similar context calls "the most
wonderful preestablished harmony."[72] Perhaps Barth had ideas
like these in mind when he said that "there are deep metaphysical
reasons why we need more Fielding-like books today, with plots
where everybody turns out to be related to everybody else."[73] The
family ties that link most of the novel's characters lead to another
symbol of coalescence: incest. While Anna and Eben come to recognize their secret lust, it is never consummated, but acts of near-
incest and quasi-incest fill the novel. Henry copulates with Eben's
sister, his half-sister, and his half-sister's mother, who was Eben's
father's mistress. Indeed, Eben himself almost loses his chastity to
Roxanna. John McEvoy also beds Henrietta as well as Joan Toast,
Eben's wife. Henry's brother, Billy Rumbly, goes to bed with
Anna, who later bears Henry's child. Even Andrew, Eben's father,
innocently pays £6 for the sexual services of his daughter-in-law,
Joan Toast. Thus these characters are linked by sexual as well as
familial relationships. Indeed, swiving itself, as Henry tells Eben,
portrays symbolically "the fruitful union of opposites: the Heavenly Twins embraced; the Two as One" (494). The "mystic mark of
redemption" is the number eight, "by virtue of its copulating cir-

cles"; thus in mythic terms Eben's seeking atonement for his sins through the act of fornication is hardly blasphemous. Doubling, like coincidence, incest, and fornication, suggests the coincidence of opposites that signifies cosmic unity. At one point Eben sees "commingled and transfused before his eyes the faces of Joan Toast and his sister Anna" (697), and indeed the two women are doubles, as are Eben and Henry, John Smith and Sir Henry Burlingame, Charley Mattassin and Billy Rumbly, John Coode and Lord Baltimore, and a host of others. Characters constantly assume one another's identities, in still another emblem of coalescence. Similarly, Mary Mungummory's richly phrased question — "Is man a salvage at heart, skinned o'er with Manners? Or is salvagery but a faint taint in the natural man's gentility, which erupts now and again like pimples on an angel's arse?" (610) — can be answered, the novel suggests, only with a paradoxical "Yes." Man's nature, as Eben concludes, "hath in germ the sum of poles and possibilities" that combined constitute "reality."

Even Barth's occasional use of language in which the metaphoric axis predominates contributes emblematically to his concern with unity. Whereas ordinary language, as Gerald Bruns explains, "differentiates experience because it is itself a system of differences, in which words derive their meanings from their opposition to one another," poetic speech "executes an abolishment of differences — executes, that is, the formation of equivalences among separate identities."[74] In substitutive contexts, that is, words function less as units of signification than as units of equivalence. This is particularly clear in the use of the leitmotif in literature. "Technically," writes Clive Hart, "the leitmotif is a highly self-conscious device. It functions primarily at the surface level, within the verbal texture. . . . We are, as a result, constantly impelled to shift our attention from the subject-matter seen through the words to the words themselves."[75] That is, leitmotifs function to shift our attention from the horizontal to the vertical axis of language activity. "Meaning" similarly shifts from referential to symbolic. What is symbolized is equivalence, each recurring motif merging with all other occurrences of that motif. In *The Sot-Weed Factor* the catalogs discussed earlier function in this respect, striving to connect with one another symbolically. To an extent, all the recurring features in the novel that we have just examined as emblems of coalescence share this feature. They suggest unity not only individually, that is, but collectively as well, "vertically" coalescing like the leitmotif.

Yet, except for occasional "poetic" flights, Barth's language is firmly rooted in the novel's horizontal level, with which the vertical dimension of his language functions in tandem. The problem with hermetic language, Barth seems to feel, is that what it really desires is the abolition of language; its secret desire is to press time and language back to the primordial blank whence language sprung, a desire which Barth addresses directly in *Lost in the Funhouse*. But a movement outside language is a movement into death — or mystical vision. In *The Sot-Weed Factor*, at least, Barth affirms the necessity of experience in the world and the orphic use of language that makes that experience possible, that expresses while it creates that world. In *Giles Goat-Boy* he will allow his protagonist to achieve at last that ineffable unity toward which his first three novels have increasingly pointed.

NOTES

1. Gado, ed., *First Person*, p. 117.
2. Barth, *Giles Goat-Boy*, p. 616.
3. See Jac Tharpe's sensitive discussion of Barth's "carnal vision" in *Barth*, pp. 5–6. See also LeClair, "Death and Black Humor," pp. 17–18.
4. Kuhn, *Structure of Scientific Revolutions*, p. 102.
5. Ibid., p. 113.
6. Barth, *The Sot-Weed Factor*, rev. ed. (Garden City, N.Y.: Doubleday, 1967), pp. 125–26. Subsequent references to this edition are noted in parentheses in the text.
7. Enck, "Interview," p. 23. Barth ascribes a similar sentiment to Eben (*Sot-Weed Factor*, p. 9).
8. Turbayne, *Myth of Metaphor*, p. 65.
9. Ibid.
10. Kuhn, *Structure of Scientific Revolutions*, p. 116.
11. Nicholson, *Breaking of the Circle*, Ch. 2.
12. Bellamy, *The New Fiction*, p. 16.
13. Nicholson, *Breaking of the Circle*, p. 81.
14. Warnke, *Versions of the Baroque*, pp. 220, 65, 81.
15. Though in a different sense, as we shall see in Ch. 8, it remains decidedly Aristotelian.
16. Watt, *Rise of the Novel*, p. 13.
17. Ibid., p. 14.

18. Ibid., p. 32.

19. Fielding, as Watt points out, generally maintains his Aristotelian bias until his last novel, *Amelia*. The "distinguishing elements" of his novels "have their roots not so much in social change as in the neo-classical literary tradition" (*Rise of the Novel*, p. 239). That tradition, as David Vieth maintains, remains essentially Aristotelian in its operating assumptions: "To be sure, the Aristotelian tradition remains primary and the anti-Aristotelian secondary, for the latter cannot subsist without a lively consciousness of the former. Thus it is a paradox—scarcely surprising, however, to those acquainted with the humor inseparable from the anti-Aristotelian response—that so many major works of Augustan literature belong to the secondary tradition, whereas the primary tradition is better represented by minor works" ("Toward an Anti-Aristotelian Poetic," p. 124). Among those major works Vieth lists are Swift's *Tale of a Tub*, Gay's *Beggar's Opera*, and of course Sterne's *Tristram Shandy*. The Aristotelian bias of Fielding's *Tom Jones*, the novel Barth has in mind as a model for the plot of *The Sot-Weed Factor*, has been examined by Battestin in *Twentieth Century Interpretations of Tom Jones*, pp. 10–15. As I have pointed out elsewhere, the eighteenth-century idea of order is also under parodic attack in Barth's novel (*Contemporary American Novelists of the Absurd*, pp. 116–19).

20. Bellamy, *The New Fiction*, p. 6.

21. Prince, "Interview," p. 48.

22. Jakobson and Halle, *Fundamentals of Language*, p. 58.

23. Bruns, *Modern Poetry*, p. 139.

24. Dembo and Pondrom, *Contemporary Writer*, p. 22.

25. Stark, *Literature of Exhaustion*, p. 161.

26. Morrell, *Barth*, p. 47.

27. Mukarovský, "Standard Language and Poetic Language," in Garvin, ed. and trans., *A Prague School Reader*, p. 19. Tanner says he first found the term in G. B. Tennyson's book on *Sartor Resartus*; see *City of Words*, p. 20.

28. Maurice Blanchot, quoted in Bruns, *Modern Poetry*, pp. 148–49. Barth attributes the term to Borges in Bellamy, *The New Fiction*, p. 4.

29. Gass, *Fiction and the Figures of Life*, p. 27.

30. Bruns, *Modern Poetry*, p. 148.

31. The novelist, says Gass, "is ceasing to pretend that his business is to render the world; he knows, more often now, that his business is to *make* one, and to make one from the only medium of which he is a master—language" (*Fiction and the Figures of Life*, p. 24).

32. Enck, "Interview," p. 21.

33. "Terministic screens" is Kenneth Burke's phrase; see *Language as Symbolic Action*, pp. 44–63.

34. McKenzie, ed., "Pole-Vaulting in Top Hats," p. 151.

35. Ibid.

36. Olderman, *Beyond the Waste Land*, p. 2.

37. Tanner, *City of Words*, p. 246.

38. Jameson, *Prison-House of Language*, p. 37.

39. Barth, *Chimera*, p. 203.

40. Young, *Three Bags Full*, pp. 175–203. See Weixlmann's full account of Barth's use of Smith's journals in "Use and Abuse of Smith's *General Historie.*"

41. Diser, "Historical Ebenezer Cooke," and Morrell, *Barth*, pp. 27–48. See also Alan Holder, " 'What Marvelous Plot Was Afoot?' "

42. Spencer, *Space, Time, and Structure*, p. 52.

43. Ewell, "Barth," pp. 40–41.

44. Gado, ed., *First Person*, p. 132.

45. Glasheen, *Third Census of Finnegans Wake*, pp. lxxii–lxxxvi.

46. Bruns, *Modern Poetry*, p. 159.

47. Locke, *Essay Concerning Human Understanding*, II, 27.

48. Hume, *Treatise of Human Nature*, I, iv, 6.

49. Schulz, *Black Humor Fiction*, p. 19; Diser, "Historical Ebenezer Cooke," p. 58; Zavarzadeh, *Mythopoeic Reality*, p. 3.

50. Kaplan, *Passive Voice*, pp. 19, 192–93.

51. Ibid., p. 99.

52. Nahal, *Narrative Pattern in Hemingway*, pp. 36–38.

53. Ibid., p. 44.

54. Ewell, "Barth," p. 37.

55. Saussure, *Cours de linguistique générale*.

56. Cf. Robert R. Magliola's discussion of Heidegger's theory of language, a theory (as I point out in Chs. 6 and 8 and which I suggest throughout the present chapter) that Barth's own theory of language seems to resemble closely. Heidegger's theory, Magliola writes, "strikes middle ground between the radical structuralist position and that of the more conventional linguistic schools. For a pure structuralist, written or spoken words *(parole)* refer only to each other and do so through couplings of sound and sense determined by the grammar and lexic of a people's language *(langue)*. The system of language (which is a 'blank' of arbitrary correlations between sound and sense) is thus self-enclosed and does not recognize references to the real world. On the other hand, conventional linguistics has interpreted language as 'sign or cipher' . . . and has considered language referential: words point to the real world, and according to some linguists even correspond to the real form of that world. Martin Heidegger denies that poetic language is referential in the ordinary sense, that of pointing towards the outside. But . . . he does not exclude referentiality in a broader sense, that of language referring to a prelinguistic

world. Rather, language refers to Being by making it 'present' within words. Heidegger takes the 'outside' and brings it 'inside' the house of language." (*Phenomenology and Literature*, p. 69). On "orphic" as opposed to "hermetic" theories of language, see Bruns, *Modern Poetry*, p. 2.

57. Roland Barthes, "To Write: An Intransitive Verb?," in DeGeorge, ed., *The Structuralists*, pp. 155–67.

58. Barth, *The Floating Opera*, p. 58.

59. Jameson, *Prison-House of Language*, pp. 122–23.

60. Turbayne, *Myth of Metaphor*, p. 216.

61. Ryle, *Concept of Mind*, p. 8.

62. On this matter Barth writes: "the difference between the fantasy we call reality and the fantasies we call fantasy has to do with cultural consensus and with one's manner of relating to the concept-structure involved: what we call the real world, we relate to as if it were the case" ("Tales within Tales within Tales," p. 45).

63. Turbayne, *Myth of Metaphor*, pp. 22, 8, 69.

64. Klein, "The Tower and the Muse."

65. Fiedler, *Love and Death in the American Novel*, pp. 10–11.

66. Friedman, *The Turn of the Novel*, Ch. 2.

67. Dryden, *Melville's Thematics of Form*, p. 211.

68. Barthes, "To Write," in DeGeorge, ed., *The Structuralists*, p. 166.

69. Himself an opposite-sex fraternal twin, Barth attributes much of his interest in language as well as in the dualism/unity question to the fact of his twinness. See "Some Reasons Why I Tell the Stories I Tell."

70. Henry has attained that unified state of consciousness the Heideggerian psychoanalyst Ludwig Binswanger terms *koinonia*, which, roughly translated, means "alliance" or "interrelationship." *Koinonia* assumes three functions: the alliance between human existence *(Dasein)* and the world of things *(Seienden)*, the integration or interpenetration of body and "soul," and the temporal alliance between past and future, life and death. "The self of existence," Binswanger writes of this latter function, "has to be 'as it is and can be.' Its being . . . is always already in *advance* of itself. This being in advance of itself also concerns the whole of *Dasein's* structure. [The "meaning" of *Dasein*, says Heidegger, is temporal; its "structure" is "Care."] Corresponding to all that we know of its throwness (as already-being-in-the-world), the being-in-advance-of-itself of the Dasein, its futurity, is through and through implicated with its past. Out of both the temporal 'ecstasies' the authentic present temporalizes itself" (in Gras, ed., *European Literary Theory and Practice*, p. 51). Only near the novel's close does Henry locate his place in history, which satisfies the third function of *koinonia*, thus making his future possible — a fact symbolized in the novel by Henry's use of the eggplant recipe, a representative of the past, to sire a son.

71. See my analysis of Barth's parody of the eighteenth-century use of coincidence in *Contemporary American Novelists of the Absurd*, pp. 116–18.

72. Quoted in Koestler, *Roots of Coincidence*, p. 108. Koestler's discussion of synchronicity and seriality is stimulating and accurate.

73. Murphy, "In Print: Barth," p. 37. More recently, Barth has said he does not remember making this remark; see Bellamy, *The New Fiction*, p. 14.

74. Bruns, *Modern Poetry*, p. 161.

75. Hart, *Structure and Motif in Finnegans Wake*, pp. 166–67.

5
Synthesis Gained:
Giles Goat-Boy

"I'm not sure that synthesis is possible," Barth told an interviewer. "And I'm not terribly interested in it anyhow."[1] One detects a bit of Todd Andrews in that statement, for it is at best half-true. Barth may not believe synthesis possible, but his interest in it grows increasingly evident through the first three novels. In *Giles Goat-Boy* (1966) that interest becomes a preoccupation. All but the final forty pages concern the heroic struggle of George Giles to decide the ostensibly antithetical nature of Flunkedness and Passedness, good and evil. In those final pages, however, George transcends the disparate nature of things and arrives at an awareness of the unity of an apparently various universe. His moment of illumination occurs during his third descent into WESCAC's belly. Coupled with Anastasia, his head covered by his mother's purse, George perceives "the University whole and clear." Like Oedipus he sees "in the darkness blinding light! The end of the University! Commencement Day!"[2] As Robert Scholes phrases it, George discovers "Synthesis. Passage and Failure are distinct but interdependent. They define one another and are as necessary as North and South or male and female to the functioning of the universe."[3] In this crucial scene not only does George attain a vision of cosmic synthesis, but the multiple strands of Barth's intricate artifice are themselves reconciled into an artistic whole.

Several critics have detected certain facets of the novel's unity. In his perceptive discussion of the linguistic richness of Barth's book, for instance, Peter Mercer observes that the narrating rhetoric used by Giles constitutes a synthesis of various "rhetorical registers" that refer to separate dimensions of human experience. Expansive and inclusive, Giles's language metaphorically yokes the novel's apparent incongruities as reflected in its multiple rhetorics. Also emphasizing the principle of synthesis is John Tilton, who discusses the confluence in the novel of three mythological components: the myth of the hero, the myth of Satan, and the mythopoeic implications of the differences between oriental and occidental responses to life. Though operative at different levels, these three myths ultimately merge, forming a thematic unity. In *The Fabulators* Scholes discerns a dialectical structure in *Giles Goat-Boy*, observing that the novel's "three main phases — thesis, antithesis, and synthesis — are unmistakable. They are correlated in the narrative with George's three descents to WESCAC's belly, and all the actions and advice associated with those three descents." Though focusing respectively on language, theme, and structure, each critic locates the novel's matrix of meaning in synthesis. [4]

By far the most comprehensive statement of the principle of synthesis in the novel is provided by Jac Tharpe, who analyzes in precise detail the elaborate system of polarities running in dialectical confrontation. "*Giles*," Tharpe summarizes, "is built on a series of parallels between WESCAC and EASCAC, Russia and America, East and West, pacifism and activity, light and dark, Stoker and Rexford, Giles and Bray, mystery and knowledge, natural and supernatural, Max and Eierkopf, Croaker and Eierkopf, among many others." Yet Tharpe's conclusion that "the novel apparently ends with a statement of synthesis that derives from Hegel"[5] requires some modification. Hegel saw history as an ongoing dynamic process in which everything is eventually transformed into its opposite, thesis becoming antithesis until both merge into a new whole, a synthesis that retains the elements of the prior phases but in an altered or elevated (Hegel's word is *aufgehoben)* state. As this dialectical process unfolds, man potentially achieves higher and higher levels of freedom and consciousness. Yet, as Gordon E. Slethaug demonstrates, Barth has little faith in the idea of progress.[6] Accordingly, the dialectical presentation of *Giles Goat-Boy* resembles Hegel's system less than the presentational mode that Stanley Fish finds characteristic of much seventeenth-century literature.

Fish distinguishes between two kinds of literary presentation: the rhetorical, which "satisfies" the reader in its confirmation of

"the categories and assumptions of received systems of knowledge," and the dialectical, which tends to subvert those received
systems. Each mode of presentation represents a different way of
perceiving the world. The rhetorical affirms discursive or rational
epistemologies; "its characteristic motion is one of distinguishing,
and the world it delivers is one of separable and discrete entities
where everything is in its proper place." The dialectical, on the
other hand, is anti-discursive and anti-rational, resolving rather
than distinguishing, "and in the world it delivers the lines of de-
marcation between places and things fade in the light of an all-
embracing unity."[7] In his study of seventeenth-century literature,
Frank Warnke similarly refers to the "conviction, expressed in various ways, that ultimate reality is some kind of all-embracing unity."[8] Having lost its faith in the reality of the phenomenal world, a
world of discrete and changing entities, the Baroque period displayed obsessive desire for the unchanging One. The realm of ultimate unity exceeds man's powers of articulation, since words force
distinctions. Referring to the difficulties in writing a sermon based
on Augustine's *On Christian Doctrine*, Fish states: "The simplest
syntactical string — subject-object-verb — assumes distinctions a
sacramental [i.e., holistic] view of the world denies, and one cannot write a sentence without placing the objects to which its words
refer in relationships of subordination and dependence." How,
then, can a writer use words, his only medium, "to frustrate these
dividing and distinguishing tendencies of language"? The answer:
through the strategic use of a dialectical presentation which by its
very processes *cancels itself out.* Paradoxically, such presentation
succeeds best when it fails, "when it points *away* from itself to
something its forms cannot capture." Art thus becomes "self-
consuming," for "by conveying those who experience it to a point
where they are beyond the aid that discursive or rational forms
can offer, it becomes the vehicle of its own abandonment," moving
the reader beyond the artifact that cannot contain ineffable Truth
to personal confrontation with that Truth.[9]

Such conceptions are by no means limited to the seventeenth
century. Wittgenstein, for example, speaking of the *Tractatus*, his
own "self-consuming artifact," writes, "My propositions serve as
elucidations in the following way: anyone who understands me
eventually recognizes them as nonsensical, when he has used
them — as steps — to climb up beyond them. (He must, so to speak,

throw away the ladder after he has climbed up it)."[10] Truth, to
paraphrase Fish, is not brought to man by such artifacts, but man
to the Truth. The synthesis toward which the dialectical movement of these artifacts proceeds is not achieved *within* the artifact
itself; rather, it lies outside the artwork, outside language — in
Wittgenstein's words, "outside the world."[11] Nietzsche also envi-
sions an un-Hegelian synthesis, one that remains ever-present, discoverable at any moment by great individuals.[12] This is not to say
that Creation itself lacks shift and flux; to the contrary, change
defines reality. But flux and opposition form part of a larger unity.
"Is the world full of guilt, injustice, contradiction, and suffering?"
Nietzsche asks. "Yes . . . but only for the limited man who does
not see the total design; . . . for [the unlimited man] all contradiction is harmonized."[13] Correctly perceived, Creation is a vast unity
of interconnected polarities. That man who apprehends this identity of opposites Nietzsche calls Dionysian: "What he [wants is]
totality; he [fights] the mutual extraneousness of reason, senses,
feeling, and will . . . he discipline[s] himself to wholeness, he
create[s] himself. . . . Such a spirit . . . stands amid the cosmos
with a joyous and trusting fatalism, in the *faith* that only the particular is loathesome, and that all is redeemed and affirmed in the
whole — *he does not negate anymore.* Such a faith . . . is the
highest of all possible faiths: I have baptized it with the name of
Dionysus."[14] Nietzsche has Goethe in mind in the preceding passage, but he could as easily be speaking of Henry Burlingame.
While clearly mythic, Nietzsche's vision is less mystical than either
Wittgenstein's or that of the seventeenth-century writers Fish examines. Consequently, the art he most admires does not deny itself
through a self-consuming process, but embodies that synthesis of
opposites he calls Dionysian. Greek tragedy, particularly in the
hands of Sophocles and Aeschylus, represents Dionysian art at its
highest. Such tragedy, "by its fusion of dialogue and chorus, image
and music, exhibits for Nietzsche the union of the Apollonian
and Dionysian, a union in which Dionysian passion and dithyram-
bic madness merge with Apollonian measure and lucidity."[15]
Translated into Barthian terms, Dionysian art achieves passionate
virtuosity.

   While it would prove difficult to establish a direct influence of
these ideas on Barth's fiction, as analogs their relevance should be
evident. In his transcension of categories Giles enters the realm be-

yond language that Wittgenstein terms the "mystical," just as his realization that all opposites ultimately coincide resembles the vision of synthesis that Nietzsche calls Dionysian. One need turn neither to Nietzsche nor to Wittgenstein for analogs to George's illumination, since a more relevant parallel (indeed, the primary source for Barth's handling of the scene) is Joseph Campbell's treatment of the hero myth in *The Hero with a Thousand Faces*. On the other hand, Nietzsche's conception of Dionysian art and Fish's examination of self-consuming artifacts are quite pertinent to the formal properties of *Giles Goat-Boy*. The manifold allusions informing the novel's various frames of reference — the historical, theological, mythological, sociological, philosophical, and literary, among others, each in keeping with the novel's controlling metaphor: the universe as university — lead nowhere if tracked individually. Indeed, they serve as a parody of the rhetorical (that is, the discursive or rational) approach to experience, each allusion representing a separate version of "reality" constructed by man. The novel's allegorical dimension plus its self-reflexive nature, its insistence that it is nothing more than artifice, constitute a form of self-invalidation or, to use Fish's term, self-consumption. At the same time, the fact that the novel's various strands, if viewed from a larger perspective, reconcile themselves into a meaningful whole (as Mercer, Tilton, Scholes, and Tharpe have demonstrated) suggests the Dionysian synthesis Nietzsche finds in Greek tragedy. In this respect the book itself serves as a metaphor for the unified cosmos Giles perceives, just as Giles's relationship to that cosmos parallels the reader's relationship to Barth's novel. As Giles must transcend the shift and flux of human experience to see the University whole, so must the reader see Barth's labyrinthian novel whole if he is to avoid becoming lost in its Baroque passageways.

George's character embodies elements that reflect that unity he ultimately perceives and the novel itself embodies. The fact that George is a goat-boy and possibly divine, for example, suggests the goat-god Pan. In fact, in her revealing study of Pan, Patricia Merivale calls Giles "the best-known contemporary goatish superman." The "very core" of Pan's identity, Merivale writes, is "the paradox of a being half goat and half god."[16] In him the "attributes of malevolence are combined with the essence of benevolence." In classical antiquity Pan's form was extended "to include the heavens, the sea, earth, and fire — universal Nature"; he became "Supreme

Governor or 'soul' of the World."[17] In short, Pan's very identity depends upon synthesis, a fact reflected in the apparent (though probably spurious) derivation of his name from the Greek *pan*, meaning "all."

A further clue to the synthetic nature of George and his heroic mission is supplied by Campbell's *Hero with a Thousand Faces*, the influence of which upon *Giles Goat-Boy* Barth has publicly acknowledged.[18] Campbell establishes in his book a composite hero, a synthesis of various heroes from myth and folklore. In tracing that hero's adventures Campbell constructs what he terms a *monomyth*, itself a synthesis of "the basic truths by which man has lived throughout the millenniums of his residence on the planet." Giles's mission is to reenact the traditional phases of the archetypal heroic experience against the novel's comic-allegorical backdrop. That he does so in a manner closely paralleling the pattern Campbell describes has been demonstrated elsewhere and need not be repeated here.[19] Suffice it to say that, as antitype of the "monohero," Giles recapitulates the monomyth in modern times, becoming in the process a synthesis of man's endless quest for truth as well as an embodiment of the synthetic nature of that truth.

Even the circumstances of George's birth reinforce the unity he represents. Although sired by WESCAC, George's real father is mankind. As he explains, "The eugenical specimen whereof I was the issue had been drawn as it were from all studentdom, whose scion therefore I was; WESCAC's role had merely been that of an inseminatory instrument" (638). Giles is literally the son of man, a synthesis of "studentdom's" various genes. Conceived at exactly midnight, March twenty-first, Giles is born 275 days later, also at midnight, on December twenty-first (507). Moreover, his illumination seems to occur on his twenty-first birthday moment.[20] All three dates fall on cusps, those first days of an astrological house which contain characteristics of the house preceding it — days, that is, which form a *synthesis* of two separate astrological houses. Similarly, midnight is neither yesterday, today, nor quite yet tomorrow, but a synthesis of all three. George's conception, birth, and illumination (itself containing conception, in the sense of knowing or realization, and rebirth) occur at midnight and on cusps, the cusp and midnight serving as symbols for that unity of opposites embodied in synthesis. Fathered by a computer out of a human virgin and reared his first thirteen years as a goat, George serves as organic compendium of the three chief elements of the physical realm: the mechanical or technological, the human, and the animal or natural. Further linked by his vision to the metaphysical realm, George incorporates in his very essence both physical and metaphysical reality. The circumstances of his birth, the nature of his experiences, and the mythic precedents these evoke combine to make George a living symbol of the synthetic vision he ultimately perceives.

Other characters in the novel fall short of his synthetic vision. Concentrating on portions of the Whole, they gain only partial truths. Exemplifying this addiction to details is Eblis Eierkopf, who carries his reductive empiricism to such extremes that his major project involves measuring that point in clock time "where Tick becomes Tock" (434). In his zeal to order and schematize "reality" Eierkopf actually distorts it, producing scientific "truths" that reflect the "reality" they describe far less than the mind which formulates them. This tendency is further parodied when each major character offers his own definition of "Graduation," equivalent in the novel to spiritual salvation.[21] Perspectivism thus becomes a key theme in Barth's book, a theme emphasized by the many references to mirrors, scopes, and lenses. Exemplifying this addiction to lenses is, once again, Eblis Eierkopf, who tells Giles, "There aren't any mysteries, just ignorance. When something looks miraculous it's because we're using the wrong lenses. . . . Mirrors and lenses are my favorite things" (336). Later, when Giles attempts to examine a gift from Sear through one of Eierkopf's lenses, he sees only "the magnified reflection" of his own eye (361). The point, of course, is that too great a reliance upon seeing as a way of knowing results in a kind of blindness (another recurring motif in the novel). "Truth" thus becomes a matter of perspective, and the number of perspectives from which "reality" can be viewed varies infinitely, each perspective constructing a separate "reality."

Before his moment of illumination George must also view "reality" partially. At that moment, however, George transcends the categories into which he and others divide "reality." He views simultaneously its various parts—indeed, merges with, *becomes*, that reality—and, from a perspective of higher subjectivity, views Reality objectively. In George's ephiphanic vision objectivity and subjectivity merge, just as he and the University become One.[22]

George receives his "Assignment" on a computer printout presented when he attempts to pass through Scrape-goat Grate. At the top of this printout is the "Pass-All/Fail-All" paradox of George's PAT-card; below that paradox are listed the requisites of his Assignment:

To Be Done At Once, In No Time
1) Fix the Clock
2) End the Boundary Dispute
3) Overcome Your Infirmity
4) See Through Your Ladyship
5) Re-place the Founder's Scroll
6) Pass the Finals
7) Present Your ID-card, Appropriately Signed, to the Proper Authority. [383]

The Assignment overwhelms George, particularly the injunction "To Be Done At Once, In No Time." "And ay, and ay," George cries to himself, "so short a term!" (384). Unwittingly he predicts his own subsequent errors, for George does not extend the terms, the very *language*, of his Assignment far enough. He confuses the *terms* of his Assignment, its language, with the various referents with which he associates each term. Only when he realizes that Truth lies outside words will he be able to "let go" of the linguistic categories into which man subdivides the world. His problem is actually a linguistic conundrum, the solution to which requires him to transcend language. Instead, George interprets his Assignment in light of the allegory of which he is a part.

In allegory, as John Vernon has pointed out, "a figure represents a quality that exists in a different space from that of the figure itself," thus implying "that the identity of the [allegorical] symbol and its referent is not, in fact, an identity, but an external connection that preserves the discreteness of the two terms in question."[23] Seen in these terms, the allegorical mode of Barth's novel stands as metaphor for the kind of schizophrenic vision George must transcend, a vision which categorizes reality and separates it into various parts. George's "basic problem in the narrative," as Campbell Tatham has perceived, "is his failure to distinguish between artificially constructed allegories, mere ways of speaking . . . and the fluctuating realities which surround him."[24] Giles tries to fulfill the Assignment by confronting reality *partially*. He interprets the terms of his Assignment in a *particular* or *topical* sense, rather than a holistic or universal sense.

For example, George initially thinks his second task, "End the Boundary Dispute," refers to the frontier contention between New Tammany College and Nikolay College. Giles first advises widening the Boundary, then advises narrowing it, but in both cases he merely compounds the problem. At his moment of epiphany George realizes that, to end the boundary dispute once and for all, that power which separates things must be dissolved. Symbolizing this power is WESCAC. "Its power," says Max Spielman, "is the same that keeps the campus going . . . it's the first energy of the University: the Mind-force . . . [the] thing that tells you there's a *you*, that's different from *me*, and separates the goats from the sheeps" (50).[25] Just as Max bears a burlesque resemblance to Carl Jung, so does his concept of the "mind force" bear a resemblance to Jung's concept of consciousness. Until a certain stage in his development Jung sees man as existing in a state of "childlike unconsciousness and trust in nature." His every action determined by instinct — which, according to Jung, "is nature" — man in this childlike state has no problems. Indeed, "it is the growth of consciousness which we must thank for the existence of problems; they are the Danaan gift of civilization. It is just man's turning away from instinct — his opposing himself to instinct — that creates consciousness." With consciousness comes the crisis of differentiation. "The individual is faced with the necessity of recognizing and accepting what is different and strange as part of his own life, as a kind of 'also-I.'"[26] Jung's analysis of the fall into consciousness roughly parallels George's fall (as well as, the implication seems to be, the fall of West Campus) from a state of primal harmony with the environment into a world of differentiation and boundaries.

At the height of George's vision, however, all boundaries dissolve, and WESCAC, the symbol of differentiation, is significantly short circuited.

In the sweet place that contained me [says Giles] there was no East, no West, but an entire, single, seamless campus: Turnstile, Scrape-goat Grate, the Mall, the barns, the awful fires of the Powerhouse, the balmy heights of Founder's Hill — I saw them all; rank jungles of Frumentius, Nikolay's cold fastness, teeming T'ang — all one, and one with me. *Here* lay with *there*, *tick* clipped *tock*, all serviced *nothing;* I and my Ladyship, all, were one. [673]

At this moment of symbolic and actual fusion with Anastasia, George moves into the transcendent, thus ending the boundary dispute by destroying the very concept of boundaries.

At the instant when George accomplishes his second task he also completes his first one. He "fixes" the clock — but not by repairing it, as he originally believed the Assignment required. Giles again had missed the point by focusing on the partial rather than the total picture. Clock time, he discovers, is but the portioning out of that which is fluid and by its very nature indivisible. George accomplishes his task, rather, by moving *outside* time, thus "fixing," or securing against movement, clock time. "No bells toll where we were," Giles describes the place where he and Anastasia lie embraced. "*In no time* at all we lay there forever" (674, italics mine).

The phrase "in no time at all" echoes the admonition at the top of Giles's Assignment list: "To Be Done At Once, In No Time." In his limited interpretation George reads "in no time" to mean "immediately." In WESCAC's belly, however, he moves into what Campbell calls "ceremonial time," where "time collapses . . . and what was 'then' becomes 'now.'"[27] Chronological time belongs to the "allegorical" world and, as such, attempts to "map" systematically time's irregular flux, just as physical boundaries attempt to map space. But in the sweet no-time of George's deliverance tick clips tock, then becomes now, time dissolves with space. When time ceases, *simultaneity* remains. George is thus able to perform his seven tasks, not successively, one at a time, but *simultaneously*, at once, in no time.

The first two tasks are accomplished simultaneously. Similarly, at the moment when George moves beyond the limitations of time and space he overcomes his infirmity and sees through his Ladyship, fulfilling his third and fourth tasks. His infirmity is the same incapacity that prevents him from correctly interpreting his Assignment — his propensity to see things as separate and distinct, rather than as parts of a vast whole. While still a "kid" at the Ag-Hill Goat Farm, George instinctively responded to this totality, enjoying a primal harmony with his environment. In his fourteenth year, around the traditional age of initiation, the gradual destruction of his harmony begins. He learns cruelty, when the human beings visiting the Farm kick and scream at him when he accidentally falls outside his pen (14); then hatred, when he reflects on the embarrassment these human beings caused him (14); grief, when Max is forced to hit George when he attacks Lady Creamhair (16); dissembling, when he lies to Max about his meetings with Lady Creamhair (20); lust, when he watches Harry and Chickie copulate in the buckwheat and later attempts to rape Lady Creamhair; and finally jealousy, rage, and violence as he kills Redfearn Tom (44). Initiated into the complex moral relationships of human experience, George is cut off from the synergetic concord he enjoyed with his surroundings and his fellow creatures. Saddled with Max's "mind Force" and Jung's crisis of differentiation, he feels sick and alienated: "Here was this growth called Max, utterly other than myself. . . . He was, had been, and would for a while yet be a *person*, truly as I. Very nearly I shivered at his reality, and that of the university of objects which were not myself. . . . I was filled with an overwhelming sense of the queerness of things, a woozy repugnance, and a flashing discontent" (86). He has, in short, "fallen into consciousness" in the Jungian sense, a stage which normally coincides with puberty.[28]

Most of George's newly acquired "human" traits can be associated with his newly aroused sexuality. As a result of this nascent sexuality George, before his illumination, feels lust many times—for Hedda, for Chickie, for Lady Creamhair, for Anastasia—but he never feels love. Indeed, George's sense of alienation may be seen as the result of a failure of love, not romantic love but transcendent love, Whitman's "kelson of Creation." George's fall into consciousness results in the birth of his ego, a sense of his self as separate from other selves. This sense of schism allows George to view others objectively, that is, as objects inevitably apart from his subjective self. Such objectivity leads George to misunderstand his fourth task—to see through his Ladyship—by characteristically interpreting it too literally. When Anastasia correctly advises George that "the Ladyship part of Your Assignment means You're supposed to know me so well that we'll be the same person" (617), George decides he should familiarize himself with her physical person. In one of the most extraordinary scenes in all literature, Giles closely examines his Ladyship, carefully measuring her various parts, touching her everywhere, even listening to, smelling, and tasting her wherever possible. Not stopping there, however, George determines to see through her, literally, by using Dr. Sear's fluoroscope. Thoroughly examined, Anastasia remains utterly other. "I don't understand anything," George groans, echoing his

similar cry to Max when he first perceived the otherness of things
(616, 29). George knows *about* Anastasia; he understands her no-
tionally and he has experienced her sensually, but she remains
apart from him. Only love can link them. And as surely as love
links George to Anastasia, it links him to all of Creation. "According to the mysticism of sexual love," explains Joseph Campbell,
"the ultimate experience of love is a realization that beneath the illusion of twoness dwells identity: 'each is both.' This realization
can expand into a discovery that beneath the multitudinous individualities of the whole universe . . . dwells identity."[29] George
makes this discovery when, "stirred to the marrow" by the proximity of Anastasia, he embraces her and, joined conjugally, they
tumble into WESCAC's belly and a vision of totality. "For though
the place was lightless," says George of that vision, "and my head
pursed, in Anastasia I discovered the University whole and clear.
Mother of my soul, its pulse throbbed all around us; my Father's
eye it was glowed near, whose loving inquiry I perceived through
my Ladyship" (672). His infirmity overcome, Giles sees Truth
through—that is, *by way of*—his Ladyship, fulfilling the fourth
task of his assignment. Together, George and Stacey sing what
Campbell calls "the song of universal unity": "Oh, wonderful!"
(673).[30]

George has at once transcended time and space, overcome his
infirmity, and seen through His Ladyship. Simultaneously he "re-
places" the Founder's Scroll, not by putting it back in its cabinet, as
the task seen in terms of the novel's allegorical framework seems to
require, but by realizing—indeed, by *becoming*—the essential
Truth the Scroll professes to teach. He has *taken the place* of the
Scroll, suggesting that the Truth he encompasses cannot be tran-
scribed, though it may be realized experientially.

Earlier George had replaced the Scroll in a different sense. We
are told that originally the Founder's Scroll was "actually several
scrolls, overlapping, redundant, discrepant" (663). When a com-
mittee of scholars tries to derive a definitive text for the Scroll,
they ask Giles to give his thoughts on what should fill the lacuna
obfuscating a key phrase. Instead of supplying the needed information, Giles "re-places" the Scroll by returning it to the condition
it was in before the scholars began restructuring it: "I huffed a great
puff," says George, "sending vellum flinders in all directions, and
with a sweep of my stick scattered fragments, chemicals, note-

cards, shears, and scholars" (665). The Founder's Scroll once again becomes several scrolls, overlapping, redundant, and discrepant, suggesting the fluctuating, multidimensional nature of a reality that cannot be reduced to a single formulated doctrine.

What the scholars want to know is whether a crucial sentence "ought to be translated *Flunkèd who would Pass* or *Passèd are the Flunked.*" Upon this sentence "depended whole systems of others, perhaps even the overall sense of the Founder's Scroll" (664). Upon it is "constructed the whole mad edifice of campus history, for a clear understanding whereof it was absolutely essential to have accurate texts" (665). George is asked to provide a final answer to the question concerning man's final judgment: What must man do to be saved? One sentence would complete the hermetic circle of language into which these scholars and their society could then retreat, content that they had discovered when indeed they had constructed "reality." But George, like Barth, *passes by* final solutions, declining comment. He thus anticipates his mystical illumination in WESCAC's belly, when he similarly bypasses finals, both in the sense of ends (which are boundaries of sorts) and answers (which in their finality and certitude not only offer conclusions but involve formulations that by their very nature are reductive and distortive). "'I knew what studentdom was pleased to call 'The Answer,'" says George near the novel's end, "though that term — indeed the whole proposition — was as misleading as any other (and thus as satisfactory), since what I 'knew' neither 'I' nor anyone could 'teach'" (703).

George encloses "The Answer," "knew," "I," and "teach" in quotation marks because the terms only approximate their referents, are mere manners of speaking — are, in short, inaccurate, since each term implies separation, the Other; and at the height of his vision the Other dissolved. George has discovered what Todd Andrews suspected, that "to understand one thing entirely, no matter how minute, requires the understanding of every other thing in the world."[31] George bypasses the finals because he cannot communicate the truth his metavision supplies. Having achieved experientially the coalescence Burlingame craves, George finds impossible what Joseph Campbell says all heroes find difficult: "How render back into light-world language the speech-defying pronouncements of the dark."[32] From a practical standpoint George's vision is as useless to him as existentialism was to Jake Horner. As he observes in the Posttape, his truth cannot be taught (707). Language, by its very nature, forces distinctions — indeed, as the structuralists see it, language "means" through distinction — while Truth incorporates "every . . . thing in the world," thus blotting out distinctions. "To turn experience into speech," Barth writes in another context, " — that is, to classify, to categorize, to conceptualize, to grammarize, to syntactify it — is always a betrayal of experience, a falsification of it."[33] So George sees "termless Truth" (706) but must remain incommunicado. As Wittgenstein suggests, metaphysics is impossible because the "solution of the riddle of life and space and time lies *outside* space and time," which is to say, outside language. "We feel," continues Wittgenstein, "that even when *all possible* scientific questions have been answered, the problems of life remain completely untouched. Of course there are then no questions left, and this itself is their answer. . . . The solution of the problem of life is seen in the vanishing of the problem."[34] Similarly, George has not answered WESCAC's questions; he has invalidated them, denied their legitimacy. He solves his problem, which is finally linguistic in nature, by transcending it. George's truth is "termless" in two senses: as eternal truth it transcends the limitations of time; as all-inclusive "mystical" truth it resists the reductiveness of language.

The all-inclusive nature of this Truth explains George's fulfillment of his seventh task: "Present Your ID-card, Appropriately Signed, to the Proper Authority." In his first two descents to WESCAC's belly George presents the ID-card to WESCAC, whom he takes to be the proper authority, by placing the card in a designated slot. George had signed the card in the invisible ink given him earlier by The Living Sahkyan, an Eastern holy man. George almost realizes the significance of this gift during the second descent into WESCAC's belly. Noticing the already fading signature, he proclaims, "I was not born George; I was not born anything; I had invented myself as I'd elected my name" (636). Again, however, he fails to go far enough in interpreting the terms of his Assignment. The point of the Buddha's gift is not just that George's name and identity are self-created, but that ultimately neither name, identity, nor self exists autonomously. Like all linguistic labels, names distinguish this person from that, that thing from its other. The very fact of a name, an identity, an ID-card, reflects the differentiation WESCAC symbolizes. By submitting his ID-card to WESCAC, the proper *secular* authority, Giles affirms this differentiation.

In George's final descent to the belly, however, the ID-card goes significantly unmentioned. Giles's personal autonomous identity, like his name, has disappeared. "I was the Founder," he cries; "I was WESCAC; I was not" (673). In dissolving his personality George fulfills the point made by The Living Sahkyan, whose name means "living silence."[35] The holy man embodies the living, all-encompassing silence — Campbell's "ineluctable void" — that George perceives, and he foreshadows the silence George eventually practices insofar as the Truth he learns is concerned. Moreover, in merging with The Founder, George becomes as well the "proper authority" to whom he must present himself, a living "ID-card." Thus he feeds himself to himself (673). As Campbell writes, "The hero, the waker of his own soul, is himself but the convenient means of his own dissolution. . . . God, the waker of the soul, is therewith his own immediate death. . . . God assumes the life of man and man releases the God within himself . . . — each as the other's food."[36] Finally, in achieving apotheoses, George has recapitulated the trials and achievement of the archetypal hero, thus fulfilling the requisite signs for herohood. He is therefore "appropriately signed."

So in one remarkable scene George achieves a vision of simultaneity and synthesis and the various parts of Barth's massive fiction are explained and reconciled, thus establishing the synthetic quality of the entire novel. But if Barth gives us a hero who perceives order and a novel that demonstrates it, he insists throughout that the novel is an artifice, its world militantly fictional. Like Ambrose, the artist-narrator of "Lost in the Funhouse," Barth has constructed "a truly astonishing funhouse, incredibly complex yet utterly controlled."[37] As an alternative to "reality," Barth's fictional world possesses order. The Funhouse we occupy may not. And even if it does, its order is probably like that George perceives, all-encompassing, immeasurable, inexpressible — much like chaos itself. Thus Barth's elaborately ordered fictional world suggests the fictiveness of all ordered worlds. Indeed, the very elements that I have been analyzing (the hero motif, the Jungian parallels, the allegory) plus numerous others (the *Bildungsroman* form, the stock characters and situations, the classical and biblical allusions) are self-consciously "literary," their artificiality emphasized. The familiarity of these motifs and devices suggests that Barth is not imitating "reality" at all, but — as he has indicated — imitations of reality.[38] *Giles Goat-Boy* is not about the world, but about the ways we *talk* about the world.

Such "talk" is more therapeutic than mimetic, the order it creates purely esthetic, yet Barth insists upon as he affirms its necessity. If we have "come too far" (as Jake Horner asserts in *The End of the Road*) to believe any longer in the authenticity of our formulated realities, this fact changes not in the least our need to continue formulating.[39] "How to speak the unspeakable?" cries George after his epiphany, and then he demonstrates how for over 700 pages. As Campbell Tatham observes, George finds a "way of talking about the impossibility of fixing meaning,"[40] or, to put it another way, a way of talking about the impossibility of talking. He faces an ultimacy, an artistic dead end, turns it back upon itself, and produces art, a process that explains not only George's esthetic but also Barth's. The artifice in *Giles Goat-Boy* suggests that the entire novel is but a "way of speaking," an approximation of a Truth that cannot be formulated. At the same time, the novel affirms "ways of speaking" as, quite simply, the only way *to* speak. It affirms the narrative impulse, accomplishing in the process an artistic achievement of the highest magnitude.

NOTES

1. Prince, "Interview," p. 57.

2. Barth, *Giles Goat-Boy* (Garden City, N.Y.: Doubleday, 1966), p. 673. Subsequent references to this edition appear in parentheses in the text.

3. Scholes, *The Fabulators*, p. 167.

4. Mercer, "Rhetoric of *Giles Goat-Boy*"; Tilton, *Cosmic Satire*; Scholes, *The Fabulators*, p. 163.

5. Tharpe, *Barth*, pp. 55, 54.

6. Slethaug, "Barth's Refutation of the Idea of Progress."

7. Fish, *Self-Consuming Artifacts*, pp. 1–3. In *Giles* Barth preserves some of the mannerisms of *The Sot-Weed Factor*. "I was interested to notice that after my long experience of a kind of eighteenth century-ish prose," he remarks, "my prose style in some ways was marked for good, and in the Goat Boy book—which has nothing to do with the eighteenth century—certain kinds of locutions and cadences simply were there forever," particularly "the accented last syllable of the past participle" (Prince, "Interview," p. 48). Not just stylistic devices, but certain epistemological concerns carry over as well.

8. Warnke, *Versions of the Baroque*, p. 52.

9. Fish, *Self-Consuming Artifacts*, pp. 41, 94, 3.

10. Wittgenstein, *Tractatus Logico-philosophicus*, 6.54, p. 151. At this point in his tract the understanding to which Wittgenstein refers is not mystical but philosophical. But the mystical implications of the *Tractatus* are clear, as was pointed out in Ch. 3.

11. Ibid. 6.41, p. 145.

12. "Mankind," he writes, "does *not* represent a development toward something better or stronger or higher in the sense accepted today. 'Progress' is merely a modern idea, that is, a false idea" (*The Antichrist*, in Kaufmann, ed. and trans., *Portable Nietzsche*, p. 571).

13. *Nachlass*, quoted in Pfeffer, *Nietzsche*, p. 172. My discussion of Nietzsche is indebted to Pfeffer's excellent study.

14. *Twilight of the Idols*, in Kaufmann, ed. and trans., *Portable Nietzsche*, p. 554.

15. Pfeffer, *Nietzsche*, p. 51.

16. Merivale, *Pan the Goat-God*, pp. 1, 9.

17. Embodiment of Truth, Pan revealed "the inner world to those capable of perceiving it" (ibid., p. 185). The "representatives of ordinary insensitive humanity," however, feared their own "aroused unconscious," fleeing in terror and often expiring of dread (Campbell, *Hero with a Thousand Faces*, p. 81). Giles similarly instills panic; note especially the response of the crowd witnessing Giles's rout of Bray from the campus.

18. E.g., Enck, "Interview," p. 27.

19. See my *Contemporary American Novelists of the Absurd*, pp. 110–14, or Tatham's "Gilesean Monomyth."

20. In a letter to me (11 Feb. 1972) Barth confirms that Giles's illumination does occur on his twenty-first birthday moment. In the novel the last reference to time before Giles's epiphany is to 11:15; it occurs as Giles and Anastasia make their way toward the tape-lift which will lower them to WESCAC's belly (p. 669).

21. Eierkopf, for example, believes Commencement is achieved when one eliminates his passions. Maurice Stoker, satanic embodiment of energy, insists that Graduation is power. Dr. Kennard Sear, hedonistic erotopath, feels that Graduation occurs when "we've . . . rid ourselves of every trace of innocence" (313). Lucius Rexford, Kennedy-like Chancellor of West Campus, defines the Graduate as one who has "the best mind in the best body he can manage. . . . An All-College halfback, say, with a Ph.D.!" (368). The wealthy capitalist Ira Hector rejects the concept of Graduation altogether as a "day-dream of fools and bankrupts, worth nothing on the . . . market" (393).

22. George achieves what John Vernon calls "garden consciousness" in *The Garden and the Map*. Vernon's thesis is that what he terms "map

consciousness," the propensity to see "reality" in terms of opposites (inner and outer, fantasy and reality, Being and Nonbeing, Good and Evil, etc.), is gradually giving way to "garden consciousness," the ability to perceive "reality" as integrated and whole. Garden consciousness belongs to primitive man, to children, and to Eastern culture; map consciousness, on the other hand, is the defining characteristic of Western culture. The latter, argues Vernon, is "schizophrenic, in that it chooses to fragment its experience and seal certain areas off from each other. It drains the fantastic, the mad, and the subjective out of their unity with the self and the world, out of the condition by which they are not even differentiated yet, and locks them in a common inaccessible space" (p. xi). Remaining is a partial reality that the schizophrenic mind sees as the whole reality, the only reality. Thus restricted, "reality" becomes more manageable, more predictable. In the garden consciousness, however, all "opposites" merge into a "dynamic unity of external and internal, of subjective, and objective" (p. 159).

23. Ibid., p. 116.

24. Tatham, "Barth and the Aesthetics of Artifice," p. 71. Tatham's discussion of "Counter-allegory" in the novel is especially illuminating (pp. 69–72).

25. In the novel's mythic dimension, WESCAC of course represents the father. On this point cf. Campbell: "In the father are contained and from him proceed the contradictions, good and evil, death and life, pain and pleasure, boons and deprivation. As the person of the sun door, he is the fountainhead of all the pairs of opposites" (*The Hero with a Thousand Faces*, p. 145).

26. Campbell, ed., *Portable Jung*, pp. 5, 4, 10. From *The Structure and Dynamics of the Psyche*.

27. Campbell, *Masks of God*, p. 170.

28. Campbell, ed., *Portable Jung*, p. 7.

29. Campbell, *Hero with a Thousand Faces*, p. 280.

30. Ibid.

31. Barth, *The Floating Opera*, pp. 6–7.

32. Campbell, *Hero with a Thousand Faces*, p. 218.

33. Barth, *The End of the Road*, p. 112.

34. Wittgenstein, *Tractatus Logico-philosophicus*, 6.4312, 6.52, 6.521, pp. 147–49. Nietzsche also questioned the reliability of language as a source of Truth: "What about these conventions of language? Are they really the products of knowledge, or the sense of truth? Do the designations and the things coincide? Is language the adequate expression of all realities?" (*On Truth and Lie in an Extra-Moral Sense*, in Kaufmann, ed. and trans., *Portable Nietzsche*, p. 45).

35. Campbell, *Hero with a Thousand Faces*, p. 34n. One of the titles of Gautama Buddha, writes Campbell, is *Sakyamun*, "The silent one or sage *(muni)*. Though he is the founder of a widely taught world religion, the ultimate core of his doctrine remains concealed, necessarily, in silence."

36. Ibid., p. 260. " 'When the envelopment of consciousness has been annihilated,' " Campbell quotes from an Eastern holy book, " 'then [man] becomes free of all fear.' This is the release potential within us all, and which anyone can attain — through herohood; for, as we read: 'All things are Buddha-things' . . . or again (and this is the other way of making the same statement): 'All beings are without self' " (p. 151).

37. Barth, *Lost in the Funhouse*, p. 97.

38. Barth, "The Literature of Exhaustion," p. 33. On the use of artifice Barth has said, "A different way to come to terms with the discrepancy between art and the Real Thing is to affirm the artificial element in art (you can't get rid of it anyway), and make the artifice part of your point" (Enck, "Interview," p. 21).

39. Near the end of the novel Jacob finds himself bound "by the serpents Knowledge and Imagination, which, grown great in the fullness of time, no longer tempt but annihilate" (187). The implication is that knowledge prevents formulations that oversimplify; imagination poses infinite possibilities. In Jake's case, the confluence of these attributes causes "cosmopsis," paralysis; in Barth's case, the result is *Giles Goat-Boy*.

40. Tatham, "Barth and the Aesthetics of Artifice," p. 71.

6

"A Continuing, Strange Love Letter": Sex and Language in
Lost in the Funhouse

One of John Barth's major concerns is the mysterious re-lationship between sex and other forms of human experience. While implicit in Barth's fiction from the beginning, this relation-ship receives its first explicit reference in *The End of the Road* when Jacob Horner makes the following observation:

> If one had no other reason for choosing to subscribe to Freud, what could be more charming than to believe that the whole vaudeville of the world, the entire dizzy circus of history, is but a fancy mating dance. . . . Who would not delight in tell-ing some extragalactic tourist, "On our planet, sir, males and females copulate. Moreover, they enjoy copulating. But for various reasons they cannot do this whenever, wherever, and with whomever they choose. Hence all this running around that you observe. Hence the world"?[1]

Ambrose, the narrator/protagonist of *Lost in the Funhouse* (1968), reaches a similar conclusion. Reflecting upon the funhouse tumbling-barrel which upends girls so that "their boyfriends and others could see up their dresses," Ambrose suddenly realizes that such apparent sexual byplay is really "the whole point . . . [of] the entire funhouse!"[2] All that normally shows, he continues, "like res-taurants and dance halls and clothing and test-your-strength machines, was merely preparation and intermission" (89). Since the funhouse stands for the universe, Barth's meaning becomes clear. At the center of all human activity lies sex, that "shluppish whisper, continuous as seawash round the globe" (80). At one point Ambrose even goes so far as to wonder whether his story contains any other "sound besides the little slap slap of thigh on ham, like water sucking at the chine-boards of a skiff" (88).

Observations such as the latter suggest what is perhaps the major concern of *Lost in the Funhouse*, the relationship between sex and language — ultimately, between sex and art. Barth's familiarity with the Freudian notion of language as sublimated sexuality receives specific attention in *Chimera* when Dunyazade comments on the comparisons between narrative and sexual art made by Scheherazade and the Genie: "The Genie declared that in his time and place there were scientists of the passions who maintained that language itself, on the one hand, originated in 'infantile pregenital erotic exuberance, polymorphously perverse,' and that conscious attention, on the other, was a 'libidinal hypercathexis' — by which magic phrases they seemed to mean that writing and reading, or telling and listening, were literally ways of making love."[3] A form of substitute gratification, narrative, in Norman O. Brown's phrase, is "made out of love."[4]

For Ambrose, however, art fails to gratify. He would much prefer to be among the lovers for whom the funhouse is fun, but the exuberant spontaneity necessary to young love (witness the antics of Peter and Magda) is checked in Ambrose by an almost paralyzing artistic self-consciousness. Even when Magda kneels to initiate the ten-year-old Ambrose into sex, his self-consciousness prevents his full enjoyment: "though he had breathed heavily, groaned as if ecstatic, what he'd really felt throughout was an odd detachment, as though someone else were Master. Strive as he might to be transported, he heard his mind take notes upon the scene: *This is what they call* passion. *I am experiencing it*" (84). Even at the height of pleasure Ambrose must watch himself react, must convert the experience into language.

Other protagonists in *Funhouse* (each a mask for Ambrose, the true protagonist and "author" of the book[5]) suffer similarly. The narrator's difficulty in composing "Title," for example, comes between him and his understandably frustrated mistress. Words replace deeds in their relationship, and she at one point exclaims, "Is this what we're going to talk about, our obscene verbal problem?"

(106). While composing "Life-Story" the narrator is interrupted by his mistress, who declares, "The passion of love . . . does not in fact play in your life a role of sufficient importance to sustain my presence here. It plays in fact little role at all outside your imaginative and/or ary life" (123). The commitment to art obstructs even the love of the "Anonymiad"'s nameless minstrel for his beloved Merope, as he deserts her for experiences he believes will make him a better storyteller. Tricked by Aegisthus, however, he ends up alone on a desert island, with only imaginary experience left open to him. Each narrator (others could be named) seems destined by artistic temperament to be a partial participant in life. Like Mann's Tonio Kröger, each stands apart from experience, observing and ordering it for others. As Ambrose sadly concludes the title story of *Funhouse*, "he will construct funhouses for others and be their secret operator — though he would rather be among the lovers for whom funhouses are designed" (97).

Unfortunately, the same self-consciousness responsible for Ambrose's failure as a lover also inhibits his success at storytelling. A certain degree of innocent spontaneity, it seems, is necessary for literature as well as for love. Yet Ambrose stands at what he supposes is the end of a long history of narrative literature. And, as the narrator of "Title" avers, "Historicity and self-awareness . . . while ineluctable and even greatly to be prized, are always fatal to innocence and spontaneity" (110). Condemned to write, unfit by temperament simply to repeat what has already been written, yet aware that little hope exists for producing something new, Ambrose faces the dreary prospect articulated by the narrator of "Life-Story": "He rather suspected that the medium and genre in which he worked — the only ones for which he felt any vocation — were moribund if not already dead" (121). A paragraph later the same somber observation is applied to Western society. For Ambrose, culture and art, like his personal life, seem bereft of meaningful possibilities.

In "The Literature of Exhaustion," published the year before *Funhouse*, Barth expresses general agreement with this assessment, at least as it applies to narrative. Yet he refuses to let the apocalyptic ambience immobilize him as an artist. "The man or woman whose style I admire most," he has said, "is the one who has a sophisticated awareness of alternatives; who knows the tragic futility of actions, yet doesn't yield to castration by all his sophistication."⁶ Barth demonstrates his own sophisticated awareness of alternatives by examining several in *Funhouse.* The one he chooses to employ involves turning "ultimacy, exhaustion, paralyzing self-consciousness and the adjective-weight of accumulated history . . . against itself to make something new and valid, the essence whereof would be the impossibility of making something new" (109), which is of course the alternative explored in "The Literature of Exhaustion." But Barth adopts yet another tactic in confronting the dilemma. While unmentioned though employed in *Funhouse,* this tactic receives specific comment in *Chimera.* The Barth-genie tells Scheherazade and Dunyazade that his literary career "had reached a hiatus which he would have been pleased to call a turning-point if he could have espied any way to turn: he wished neither to repudiate nor to repeat his past performances; he aspired to go beyond them toward a future they were not attuned to and, by some magic, at the same time go back to the original springs of narrative."⁷ Barth, that is, wishes to mine the riches of a still usable past without ignoring the present and future, a gesture he has described as "having it both ways."⁸

One method that allows Barth to have it both ways in *Funhouse* is his return to oral narrative via the tape recorder. He slyly suggests the nature and function of this regression by naming his protagonist Ambrose. Ambrose is named after the fourth-century saint because bees swarmed about both their faces while they were infants. But St. Ambrose is significant to Barth's purposes for yet another reason. In *The Gutenberg Galaxy* Marshall McLuhan, with whose theories Barth is familiar, discusses the wonderment described by Augustine when he saw St. Ambrose reading silently.⁹ In antiquity through the Middle Ages, McLuhan reminds us, reading necessarily meant reading aloud. The reason for monk's carrels in monasteries was not to insure the reader's privacy but to prevent his oral reading from disturbing others. St. Ambrose's silent reading represented a significant stage in the transition from oral to print-oriented literary cultures. Similarly, Ambrose Mensch's experiments with tape represent a transition from visual media back to the oral and auditory. Thus the bees land on his eyes and ears, rather than on his mouth. Print, according to McLuhan, is an extension of the eyes, the tape recorder an extension of the ear. By landing about Ambrose's eyes and ears, the bees predict his dual use of print and tape.

The naming of Ambrose is significant in yet another sense. It co-incides with his weaning, since the bees that inspire his name also sting his mother's breast, an event so painfully traumatic that Andrea will have little more to do with the infant Ambrose. Ambrose's naming, his initiation into a world of words, thus coincides with his forced separation from his mother. Psychologists have often associated weaning with the crisis of differentiation, the infantile trauma at which point the child suddenly becomes aware that he is distinct from others. Barth's association of this crisis with naming—thus with language—suggests the theories of Jacques Lacan, the relationship of whose thought to *Lost in the Funhouse* has been persuasively argued by Christopher D. Morris.[10] According to Lacan, a newborn child exists as an "absolute subject"; his relationship to a world he cannot yet distinguish from himself is purely intransitive. At some point in his early development, presumably around the time of weaning, he becomes aware of a lack, an absence of something (the mother's breast?), which disturbs the state of seamless concord he had previously enjoyed. For the first time the child conceives of himself as a self, an "I" apart from the Other. Language becomes the mode by which he attempts to reappropriate the Other and restore his lost sense of unity. As Anthony Wilden explains, "Lacan views speech as a movement toward something, an attempt to fill the gap, without which speech could not be articulated."[11] Paradoxically, language leads both toward and away from that holistic state man wishes to reattain. It leads to that state because its secret motivation is the desire for annihilation, the end to all distinctions; it leads away because language by its very nature is a spatializing and temporalizing medium, thus is responsible for the very world of distinctions it secretly wishes to dissolve. "Reality," that is, is essentially a linguistic construct of our own creation—a Schopenhauerian as well as Nietzschean notion Barth has called "unexceptionable."[12]

Language, as well as the "reality" it fashions, cuts us off from our lost "authentic" self as surely as it signals that separation. The mythic desire to return to origins is at base the desire to rediscover the authentic self that existed in a state before ego, before language. "Since the discovery of the lack of object is for Lacan the condition and the cause of desire," explains Anthony Wilden, "the adult quest for transcendence, lost time, lost paradise, or any of the myriad forms the lack of object may take . . . can be reduced, if one wishes, to the . . . question asked by Oedipus: 'Who (or what) am I?'" Yet, Wilden continues, the very fact that this question is asked verifies the subject's recognition "that he is neither who he thinks he is nor what he wants to be, since at the level of the *parole vide* he will always find that he is another."[13] The ego, the only "self" we and others acknowledge, is a linguistic category constructed of a medium appropriated from another. As Ambrose muses, "I and my sign are neither one nor quite two" (34). Moreover, not only is our language the "discourse of the other," but our identity is no more than the "internalization of the other through identification."[14] We locate the self in the other; thus our "I", our ego, is another self, fundamentally objective rather than subjective, pure subjectivity lying only in the prenatal state before our fall into language and consciousness.

It is for this reason in "Echo" that Narcissus' self-knowledge must remain partial: "it was never himself Narcissus craved, *but his reflection*, the Echo of his fancy" (103, italics mine). We linger forever "on the autognostic verge" because the self we hope to know is always an *other*, a reflection of the other internalized through identification, just as the language we speak is always ultimately the discourse of the other from which it has been appropriated. The voice which leads Narcissus to the Donaconan spring, while resembling his own, is really another's, Echo's, whose own voice is similarly the appropriation of another's. Both Narcissus and Echo seek self-effacement — yet the self they wish to efface is really a reflection of another. So long as they remain in a world of words, they remain locked into the discourse of the other. Narcissus and Echo, despite their apparent differences, "come to the same" (103).

In his attempt to embrace his reflected self, Narcissus plunges into water. Throughout *Funhouse* water is associated with language, which (like the sea) envelops mankind. Messages are received from the sea in two stories; the sperm cell, himself a message ("both vessel and contents"), journeys a night sea; Ambrose struggles with his story at Ocean City and wonders if that story is nothing more than the "slap slap of thigh on ham, like water sucking at the chineboards of a skiff"; and bodies of water figure in "Menelaiad," "Two Meditations," even "Petition" (Prajadhipok is Supreme Arbiter of the Ebb and Flow of the Tide). But if water in *Funhouse* suggests language, that autotelic, self-referential medium in which man is awash, it has another significance as well. Archetypally, water signifies the return to the preformal, holistic state before words and world. In this more obvious yet perhaps more basic sense, water reinforces the motif of the return to origins so important to *Funhouse*. Thus water as symbol contains both poles that comprise the essence of language. Language fundamentally seeks to close all subject-object dichotomies and to relocate single, holistic selfhood, yet by its very nature it creates distinctions, confirming the other from which it has been appropriated and with which it would merge.

Narcissism contains a similar ambivalence, which may partially explain Barth's decision to retell the Narcissus-Echo myth. In Norman O. Brown's formulation, narcissism is not restricted to self-love but ultimately represents a desire to recover the state of primal narcissism when the self was indistinguishable from "a world of love and pleasure." The development of the ego forces a departure from this holistic state, which in turn results in "a vigorous attempt to recover it." Self-love, then, like Eros in general, is "fundamentally a desire for union (being one) with objects in the world."[15] What manifests itself as an intensely inner-directed love really conceals a passion to re-collect the world of objects and others into a holistic and pre-predicative selfhood.[16]

Barth, then, seems to have chosen the Narcissus-Echo myth because of its relevance to selfhood, language, and the return to origins. But one other implication of the myth appealed to Barth as well. In her various authorial stages, Echo's history parallels the history of narrative literature. As a teller of tales she at first had a body (i.e., an authorial "presence") and her own voice (i.e., she could re-invent "reality" to suit her artistic purposes). After Hera's punishment she retains her body and voice, but now she can only repeat the words of others, a state roughly equivalent to representationalism or realism. In love with Narcissus, she pines away until only her mimetic voice remains, moving into the next state: the "dehumanized" art of the self-effaced narrator. In Barth's story even her voice has ceased to be hers, as it imitates not just the words but the actual voices of others. She has become what Barth calls a "proto-Ampex."[17]

Part of Barth's point seems to be that narrative history represents a progressive movement away from that mythic stage when story, and thus world, was fresh and seemingly inexhaustible. At the cosmogonic moment all "reality" remained to be created; out of the pregnant, primeval condition, poet-magi called the world. Once established, however, the world-become-fact replaced the mythic time of origins. Rather than invent "reality," artists represented an already invented world. Literature relinquished its role as creator of realities, becoming instead a validator of "preexistent," "objective" reality. Objectivity became an esthetic value, as did impersonality. Total absence of authorial presence became a goal. Yet even the super-realism of a Robbe-Grillet, say, still suffers "overmuch presence." As "sharp-eyed Tiresias" espies, "one may yet distinguish narrator from narrative, medium from message. One lesson remains to be learned" (101). Echo learns that lesson as she takes the final step on the long road away from subjectivity. Radically mimetic, she becomes an organic tape recorder. This point having been reached, Tiresias speculates, "perhaps the narrative proper may resume" (101).

Barth's implication seems to be that behind the development of narrative literature lies a desire to exhaust literary possibilities, to extend to the limits the boundaries of objective presentation so narrative can at last collapse back into the subjectivity of the mythic moment. "What the mind finally seeks," writes Carter Wheelock, "is a new arrangement of reality, and to achieve this it must go back to the mythical condition prior to the gods, before language; for out of that pregnancy some more adequate Gods, some better language may come, though it be faceless and wordless."[18] Before this radical regress becomes possible, however, the full potential of the present must be depleted. Thus the extreme nature of Echo's final act of self-effacement, like the radically innovative nature of the experimental fictions in *Funhouse*, is fundamentally eschatological. As Eliade maintains, "Eschatology is only the prefiguration of a cosmogony to come. But every eschatology insists on this fact: the New Creation cannot take place before this world is abolished once and for all."[19]

Barth's stories are never seriously eschatological any more than they offer themselves as new cosmogonies. But Barth uses both notions metaphorically; he propels Echo forward toward some eschatological finale while himself moving backward toward origins through his use of ancient myths and an appropriately fabulative mode. Thus he acknowledges both horns of the contemporary writer's dilemma: the inexhaustibility of the narrative impulse on the one hand, and the seeming exhaustion of narrative resources on the other. In the process he constructs an ingenious emblem for the present predicament of narrative art while managing to go "on with the story."

"Echo" is emblematic of the conditions of contemporary fiction in yet another sense. In his "Seven Additional Author's Notes" Barth offers the following description of point of view in "Echo": "Inasmuch as the nymph in her ultimate condition repeats the words of others in their own voices, the words of 'Echo' on the tape or the page may be regarded validly as hers, Narcissus's, Tiresias's, mine, or any combination or series of the four of Us's."[20] In a later interview, however, Barth concedes that "Finally, of course, it's the *author's* voice you're hearing and the author is always all of those things he makes up."[21] The deeper implications of this statement reverberate after its surface meaning registers. Barth often refers to Borges's idea that fictions about fictions disturb us metaphysically because they remind us of the fictitious nature of our lives. Similarly, the realization that all voices in a work of fiction are ultimately a single voice, that of the artificer, resonates in both ontological directions. We are reminded of the Lacanian possibility that we, too, are but the sounds of other people's voices.

This possibility seems to explain the significance of the quotation marks enclosing "Night-Sea Journey." The narrator being quoted is a spermatozoan about to impregnate Andrea and become a fetal Ambrose. Not only will it become Ambrose in a literal, physical sense, but what Barth calls its "eschatological and other speculations"[22] will become part of Ambrose's "official Heritage" (12). The sperm cell is the "tale-bearer of a generation" (9). The fictions that comprise the realities of our age, fictions themselves built upon past fictions, the entire construct, as Nietzsche saw, forming the a priori beliefs of our time—these, too, Ambrose inherits. Had the narrator of the story been the fish that early reviewers mistook him to be, his eschatological murmurings, Barth concedes, would indeed have been trite. Given "his actual nature, they are merely correct."[23] Whether the sperm cell is alluding to Ginsberg's *Howl* or to Barth's own *Floating Opera*, or whether he's summarizing "the history of philosophical speculation about ontology,"[24] his concerns and formulations are among the pertinent concerns and formulations of our time. Ambrose is an outgrowth of the collected story of his race.

Language does not belong to Ambrose so much as he belongs to it. His utterances are controlled by the limitations of the medium in which he writes, thinks, and lives. Barth quotes one of Borges's editors to the effect that "For [Borges] no one has claim to original-ity in literature; all writers are more or less faithful amanuenses of the spirit, translators and annotators of pre-existing archetypes."[25] Italo Calvino, whose fiction Barth greatly admires, goes a step fur-ther: "I believe that all of literature is implicit in language — that lit-erature itself is merely the permutation of a finite set of elements and functions."[26] Just as the self-recorded fiction of "Autobiogra-phy" echoes the words of its Father/Creator ("My first words weren't my first words"), so Ambrose, presumably that Father/ Creator, echoes the words of Barth, who in turn permutates the elements and functions he has inherited from his precursors. And so on. Yet Ambrose (like Barth) is born at a time when the possible permutations of the finite have apparently been used up. "Every-thing's been said already, over and over" (105), the artist in "Title" complains. Consequently, the desire to squelch the narrative im-pulse becomes strong. The spermatozoan of "Night-Sea Journey," the self-recorded fiction in "Autobiography," and several other narrators long to stop talking. But all seem to realize, if only im-plicitly, that to lift the mask of words is to end up like Ahab, lashed to nothingness.

This nothingness, while disturbing enough to Ambrose and his various avatars, is not necessarily viewed by Barth as a Kurtzian horror. Rather, it coincides with that pre-linguistic state the sepa-ration from which generated language and the return to which all human activity, language included, secretly inclines. Like Borges, however, Barth believes that a complete return to this primal state is impossible (except perhaps for mystics). Man simply cannot leap outside language.[27] Even if he does, the mystic moment of all-in-one, one-in-all inclusiveness is temporary; one must inevitably re-turn to the world of words and men. Once back, as Giles learns, the ineffable remains unspeakable. Thus the admonition "Let go!" that recurs throughout *Giles Goat-Boy* and which demands the abandonment of the world of perceptual and conceptual categories is replaced in *Funhouse* by the imperative "Hold on!" By recasting ancient tales and myths in modern terms, Barth is able to hold onto the demands and concerns of the present while metaphorically returning to literary origins. Barth thus acknowledges the history that contains him, while simultaneously evoking that cosmogonic moment whence all history began.

But if Man's return to origins must be relative rather than radical, Barth remains free to use the idea of radical regression as a controlling metaphor. As Eliade has said, "The return to origins gives the hope of rebirth,"[28] and it is artistic rejuvenation Barth seeks. He builds the idea of the radical regress into the structure of many of his stories. Perhaps the best example of this tactic is found in "Menelaiad." In constructing his version of the Menelaus-Helen story, Barth has drawn from most existing versions of the myth, including Homer's *Odyssey* and *Iliad*, Stesichorus' *Palinode*, Euripides' *Trojan Women*, even Hugo von Hofmannsthal and Richard Strauss's opera *Die Aegyptische Helena*.[29] These versions are themselves layered within seven different narrative perspectives provided by Menelaus, each perspective indicated by a different number of quotation marks. In his quest for Helen, Menelaus must fight his way through all these layers of "reality." At one point he cries, "When will I reach my goal through its cloaks of story? How many veils to naked Helen?" (144). He learns the answer when, in his innermost story, he asks the Oracle at Delphi the ultimate Oedipal question: "Who am I?" The answer, almost predictable by this point in *Funhouse*, is seven sets of quotation marks enclosing nothing. Neither Menelaus nor Helen exists outside the stories that contain and create them. In a heroic regression, Menelaus has worked his way back through the multiple layers of "reality" to the primordial blank from which issues language and all its categories, "Helen" and "Menelaus" among them. Understandably, Menelaus recoils from the message—retreating like Ambrose and the nameless minstrel, both of whom also receive blank messages, back into story—now "done with questions" and determined to "never let go" of the protean guises of a reality that stands between him and the silence of annihilation.

But though Menelaus "continues to hold on," he "can no longer take the world seriously" (166), for at the point where he realized "that Proteus somewhere on the beach became Menelaus holding the Old Man of the Sea, Menelaus ceased" (167). Previously he had suspected that Helen—indeed, that "all subsequent history"—might be Proteus. But if Proteus is everything, he must also be nothing. "I understood further," says Menelaus, "how Proteus thus also was as such no more, being as possibly Menelaus's attempt to hold him, the tale of that vain attempt, the voice that tells it" (167). Not just Menelaus, but mankind, is the story of its collective story, the sound of its own voice. History, as Barth is fond of saying, is fictive if not false, "our dream, our idea,"[30] to which we must cling even when, like Menelaus, we realize its fictiveness.

Without the story there is only the blank. This blank is that sense of absence which propels man to create language, self, and civilization — each a sublimated desire to "fill in the blank." All three are made out of love, since language, which creates self and society, is essentially sexual at base in its Oedipal longing to regain the mother's breast, to fill in the blank separating self from the world. "'Love is how we call our ignorance of what whips us,'" cries the disgruntled sperm cell of "Night-Sea Journey," as he, too, despite his nihilism, plunges toward the mysterious She and "*consummation, transfiguration, Union of contraries, transcension of categories*" (11). He attains that holistic realm known to mystics and heroes.[31] But of course he will be expunged once again as Ambrose into a world of words and categories, only to return metaphorically through Ambrose's artistic regression to past forms and tales. Love, then, moves us to fill in the blank, to create our history. As Helen tells Menelaus, it is "the senseless answer to our riddle . . . mad history's secret, base-fact and footer to the fiction crazy-house our life" (165). When the teller of Menelaus' tale dies, and then is followed by the tale itself, the tale's motivation and subject, love, will remain.

But if love motivates tale and teller, what of told? Throughout *Funhouse* the importance of an audience — real or implied — to the narrative process is emphasized. Several narrators realize that they must continue speaking as long as they have readers or hearers. "You who listen give me life in a manner of speaking" (35) begins the narrator of "Autobiography," the curious spacing in his utterance making it unclear whether that utterance is indicative or imperative.[32] At least two of the stories actually insult the reader/hearer in an effort to cut off communication. As the author/narrator of "Life-Story," addressing his reader, concludes about the author-audience relationship in the story he is writing: "Don't you think he [the author of the story-within-the-story] knows who gives his creatures their lives and deaths? Do they exist except as he or others read their words? Age except we turn their pages?

And can he die until you have no more of him?" (127). Later he
answers his own not-quite-rhetorical questions. "That he continues
means that he continues, a fortiori you too. Suicide's impossible:
he can't kill himself without your help" (128). Not only does the
reader give life to the characters and situation in the author's story,
but in a real sense the reader gives the author life, since he makes
his role possible. By that same token, the writer as well as his story
makes possible the reader's role. Tale, teller, and told thus become
linked in a reciprocal process. Writing is not a monologue in which
a Godlike author creates a world which he then dispenses to a passive auditor; rather, it is—as Heidegger argues all language is—a
conversation.

"Language is not a mere tool, one of the many which man possesses," writes Heidegger in his essay on Hölderlin; "on the contrary,
it is only language that affords the very possibility of standing in the
openness of the existent. Only where there is language is there
world." But if the "being of man is founded in language . . . this only
becomes actual in conversation." Speaking and hearing are "equally fundamental" to human existence among the things of the world
made manifest by language. Moreover, conversation makes time
and history possible:

> We have been a single conversation since the time when it "is
> time." Ever since time arose, we have existed historically. . . .
> Since language really became actual as conversation, the gods
> have acquired names and a world has appeared. But again it
> should be noticed: the presence of the gods and the appear-
> ance of the world are not merely a consequence of the actuali-
> zation of language, they are contemporaneous with it. And
> this to the extent that it is precisely in the naming of the gods,
> and in the transmutation of the world into word, that the real
> conversation, which we ourselves are, consists.[33]

At this point Heidegger engages in a regression to origins of his
own. "How does this conversation, which we are, begin?" he asks.
His answer: "The poet names the gods and names all things in that
which they are." The primordial poets did not merely supply
things already known with names; "it is rather that when the poet
speaks the essential word, the existent is by this naming nominated
as what it is." In short, "Poetry is the establishing of being by
means of the word."[34] In speaking being, poetry reveals Being,
which, as Giles discovers, is One. The "blank" at the center of lan-

guage is not absence but plenum, the Being of beings, called by Heidegger the *vis primitiva activa:* the "primordial and active force." Pre-linguistic and pre-predicative, like Jung's realm of the archetype, Being — though disclosed by language — is never captured by it, remaining forever proximate: "The essence of proximity seems to consist in bringing near the Near, while keeping it at a distance. Proximity to the source is a mystery."[35] Poetry provides this proximity, creating being — the world of man *(Dasein)* and things *(Seienden)* — while approximating, "unconcealing," Being, the primordial source of being, at the same time.

Poetry was the *Ursprache,* the "primitive language of a historical people."[36] In time, of course, the poetic hardened into the vernacular, the mythic into the ritualistic, then the mundane. But the truly original poet's task remains the same: he must return to origins, recapitulating in the moment of creation that primordial creation when the first poet-magi called a world out of darkness. In the words of Eliade, "All poetry is an effort to *re-create* the language; in other words, to abolish current language, that of every day, and to invent a new, private and personal speech. . . . But poetic creation, like linguistic creation, implies the abolition of time — of the history concentrated in language — and tends toward the recovery of the paradisiac, primordial situation . . . when one could *create spontaneously.* . . . From a certain point of view, we may say that every great poet is *re-making* the world."[37]

For this crucial reason, despite the reciprocity of the reader-writer process, the reader's need for the writer may be greater than vice versa — far greater perhaps than most readers would be comfortable knowing. The truly serious poet in his various guises continues to invent our universe. In the process he perhaps teaches the reader how to invent his world, which is what Ronald Sukenick calls "the main didactic job of the contemporary novelist."[38] The artist keeps the necessary conversation vital by refusing to allow it to harden into meaningless cliché. This is one reason why Barth and his artist-protagonists are so concerned with originality. If language forms our a priori beliefs, if it is the filter through which our "realities" are perceived, then the freshness and significance of those realities depend upon the health of the language. "Where language is corrupted or bastardized," writes George Steiner, "there will be a corresponding decline in the character and fortunes of the body politic."[39] And when language falls into silence, spiritual if

not actual self-extinction follows. "If Sinbad sinks it's Scheherazade who drowns," writes the narrator of "Life-Story." "Whose
neck one wonders is on her line?" (121). The answer, of course, is
our own.

The reader's dependence upon the writer—though often unac-
knowledged, as Shelley noted—becomes the writer's most pressing
obligation. The act of writing, of reaching out to another for understanding and acceptance, is frequently painful since the writer
can never be sure he will make contact. "Are you there?" (35) asks
the self-recorded fiction of "Autobiography," a question echoed by
Menelaus' "Anyone there?" (130) and implicitly or explicitly repeated throughout *Funhouse*. More awesome still is the realization
that someone may be reaching out to the writer. "To love is easy,"
speaks Menelaus; "to be loved, as if one were real, on the order of
others: fearsome mystery!" (156). This realization confirms the
writer's participation in the ontological conversation, thus verify-
ing his existence in the symbolic order that man calls reality. More
important, perhaps, it forces the writer to acknowledge his role as
poet and the obligations that role entails.

A message from the sea launches Ambrose's role as writer. Similarly, a sea-message resuscitates the moribund narrative impulse of
the minstrel in "Anonymiad." Marooned on an island, the minstrel
invents written narrative, then muse by muse exhausts its possibilities. Like Echo, he rehearses the various stages of the narrative
tradition; having reached its final stage, he faces a depletion of narrative resources: "Was there any new thing to say, new way to say
the old?" (195). Just as Ambrose's sea message is blank, the
medium forming its sole message, so the minstrel's message is all
but blank. But the renewed creativity inspired by the message
comes "as much from the lacunae as from the rest" (196). Whereas
he had thought himself "the only stranded spirit, and had survived
by sending messages to whom they might concern," he now realizes the world "might be astrew with isled souls, *become minstrels
perforce*, and the sea a-clink with literature!" (196). The phrase I
have italicized suggests a causal relationship between isolation and
art, which is precisely the point I have been making. Language
issues from the ontogenetic and phylogenic realization of separation. It represents an attempt to fill in the blank sensed by the individual at the point of the infantile trauma and by ancient man at
the time of the "catastrophe" or expulsion from paradise.[40] The

realization that another is similarly isolated and simultaneously reaching out for understanding and love confirms the existence of a continuing conversation, which Heidegger sees as the ground of being. Thus messaged, the minstrel continues the exchange, realizing now that this "Anonymiad" as well as "all its predecessors" are a "continuing, strange love letter" (200).

The minstrel's — thus Ambrose's — realization that art, like language itself, is fundamentally a conversation casts light on a previous statement by the narrator of "Life-Story." Concluding that "the old analogy between Author and God, novel and world, can no longer be employed unless deliberately as a false analogy," the narrator lists among the possible fictional responses to this fact the following: fiction must "establish some other, acceptable relation between itself, its author, its reader" (128). This new relation is one of reciprocity. The text is not solely the creation of the author but (to paraphrase "Autobiography") the sum of the author and reader's conjoined efforts. By that same token, the language employed by the author exists prior to its use by that author; thus artistic *parole*, no matter how novel in its permutations, is controlled by the *langue* from which it is selected and which forms the context that gives it sense. Thus all three — teller, tale, and told — are inextricably linked and mutually interdependent.

The artist's obligation to keep the ontological conversation going is manifested in various ways in *Funhouse*. The need to "hold on" to reality's various guises, for example, becomes even more essential when the artist realizes that those forms and guises — our cognitive and perceptual "realities" — depend for their existence on the conversation which actualized them. This conversation, according to Heidegger, is a single one; it has existed continuously since its inception and cannot be interrupted without plunging man and his world back into the void. And while there is throughout *Funhouse* a persistent impulse toward the Baroque, that impulse to get it all said, to exhaust the possible permutations of words and yield at last to the all-encompassing silence, this eschatological tendency is counteracted by a stronger if paradoxically weary desire to continue filling in the blank.

These twin impulses are especially evident in the triptych formed by "Autobiography," "Title," and "Life-Story." While all three stories are concerned with the relationship between reader, writer, and story, each story focuses primarily on one element of the relationship: "Autobiography," narrated by itself, focuses obviously on the tale; "Title," concerned with the author-narrator's difficulties in composing his story, focuses on the teller; "Life-Story," particularly the last two sections, focuses primarily on the audience. Each story is radically reflexive, its form not "contentless" (as the narrator of "Autobiography" complains) so much as comprising content. The stories' discourse, their very processes, form their substance. "You tell me it's self-defeating to talk about it instead of just up and doing it," explains the narrator of "Title," "but to acknowledge what I'm doing while I'm doing it is exactly the point" (111). Yet even this novel approach soon grows hackneyed. "Another story about a writer writing a story!" complains the narrator of "Life-Story." "Another regressus in infinitum! Who doesn't prefer art that at least overtly imitates something other than its own processes?" (117). Despite the curse of exhaustion and apparent meaninglessness, these tales, in the words of "Autobiography," "continue the tale of [their] forebears" (37), refusing (perhaps unable) to end, as indicated by the absence of periods concluding "Autobiography" and "Title." In this respect these two stories resemble the types of narrative Beckett has described: "It's an unbroken flow of words and tears. . . . it's for ever the same murmur, flowing unbroken, like a single endless word and therefore meaningless, *for it's the end gives the meaning to words.*"[41]

"Life-Story" does end, however, at least in a relative sense. Indeed, it closes with a pair of periods, the second larger than the first. The narrator of "Life-Story" is writing a story about a writer writing a story, both stories concluding almost simultaneously, which may explain the twin periods. But the second, larger period may also apply retroactively to the unconcluded initial stories in the triptych. Significantly, "Life-Story" closes when the narrator is led to bed and sex by his playful but determined wife. Narrative, the sexual surrogate, gives way to actual sex. Since this occurs on the narrator's birthday, a regress of sorts also occurs, the act of sex symbolically restoring that harmony interrupted by the birth trauma thirty-six years before. Sex, at its climactic moment, returns us symbolically and perhaps psychologically to Eliade's *illud tempus,* that time before time, before man's fall into consciousness and categories. In the "dizzy instant of coitus," writes Borges, "all men are one man."[42] Moreover, just as the sexual orgy provided ancient man with a ritual for regressing psychically to primal chaos (the mythic state), so do the distractions of modern man, particularly reading, provide the same function. Such is the "mythological function of reading," according to Eliade. "For the modern man it is the supreme 'distraction,' yielding him the illusion of *a mastery of Time* which, we may well suspect, gratifies a secret desire to withdraw from the implacable becoming that leads toward death."[43] Like the act of sex, the acts of reading and writing are forms of love—love in the mythic sense, love as the desire to overcome all dualisms and to heal permanently the primordial breach between man and the other. Thus the narrator of "Life-Story" doesn't stop the ontological conversation, even though he does cap his pen. His "ending story" remains "endless by interruption," that interruption causing merely a shift of media, an exchange of the flesh for the word, both of which symbolize the human desire to abolish all distinctions.

Nor does *Funhouse* conclude with the minstrel's affirmative "Wrote it." These words, we understand, apply to the "Anonymiad" itself; that realization sends us back to the beginning of that story and, since "Anonymiad" forms the final fiction in the series composed by Ambrose, back to the beginning of *Funhouse* as well. The structure of *Funhouse* is therefore cyclic, a fitting shape for a narrative concerned with regressions to origins. But the nature of the cycle, as "Frame-Tale" promises, is spiraling, not spheric.[44] "Anonymiad" echoes "Night-Sea Journey" but with a crucial difference: whereas the spermatozoan is propelled unwillingly by Love, the nameless minstrel, after some recalcitrance, yields enthusiastically. Addressing an absent Merope in terms deliberately reminiscent of "Night-Sea Journey," the minstrel proclaims, "I wish you were here. The water's fine; in the intervals of this composition I've taught myself to swim, and if some night your voice recalls me, by a new name, I'll commit myself to it, paddling and resting, drifting like my amphorae, to attain you or to drown" (200). The new name, of course, will be Ambrose. And the call will be to art, not to physical love. But the subject of Ambrose's fiction will be love, what goes on between men and women remaining "not only the most interesting but the most important thing in the bloody murderous world" (113). And the art Ambrose fashions will demand a reciprocal relationship between reader, writer, and story that resembles love. Moreover, by this point in his narrative Ambrose has perhaps learned that if art is a sexual substitute, the act of sex is

itself a substitute, pointing like language to that holistic, primordial state man struggles to reattain. As a record of that struggle, art
remains as vitally necessary to the survival of the human race as
does sex. "A continuing, strange love letter," it preserves the ontological conversation that is man.

NOTES

1. Barth, *The End of the Road*, p. 87.
2. Barth, *Lost in the Funhouse* (Garden City, N.Y.: Doubleday, 1968),
p. 89. Subsequent references to this edition appear in parentheses in the
text.
3. Barth, *Chimera*, p. 24.
4. Brown, *Life against Death*, p. 69.
5. Robert Kiernan argues this point convincingly in "Barth's Artist in
the Fun House"; see especially pp. 373–74.
6. Gado, ed., *First Person*, p. 138.
7. Barth, *Chimera*, pp. 9–10, italics mine. Max F. Schulz examines this
idea in "Characters (Contra Characterization)," pp. 141–54.
8. Bellamy, *The New Fiction*, pp. 4–5.
9. McLuhan, *Gutenberg Galaxy*, pp. 107–8. Barth confesses that
McLuhan has influenced his work, but he insists that he has never read
McLuhan. "These ideas are in the air, you know, and you gather what
certain people are talking about without having read them" (Prince, "Interview," p. 46). Nonetheless, Barth includes references to McLuhan in
his books and essays, and he has frequently mentioned him in interviews – so one cannot be completely sure that Barth is not playing Todd
Andrews in denying familiarity with McLuhan's books, particularly
when textual evidence suggests such a familiarity.
10. Morris, "Barth and Lacan."
11. Anthony Wilde, "Lacan and the Discourse of the Other," in Lacan,
Language of the Self, p. 164.
12. Bellamy, *The New Fiction*, p. 10. More recently Barth has said
"that the difference between the fantasy we call reality and the fantasies
we call fantasy has to do with cultural consensus" ("Tales within Tales
within Tales," p. 47).
13. Lacan, *Language of the Self*, p. 169.
14. Ibid., p. 160.
15. Brown, *Life against Death*, pp. 46, 44.
16. I am indebted here to Harris, "Criticism and the Incorporative
Consciousness." While concerned with the cultural context of recent
American poetry, many of Harris's insights have relevance to the state of
contemporary literature in general.

17. Bellamy, *The New Fiction*, p. 9.

18. Wheelock, *The Mythmaker*, p. 46.

19. Eliade, *Myth and Reality*, pp. 51–52.

20. Barth, *Lost in the Funhouse* (New York: Bantam, 1969), p. x.

21. Bellamy, *The New Fiction*, pp. 9–10.

22. Barth, "Seven Additional Author's Notes," p. x.

23. Ibid.

24. Tharpe, *Barth*, p. 93.

25. Barth, "The Literature of Exhaustion," p. 33.

26. Italo Calvino, "Myth in the Narrative," in Federman, ed., *Surfiction*, p. 76. In the Gado interview Barth refers to Calvino as "a contemporary Italian I find terribly exciting" *(First Person*, p. 125). Also see Barth's comments on Calvino in "The Literature of Replenishment."

27. Cf. Wheelock, *The Mythmaker*, p. 17: "Men are doomed to possess their world as language which cannot bespeak the objective order but can only reflect the imperfect memories of the mind. Experiences of the pregnant moments do not remain as full-blown images, but as mere language that stands where reality used to be." See also Steiner, *After Babel*; discussing the cognitive substances of our being, Steiner writes, "The sole mediate, truly external view of them conceivable is that of a total leap out of language, which is death" (p. 111).

28. Eliade, *Myth and Reality*, p. 30.

29. For this observation I am indebted to an unpublished essay by Harold Farwell entitled "The Absurd, Unending Possibility of Love." Presented at an MLA conference seminar in 1972, the paper was later published in a much revised version as "Barth's Tenuous Affirmation."

30. Barth, "The Literature of Exhaustion," p. 34.

31. Which may be what Barth has in mind when he suggests that "Night-Sea Journey" may "illumine certain speculations of Lord Raglan, Carl Jung, and Joseph Campbell" ("Seven Additional Author's Notes," p. x).

32. Written for tape, the first line when heard could be: "Yoo hoo! Listen. Give me life in a manner of speaking."

33. Martin Heidegger, "Hölderlin and the Essence of Poetry," in Gras, ed., *European Literary Theory and Practice*, pp. 31, 32, 33, italics mine.

34. Ibid., p. 33.

35. Heidegger, *Being and Time*, p. 184.

36. Gras, ed., *European Literary Theory and Practice*, p. 35.

37. Eliade, *Myths, Dreams, and Mysteries*, pp. 35–36. Cf. Barth's early statement, "If you are a novelist of a certain type of temperament, then what you really want to do is re-invent the world" (Enck, "Interview," p. 23).

38. Ronald Sukenick, "The New Tradition in Fiction," in Federman, ed., *Surfiction*, p. 41.

39. Steiner, *After Babel*, p. 78.

40. Cf. Eliade, *Myths, Dreams, and Mysteries*, p. 54.

41. Beckett, *Stories and Texts for Nothing*, p. 111, italics mine.

42. Borges, *Labyrinths*, p. 12.

43. Eliade, *Myths, Dreams, and Mysteries*, p. 36.

44. Cf., Slethaug, "Barth's Refutation of the Idea of Progress." Describing the Moebius strip, Slethaug writes, "if an individual were to begin at point A and walk along the surface of this Moebius strip on the right-hand side, he would, upon returning to point A, be upside-down and on the left-hand side. In terms of Barth's theory of cycles, an individual such as Ambrose might well begin his life journey and later return to approximately the same position as he began, but he would not be quite the same person; he would have moved from innocence to experience or self-knowledge" (pp. 26–27). The best analysis to date of Barth's use of the Moebius strip in *Funhouse* is Vintanza, "The Novelist as Topologist."

7

The New Medusa: Feminism and the Uses of Myth
in *Chimera*

From the beginning Barth has avoided social criticism in his novels. "I can't in fiction get very interested in such things," he told John Enck. "My argument is with the facts of life, not the conditions of it."[1] In a more recent interview, however, Barth not only confesses his preoccupation "as a private citizen" with the women's liberation movement, but concedes that the woman's question is one of the themes that holds *Chimera* together. Yet, he quickly adds, only a "simple-minded critic could say my trio of novellas is about women's lib. . . . That's not at all what it's about for me."[2] Barth is too careful a craftsman to include anything in his fiction that does not contribute to that fiction as a whole, so the references to women's liberation in *Chimera* are of considerable consequence. Yet he is not playing games when he insists that the novel is not *about* the women's movement. Rather, women's liberation provides a clue to the significance of Barth's more general use of myth in the novel. Concerning myth Barth has said:

> I always felt it was a bad idea on the face of it . . . to write a more or less realistic piece of fiction, one dimension of which keeps pointing to the classical myths — like John Updike's *Centaur*, or Joyce's *Ulysses*, or Malamud's *The Natural*. Much as one may admire those novels in other respects, their authors have hold of the wrong end of the mythopoeic stick. The

myths themselves are produced by the collective narrative imagination (or whatever), partly to point down at our daily reality; and so to write about our daily experiences in order to point up to the myths seems to me mythopoeically retrograde. I think it's a more interesting thing to do . . . to address them directly.[3]

In his treatment of the myths of Scheherazade, Perseus, and Bellerophon, Barth does address the myths directly; in his scattered references to women's liberation he suggests an aspect of daily reality to which these myths point. The interrelationship of myth and daily reality becomes Barth's concern. *Chimera* is not about the woman's question, but about the larger historical, psychological, and esthetic concerns that the woman's question embodies.

Accordingly Barth chooses for *Chimera* myths that are associated with that point in antiquity when patriarchal control began to emerge. Most authorities still agree with Frazer's contention that "as the result of a social system in which maternity counted for more than paternity," in ancient times "descent [was] traced and property handed down through women rather than through men."[4] A few go so far as to argue that a thoroughgoing matriarchy also existed. Among these is Robert Graves, whose book *The Greek Myths* Barth used as a source for the Perseus and Bellerophon stories in *Chimera*. According to Graves, pre-Homeric Greece was ruled not by the familiar pantheon of gods and goddesses headed by Zeus, but by a single female deity. During the reign of the Great Goddess tribal rule was matriarchal and queenly succession matrilineal. Kingship appeared only after procreation became associated with coition.[5] Chosen by the tribal nymph as a symbol of fertility, the king ruled a short time, then was sacrificed and replaced by another lover for the queen. Early Greek mythology, Graves contends, "is concerned, *above all else,* with the changing relations between the queen and her lovers, which began with their yearly or twice-yearly sacrifices, and end . . . with her eclipse by an unlimited male monarchy."[6] The Perseus myth provides a key iconograph for this eclipse. Originally Medusa was a moon goddess whose priestesses wore gorgon masks to frighten the profane from trespassing on her mysteries. The Perseus myth records that ancient occurrence when, around 1290 B.C., patriarchal Hellenes invaded the goddess's shrines and stripped the priestesses of their prophylactic masks. Joseph Campbell agrees with

Graves's account: "If Perseus was indeed the founder of a new dynasty at Mycenae . . . his violation of the neighboring goddess's grove must have marked the end of an ancient rite—*possibly of regicide*—there practiced. The myth of his miraculous birth from the golden shower of Zeus then would have been of great moment, as validating his act in terms of a divine patriarchal order of belief that was now to supplant the old, of the mother-goddess in whom death is life."[7]

The Bellerophon myth is a variant iconograph of the same legend,[8] but what of the Scheherazade story? Barth has told David Morrell that he chose the myth because it jars with the "Greek nature" of the other stories, thus reinforcing "the monstrous, mixed-metaphor notion that the book's title . . . represented."[9] But according to Campbell the Scheherazade story also has ancient connections with the ritual of regicide. In *The Masks of God: Primitive Mythology* Campbell compares the famous frame tale of the *1001 Nights* with an obscure tale told in 1912 in the marketplace of the capital of Kordofan. In this tale an ancient king of Sudan and his sister, Sali, are saved from immolation by a poet-slave named Far-li-mas, whose eloquent storytelling first diverts and then destroys the priests responsible for determining the exact date of the regicide. "And since that day," the tale concludes, "there have been no more human sacrifices in Napata."[10] The Scheherazade story is a later version of this tale, both of which, like the myths of Perseus and Bellerophon, may reflect an actual prehistoric occurrence. "There is reason to believe," Campbell concludes, "that the tales both of the King's sister-in-death, Sali, and of Shehrzad [*sic*], the King's bride who was to have died on her wedding night, must be echoes of a dim, dark past that was, after all, neither so dim nor dark in the memory of the world in which the tales were [originally] told."[11] Historically, then, each of the three myths Barth includes in *Chimera* records in some fashion the demise of the matriarchy and the consciousness with which it is associated.

Barth's primary concern, however, is less with the historical dimensions of the myths he has chosen to retell than with the psychological and esthetic implications of those primordial fictions. Indeed, Barth's "recycling" of ancient narratives itself represents his desire to return, at least metaphorically, to the creative springs of all story and literally to the sources of creativity in the human mind. Like the genie in "Dunyazadiad," Barth suffered a serious

writer's block in 1969.[12] Also like the genie, Barth "found his way
out of that slough of the imagination in which he'd felt himself
bogged . . . by going back, to the very roots and springs of story":
those ancient myths of Scheherazade, Perseus, and Bellerophon.
Although an overly *self*-conscious use of ancient materials can
prove artistically inhibiting, Barth has conceded, a conscious use
of mythic patterns not only can prove fruitful as a source of artistic material but can also result in "the genuinely mythopoeic," although mythopoeia will be manifested in new and different
ways.[13] Barth seems in basic agreement with Carl Jung, who maintains, "It is . . . to be expected that the poet will turn to mythological figures in order to give suitable expression to his experience.
Nothing would be more mistaken than to suppose that he is working with second-hand material. On the contrary, *the primordial
experience is the source of his creativeness*, but it is so dark and
amorphous that it requires the related mythological imagery to
give it form."[14] Barth's use of ancient myths, then, brings him into
contact with what Jung calls "the hinterland of man's mind," that
"tremendous intuition striving for expression" which is the source
and stimulant of all story.

Especially pertinent to Barth's concerns in *Chimera* is the fact
that this mythopoeic reservoir is frequently viewed as feminine.
"The creative process," writes Jung, "has a feminine quality, and
the creative work arises from unconscious depths — we might truly
say from the realm of the Mother."[15] At least since *Giles Goat-Boy*
Barth has associated creativity, if not with the feminine, then with
the fusion of masculine and feminine consciousness. He would no
doubt agree with Erich Neumann's assessment that "all creative
cultural achievement — at least in its highest form — represents a
synthesis of receptive matriarchal and formative patriarchal consciousness."[16] The feminine unconsciousness informs; the masculine consciousness forms. What becomes necessary in art, as well
as in most human activity, is a balance between masculine and
feminine consciousness.

In "Dunyazadiad" Barth provides a superb metaphor for this reciprocal alliance. Discussing the ideal relationship between the
teller of stories and the one to whom they are told, the genie tells
Scheherazade that the "teller's role . . . regardless of his actual gender, [is] essentially masculine, the listener's or reader's feminine,
and the tale [is] the medium of their intercourse" (25–26). Though

clearly sexual, the metaphor is not sexist, for the audience, though feminine, does not assume a passive or inferior role. "A good reader of cunning tales" works, in her way, "as busily as their author" (26). Indeed, both participants can become pregnant, conceiving new images and ideas as a result of their relationship. Since this relationship is by nature a reciprocal process, Barth refuses to allow his metaphor for that process to grow static. The genie, in his role of masculine teller, relates his tales to Scheherazade, in her role as feminine auditor. But the very tales he relates are drawn from the *1001 Nights*, thus from Scheherazade, so their roles and accompanying genders are immediately reversed.[17] Since Sherry doesn't invent but recounts (29), the tales she originally tells in the *1001 Nights* — that is, those she tells the genie *before* he retells them to her — were drawn in her feminine role as auditor from the general treasury of tales extant during her time. Thus the gender roles assumed by the genie and Sherry relative to the stories they tell and/or hear continually shift, until the distinction between male and female becomes blurred in an androgynous whirl. As the genie tells Scheherazade, "it goes beyond male and female" (26).

But Barth does not allow the figure to rest even there. We learn when reaching Part 2 of "Dunyazadiad" that Part 1 — the story of Scheherazade's story — has been related to Shah Zaman by Dunyazade on their wedding night. Thus Duny — who has done little but listen to the stories up to this point — now assumes the masculine role of teller, Zaman the feminine role of auditor. Moreover, since she threatens Zaman with dismemberment throughout the telling of her tale, their political circumstances are also reversed — a fact not lost on Scheherazade, who has instructed Dunyazade in what was planned as a final scenario (37–38). After regaining and then willingly relinquishing control of the situation, Zaman tries to change Duny's mind and save his life by telling *her* a story, reversing their narrative genders once again, as well as replicating the earlier situations of Scheherazade and the genie, whose survival — literal in the case of the former, figurative in the case of the latter — also depended upon story. In an adjoining chamber, Zaman tells Dunyazade, a similar scenario is probably being enacted by Scheherazade and Sharyahr (53–54); thus the roles of the latter pair are also reversed, then re-reversed. Finally we discover as we reach Section 3 of the novella that the only voice we've been hearing all along is that of the genie, the real narrator of the novella (not Scheherazade, as one critic has suggested[18]). In his masculine role as teller the genie has related to us the "Dunyazadiad," but the source of much of that story, as well as its inspiration, has been Scheherazade, both as author of the original *1001 Nights* and as character in the story the genie relates. (She, for instance, gives him a note detailing what will happen on her and Duny's wedding night, which the genie then includes in his novella.) Thus the genie's narrative role also constantly interchanges.

We are left with a series of role reversals and replications as teller becomes told, then teller again. Much creative progress results from this constant cycling and recycling of identities and narrative guises. Sharyahr and Zaman renounce their masculine resentment and the sexist assault it provoked, accepting equality between the sexes insofar as "good public relations" allow; Sherry and Duny presumably gain their lives as well as their newly won equality; the genie regains his own creative abilities, and *Chimera* is the result. Barth's inspired metaphor suggests not only the nature of sexual balance, but also the fortuitous results of such harmony.

Indeed, it would not require a great imaginative leap to visualize the metaphor in terms of the Taoist symbol of the Great Ultimate, Yang-Yin, which plays so central a role in *Giles Goat-Boy*. Though usually diagrammed as a circle bisected by a sigmoid line, on one side of which lies the Yang or masculine force, on the other the Yin or feminine force, the symbol is not, properly speaking, a circle at all, but a helicoid. In Rene Guenon's view it is "a section of the universal whirlwind which brings opposites together and engenders perpetual motion, metamorphosis and continuity in situations characterized by contradiction."[19] This is an important distinction, for in *Chimera* the circle is almost always a symbol of sterile repetition without development or change. "I'm going in circles," the genie complains to Scheherazade, "following my own trail" (10). The circle also constitutes the main structural principle of "Bellerophoniad," the only novella in *Chimera* which concerns ultimate failure. In both "Dunyazadiad" and "Perseid," on the other hand, the primary structural principle is the spiral, although the spiral structure of each novella is perceived from a different perspective. In "Dunyazadiad" it is as if we were somehow above the "universal whirlwind," looking down at it so that it would appear to be a circle containing the whirling, interchanging, yet separate male and female principles. In "Perseid" we view the whirlwind from a horizontal perspective, watching it traverse the horizon, as it were, thus manifesting itself not as a circle but as a whirling spiral. Archetypally the spiral is frequently associated with the transformative character of the feminine,[20] so the structure of Barth's initial novellas in *Chimera* becomes emblematic of their theme: the need to recognize and to incorporate creative feminine forces into the psyche at the personal, social, and esthetic levels.

Not surprisingly, Barth reinforces the spiral structure of "Dunyazadiad" with spiral imagery. Other motifs associated with the archetypal feminine, particularly its transformative nature, also recur in the novella. For instance, the number seven, which echoes and re-echoes throughout "Dunyazadiad," plays an important role in ancient mother rites of transformation. In myths of later antiquity the journey to the underworld and its variants (the night-sea journey, entrapment in the belly of the whale, etc.), which archetypally signify a coming to terms with the feminine unconsciousness, follow the course of the sun and thus are associated with the solar number twelve. In older matriarchal myths, however, the journey to hell is always lunar, and the number seven plays a dominant role.[21] So while the first novella in *Chimera* is set clearly in a patriarchal society, Barth uses archetypal motifs which suggest earlier matriarchal cults and the consciousness associated with them.

The most meaningful pattern in "Dunyazadiad" is not the spiral or the symbolic seven but the motif of the treasure. A magic utterance, "The key to the treasure is the treasure," brings Scheherazade and the genie together in the first place, and the word "treasure" recurs in a variety of contexts throughout the novella. Nowhere, however, does Barth explicitly define the treasure. Once again, the significance of a motif in *Chimera* is derived in large part from its mythic associations. In many mythological dragon flights the hero gains "the treasure hard to attain" when he frees the female captive. Ultimately, however, the captive is herself the treasure. The treasure, that is, represents union with the feminine: creative generation. "By freeing the captive and raising the treasure," Neumann writes, "a man gains possession of his soul's treasures, which are not just 'wishes,' i.e., images of something he has not got but would like to have, but possibilities, i.e., images of something he could have and ought to have."[22] The treasure lies within; it is psychic integration of the (male) consciousness with the (female) unconsciousness, and to achieve such integration one must, quite simply, become psychologically whole. Thus the key to the treasure *is* the treasure. As Neumann concludes, "it is . . . impossible to find the treasure unless the hero has first found and redeemed his own soul, his own feminine counterpart which conceives and brings forth."[23]

Within "Dunyazadiad" the treasure is primarily associated with literature, as when the genie expresses his desire to add a new trinket to "the general treasury of civilized delights" (17), or with love, as when Shah Zaman beseeches Duny to "treasure" him (54). We have already seen how story proceeds from the realm of the Great Mother, but what of love? According to Jung, a man is often incapable of truly loving a woman until he has begun to come to terms with the feminine component in his own psyche, his anima. Until he does so he will unconsciously project his anima image onto the various women to whom he is attracted. "Naturally," writes Frieda Fordham, "this leads to endless misunderstandings, for most men are unaware that they are projecting their own inner picture of woman on to someone very different; most inexplicable love affairs and disastrous marriages arise in this way."[24] When a man represses his feminine nature in a particularly severe fashion, the dark side of the anima rises and presents itself. In cases such as these, anima projections frequently take the form of a prostitute, a seductress, or a witch. For this reason, perhaps, many of the goddess figures worshipped during the early matriarchy were transformed by the emergent patriarchy into monsters, in a process Graves calls "iconotrophy." The gorgon Medusa was once a beautiful nymph, an embodiment of the Great Goddess, before later patriarchal societies transformed her into a monster.[25]

Shah Zaman and Sharyahr exhibit symptoms of this kind of repression and its resulting anima projection. Both are shocked by their wives' adulterous reaction to husbandly neglect and punish them by death. But though the wives are dead, the projected image lives on and is attached each night to a different virgin, who is violated and then slain the following morning. Significantly, a confluence of love and art (both issues from the realm of the Mother) delivers the kings from their depression. As a result they not only forgive all women but are able to accept Sherry and Duny as individuals separate from and equal to themselves. Sharyahr, recognizing Scheherazade's libertine leanings, chooses to share equal promiscuity with her; Zaman, acknowledging Duny's essentially chaste nature (early in the novella she hints at a vow of premarital chastity), chooses equal fidelity. Each man thus sees and accepts his wife as she is, not as he unconsciously wishes her to be — a situation possible, according to Jung, only when one has recognized his anima and integrated it into his own personality. Such integration is presumably achieved by the genie as well, who not only overcomes his writer's block but, after divorce and a brace of mistresses, chooses one woman to marry.

And they lived happily ever after — or so we are tempted to add. But Barth takes his story too seriously to allow it to end sentimentally. The life story of Dunyazade and her bridegroom, like that of Scheherazade and Sharyahr and the genie and his Melissa, must end in "the night that all good mornings come to" (55). The Destroyer of Delights and Desolator of Dwelling places, inexorable death and change, are as unavoidable as life. "To be joyous in the full acceptance of this dénouement," the genie concludes his novella, "is surely to possess a treasure, the key to which is the understanding that Key and Treasure are the same" (56). The key to life's enjoyment, that is, is the acceptance of life, knowing full well its horrors and vicissitudes. This acceptance makes life a treasure; thus key and treasure are the same.

By now we should not be surprised to learn that such acceptance is itself a principal of the archetypal feminine. The rise of the patriarchy brought the rise of consciousness, with its rational and divisive functions that separate subject and object, life and death. But the aim of the earlier matriarchal mythology was "to support a state of indifference to the modalities of time and identification with the inhabiting non-dual mystery of all being."[26] We come from the Mother, "in whose being we have our death, as well as life, without fear."[27] Because Zaman understands this, "the second half of his life will be sweeter than the first" (56). He can live and love *as if* each lasts forever. Such faith is based not on delusion but on fictions which are "truer than fact" (53). Such fictions are, after all, part and parcel of the mythic impulse. Referring to the "curious game of *as if*," Campbell writes,

> Such a highly played game . . . frees our mind and spirit, on the one hand, from the presumption of theology, which pretends to know the laws of God, and, on the other, from the

bondage of reason, whose laws do not apply beyond the horizon of human experience. . . . The play state and the raptur-
ous seizures sometimes deriving from it represent, therefore, a
step rather *toward* than away from the ineluctable truth; and
belief — acquiescence in a belief that is not quite belief — is the
first step toward the deepened participation . . . in that general will to life which, in its metaphysical aspect, is antecedent
to, and the creator of, all life's laws.[28]

The treasures of love, art, and life depend upon the philosophy of
as if, which prevents them from degenerating into lifeless redun-
dancy, keeping each a dynamic flow of possibilities.

The opposite of this flow is petrifaction, the fear of which tor-
ments Perseus, self-proclaimed "protagonist and author, so to
speak" (81), of the second novel in *Chimera*. That "so to speak" is
important, for Perseus, as David Morrell points out, is really "a
character in a story . . . the central conceit of which is a constellation telling its story." But Morrell is wrong, I believe, in seeing
Polyeidus as the story's narrator. Morrell bases his assumption on
the fact that in "Bellerophoniad" shape-shifting Polyeidus turns
himself into the "Perseid" on Bellerophon's fortieth birthday. "That
is the only basis on which Barth can mix metaphors [in "Perseid"]
and have a constellation refer to its paged past and future's sentence. Perseus isn't speaking there, it's Polyeidus."[29] Moreover,
Morrell argues, Polyeidus, having transformed himself into *Chimera* at the book's conclusion, serves as the unifying medium for
the entire volume. That function became obscured when Barth
changed the original order of his novellas, which had "Dunyazadiad" concluding rather than beginning the series.

But the present arrangement of *Chimera* possesses a unifying
medium of its own. About midway through "Dunyazadiad" the
genie announces that he is at that moment in the middle of writing
a novella primarily about Dunyazade that will become part of "a
projected series of three *novellas*, longish tales which would take
their sense from one another" (28). Obviously the genie is describing
Chimera, in which Polyeidus, the shape-shifter who turns himself
into documents, is, like the constellated Perseus, another conceit.
The genie, in other words, not only narrates "Dunyzadiad" but also
is the implied narrator of "Perseid" and "Bellerophoniad." His consciousness orders the events of these novellas and serves as their unifying medium. From one perspective he may even be seen as covert

protagonist of the entire volume, since each novella dramatizes his artistic situation and concerns. In this respect he resembles Ambrose, author and protagonist of the series of stories in *Lost in the Funhouse*. Just as the early stories in *Funhouse* treat Ambrose's growth as an artist in a directly autobiographical way, so does the genie in "Dunyazadiad" treat explicitly his own artistic rebirth. Then, just as the second half of *Funhouse* concerns characters who are masks for Ambrose and whose situations in various ways replicate his own, so, too, does the genie in "Perseid" and "Bellerophoniad" recast his own artistic situation in the form of ancient myths retold.

In "Perseid," for example, Perseus, like the genie, finds himself at forty apparently burnt out, his heroic accomplishments behind him. Also like the genie, he attempts initially to overcome this immobility by repeating those past accomplishments. Both discover that mere imitation of past actions is profitless, if not impossible. The movement of one's life must be progressive — not circular, but spiraling. Like the genie, Perseus learns this lesson as a result of his relationship with two women. Just as the genie tells Scheherazade stories she had earlier told him, so Perseus tells Calyxa and Medusa stories of his life which he is reminded of by murals Calyxa painted according to instructions from Medusa. In "Perseid," then, as in "Dunyazadiad," the identities of teller and told intertwine. While not formally divided, "Perseid," like "Dunyazadiad," falls clearly into three sections. In the first Perseus tells Medusa what he told Calyxa about the first forty years of his life; in the second, after leaving Calyxa's temple, he relates to Medusa the continuation of his life's story to its end; in the third Perseus and Medusa reflect upon the just completed story, much as the genie reflects upon his never-to-be-completed story in Section 3 of "Dunyazadiad."

One more aspect of "Perseid" reflects the genie's artistic concerns as implied in "Dunyazadiad." In the earlier story the genie tells Scheherazade that he will spin from the spiral shell ring she gives him, "as from a catherine-wheel or whirling galaxy, a golden shower of fiction" (19). True to his promise, the genie fashions a novella whose title not only suggests a shower of gold[30] but whose structure is as spiral as the whirling galaxy mentioned in his not-so-idle metaphor.

In discussing this structure one need not go much beyond Barth's own description:

The structure . . . is the structure of the logarithmic spiral . . . the Fibonacci series of numbers as it manifests itself in the logarithmic spiral. The logarithmic spiral is one that expands exponentially, and it occurs all over nature. I was interested in the fact that if you unwind certain marine mollusks, like the chambered nautilus, for example, which unwinds in a logarithmic spiral, and keep unwinding the spiral in that ratio, it takes on the shape of some of the great spiral galaxies, like the galaxy M-33 in Andromeda, which is part of the Perseus series of constellations.

Beginning his novella "not *in medias res*, but *in medias* of the second half of the *res*," Barth's problem was "catching up to where [Perseus] was in the second half of his life, and at the same time reviewing the whole exposition of the first half of his life."[31] Borrowing an idea from the *Aeneid*, Barth solved the problem by having Perseus review the story of his life as it was depicted in low-relief murals on the inner walls of "a temple which unwinds in a spiral shape." "When they circle around each other," Barth continues, "the mural in back of this mural, if you had x-ray eyes and could see through the wall, would be an adventure in the second half of Perseus's life that corresponds to the adventures in the first. . . . Of course the point is that as he winds out of this temple he catches up to the story of his own life, and the implication is that he'll keep unwinding."[32]

To spiral beyond the midpoint of his life, however, Perseus, like the genie, must first come to terms with the feminine component in his psyche. This is what Medusa has in mind when she advises Perseus about his second cycle of adventures. "In general," Perseus reports, "my mode of operation in this second enterprise must be contrary to my first's: on the one hand, direct instead of indirect— no circuities, circumlocutions, reflections, or ruses—on the other, rather passive than active: beyond a certain point I must permit things to come to me instead of adventuring to them" (93–94). In short, Medusa counsels Perseus to adopt a feminine rather than masculine stance. As Erich Neumann explains, patriarchal consciousness "outstrips nature's slow process of transformation and evolution by its purposive use of experiment and calculation," whereas matriarchal consciousness "must wait for time to ripen, while with time, like sown seed, comprehension ripens too."[33]

Slow to learn Medusa's lesson, Perseus constantly reverts to his habitual masculine mode of response and almost ruins his chance for rejuvenation. On his second visit to the Graeae, for instance, he tries to conceal his true identity and is almost drowned for his indirection. Upon returning to Joppa he wastes a day prowling the city until, recalling Medusa's advice, he proceeds directly to the palace gate, announces his identity, and sits down to wait, resolving "to let come what would" (114). What comes is Cepheus, who at twice Perseus' age complains of going "round in circles," thus replicating Perseus' present plight and forecasting his future if he does not learn Medusa's lesson. Actually Cepheus' fate is the obverse of Perseus': whereas the latter, stern patriarch, adopts a dominant role in his relationship with Andromeda, the former is henpecked by Cassiopeia. In neither relationship, however, does sexual parity exist. And, as we have seen, such equality becomes possible only with acceptance of the female within.

Still too masculinely aggressive to get the point, Perseus proceeds to the Banquet Hall and, finding himself in ambush, repeats "the earlier donnybrook in that same hall" (123). He kills his half-brother Danaus in the process, thus replicating his earlier slaying of Erytus and foreshadowing Bellerophon's fratricide. Also killed in the fray are Cepheus and Cassiopeia. Perseus' masculine warriorhood has again resulted in mass deaths. But if the earlier massacre had ended when the young Perseus turned his enemies into stone, Perseus himself now faces petrifaction, spiritual if not actual. To avoid it one more death at Perseus' hands becomes necessary — not Andromeda's, as she fears, but his own. Like Todd Andrews, Barth's first protagonist, Perseus must destroy himself *symbolically* by moving from one psychological stage to another. After sneering a final sexist insult at Andromeda (his "last words") the unpleasant middle-Perseus is "promptly and forever" put to death by the "new-Medusa'd" Perseus.

Andromeda's complaint is that Perseus "had by lack of heart-deep reciprocity murdered marriage and love alike." Hopelessly self-centered, Perseus never loved Andromeda at all, "except as Mythics might mere mortals" (124). Repeating the error of Sharyahr and Zaman, he had projected onto Andromeda the role which best complemented his vision of himself, thus denying her essential otherness.[34]

Before "quite miraculous, yes blinding love" transfigured "every-thing in view" (133), Perseus fails to love in the mythic sense. The "ultimate experience of love," writes Campbell, "is a realization that beneath the illusion of two-ness dwells identity. . . . This realiza-tion can expand into a discovery that beneath the multitudinous in-dividualities of the whole surrounding universe — human, animal, vegetable, even mineral — dwells identity."[35] Such discovery, of course, represents matriarchal wisdom, "which never separates and juxtaposes opposites with the clear distinction of patriarchal con-sciousness."[36] Nor does it, like patriarchal love, become primarily associated with sexual performance, masculine *arete*. "Virtuoso per-formance is my line of work," a frustrated and impotent Perseus tells Calyxa when she chides him for equating lovemaking with "mere prolonged penetration" (70). Sex for Perseus is a covert form of masculine aggression as well as a source of masculine pride. Love in the feminine or mythic sense, on the other hand, transcends categories, including male and female; it is a form of mystical union and a source of spiritual as well as physical fulfillment, since even these dichotomies ultimately dissolve. While such union is seldom achieved, or even achievable, in "real" life, men and women must enter relationships *as if* it were possible.

It is therefore significant that Medusa passes on her advice to Per-seus in the temple of Aphrodite, not Athene, as Perseus believes. For Aphrodite, goddess of love, maintains clear links with matri-archal values, whereas Athene has been transformed almost com-pletely by the patriarchy into a reflection of its masculine values. Born not of woman but sprung fully grown from the head of Zeus, Athene is a product of that form of sublimation which Freud termed "transference upward," the male brain (rationality) replacing the female womb. As Campbell notes, "one extremely important con-sequence of this bizarre . . . aberration upward, is the notion, com-mon to all Occidental spirituality . . . that spirituality and sexuality are opposed."[37] Medusa is gorgonized in the first place because her rape by Poseidon occurs in Athene's temple. In psychological terms, Medusa's translation into gorgonhood symbolizes the patriarchal repression of the "darker" side of the Great Mother archetype which includes sex and death.

Medusa's death at the hands of Perseus represents the victory of masculine consciousness over the Great Mother and can be read as the paradigm of the Occidental hero myth in general.[38] Aided by

Hermes and Athena, deities of rational wisdom and consciousness, Perseus must use what Calyxa calls "dodge and indirection," his "conscious tactics" (80), to kill Medusa because "the power of the Great Mother is too overwhelming for any consciousness to tackle direct."[39] Perseus then presents the severed head of Medusa to Athene for display on her shield. Neumann's comments on the significance of this event deserve lengthy quotation:

> The fact that Perseus . . . gives the Gorgon's head to Athene, and that she emblazons it upon her shield, crowns this whole development as the victory of Athene over the Great Mother, of the warrior aspect which is favorable to man and consciousness. . . . The most striking feature in the figure of Athene is the defeat of the old mother goddess by the new, feminine, spiritual principle. Athene still has all the characteristics of the great Cretan goddess. . . . But the primordial power of the female has been subdued by her; she now wears the Gorgon's head as a trophy upon her shield. From quite early times she had been the patron goddess of the ruler and was worshipped in his palace, so that she came to symbolize the revolution which, in the patriarchal age, broke the power of the mother deity. Sprung from the head of Zeus, she is father-born and motherless in contrast to the mother-born, fatherless figures of ancient times; and in contrast, again, to the Terrible Mother's animosity toward all things masculine, she is the companion and helper of the masculine hero.[40]

But Aphrodite, not Athene, is Perseus' protector during the second round of his heroic cycle. To attain herohood he had to kill Medusa in her aspect as Terrible Mother; to attain selfhood he must love Medusa in her aspect as a guide. For middle-Perseus, like Odysseus on Circe's isle, has "passed to a context of initiations associated with the opposite side of the duplex Classical heritage from that represented by his earlier heroic sphere of life."[41] While the adventures of both spheres (or, to use a more Barthian metaphor, both whorls) are similar, the effect of these adventures on Perseus' psychological development must be different if complementary. Thus the goddess who in the first spiral of Perseus' adventures is, for reasons discussed, the "cannibal ogress of the Underworld" in the second whorl becomes "the guide and guardian to that realm and, as such, the giver of immortal life."[42]

The benign aspect of the goddess may be recognized by Perseus only when he has fully accepted the feminine principle within. Like Odysseus' meetings with Circe, Calypso, and Nausicaa, Perseus' encounters with Medusa represent, in Campbell's words, "psychological adventures in the mythic realm of the archetype of the soul, where the male must *experience* the import of the female before he can meet her perfectly in life."[43] This experience must be realized, not merely conceptualized; it must become an inner possession. This is why Medusa cannot relieve Perseus of his indecision over whether to join her or to kill Andromeda. "If only she'd beckon, summon, relieve me of doubt, reach forth her hand!" cries Perseus. "But of course she wouldn't, ever" (125). The principle of feminine knowledge, Medusa cannot impart that truth which may be learned but never taught. As constellated Perseus tells her, "It wasn't you who discovered your beauty to me, but I who finally unveiled it to myself" (132).[44]

Perseus' "head ego," his self-centeredness, accounts for the "childish wish for rejuvenation" (132) that initially motivated his desire to repeat the heroic cycle. "What you *really* wanted," Calyxa tells him, "was to be twenty with Andromeda again" (107). The new-Medusa'd Perseus, however, can assess himself frankly as "a reasonably healthy, no-longer-heroic mortal with more than half his life behind him, less potent and less proud than he was at twenty but still vigorous after all . . . and grown too wise to wish his time turned back" (132–33). This acceptance of time's passage, as seen at the end of "Dunyazadiad," signals acceptance of the archetypal feminine within. Paradoxically, it also leads to Perseus' immortality. As Campbell writes, "Those who . . . in some sense at least, have been themselves both male and female, know the reality from both sides that each sex experiences shadowlike from its own side; and to that extent they have assimilated what is substantial of life and are, so, eternal."[45]

Yet it is not Perseus but his "immortal part" which gains eternity. "Down there," Medusa tells him, "our mortal lives are living themselves out, or've long since done—together or apart, comic tragic, beautiful ugly. That's another story, another story; it can't be told to characters in this" (133). As myth and constellation, Perseus has undergone a dual transformation. In a suggestive analogy Jung equates constellations and myths. The "whole of mythology," he writes,

could be taken as a sort of projection of the collective unconscious. We can see this most clearly if we look at the heavenly
constellations, whose originally chaotic forms were organized
through the projection of images. This explains the influence
of the stars as asserted by astrologers. These influences are
nothing but unconscious, introspective perceptions of the activity of the collective unconscious. Just as the constellations
were projected into the heavens, similar figures were projected into legends and fairy tales or upon historical persons. [46]

In other words, the "content" of heavenly constellations, like the
content of ancient myths, consists of projections of archetypes
that, strictly speaking, have no content. Rather, archetypes are instinctive trends, not patterns so much as patterning forces in the
unconscious, the response to which results in the representations
of motifs which recur in the various world literature. As Jung explains, "The term 'archetype' is often misunderstood as meaning
certain definite mythological images or motifs. But these are nothing more than conscious representations. . . . The archetype is a
tendency to form such representations of a motif — representations
that can vary a great deal in detail without losing their basic pattern." [47] Indeed, the variations between myths are inevitable, since
mythic content is no more than the "filling out" of "pre-existent
traces" with individual experiences, experiences which bear the
stamp of the particular time and place in which they occur. As
Philonoë tells Bellerophon, "as between variants among the myths
themselves, it's in their contradictions that one may seek their
sense" (194), for only through a consideration of these variants
may one arrive at the *general* pattern, as, say, Campbell does in
Hero with a Thousand Faces. Never actually experienced, the
monomyth is an intellectual (which is to say, verbal) construct.
Archetypes are mute; myths give them voice — an idea that corresponds in part to Heidegger's theory of language as revelatory of
Being. As constellation and as myth, Perseus represents (that is,
gives verbal and conceptual content to) ineffable Truth.

A punning ambiguity thus exists in his final words to Medusa:
"I'm content." The pun suggests that Perseus is, on the one hand,
con*tent*, i.e., satisfied, with his final identity as constellation and
myth, and, on the other hand, that as constellation and myth he has
become the *content*, i.e., the vehicle, for archetypal significances.
Moreover, the very fact of the pun, its *presence* as opposed to its

content, has symbolic value. Like the various replications of incidents and character roles in *Chimera*, puns suggest the tenuous nature of autonomous identity. In a practical sense, the One and its many exemplifications in a transient and multiform existence may remain separate. But myth suggests that ultimately the One and the many are identical. The presence of certain kinds of coincidence in the world, what Jung terms "synchronicity" (and Barth's novels are filled with synchronicity), hints at the ultimate unity of all things. The "verbal emblem of coincidence," puns echo this possibility. As Richard Ellmann explains, "In a pun the component parts remain distinguishable, and yet there is a constant small excitement in their being yoked together so deftly and so improperly. An equivalence is at once asserted and questioned, sounds and senses in mutual trespass are both compared and contrasted. . . . The parts of the pun keep their identities even while these are demonstrated to be less isolating than they appeared."[48] Puns contain the hint that one thing may also be another. Can one plausibly explain the fall from favor of the pun, that "lowest form of humor," over the past two centuries as less a matter of changing tastes than of the metaphysical discomfort puns may cause a predominantly scientific age? Logos, after all, would sever things. "Archimedeses," J. Bray, inventor of scientific fictions, writes, "we lever reality by conceiving ourselves apart from its other things, them from one another, the whole from unreality" (246). And a truly scientific language strives to reduce one word to a single referent. Eros, yield of the Mother, closes dichotomies. May the pun, like the language of myth in general, be seen, at least in certain contexts, as feminine?

Other verbal devices in the "Perseid" similarly hint at a world perceived through Mother-consciousness. Its alliterative style, to which Medusa calls attention, intimates through a coincidence of sounds the secret connection among the many referents into which words fraction "reality." Another verbal stratagem that argues for the unifying flow of "reality" is Perseus' use of neologisms, particularly his conversion of nouns into verbs and verbals. Thus he awakes in heaven (actually Calyxa's temple) to think himself "beworlded" (59); he is "sea-leveled" (60) on the beach at Libya; Mother Danaë, "brazen-towered" (61) by Acrisius, is "jackpotted" (61) by Zeus with Perseus; the Gorgons in the mural in Athene's temple are "reditto'd" (62) in Calyxa's; Acrisius, killed by Perseus' discus, is "frisbee'd" (66) down to Hades; Calyxa would have "reliquaried" (69) Perseus' stool; the wound "intaglio'd" on Danaus' temple resembles "the image of his bowled foredropper" (123), and so on. Such usages imbue nouns, those solid stones of language, with the vitality of verbs, making them emblematic of the victory over petrifaction that Perseus seeks. Perseus' use of compound words, many also neologized, serves a similar purpose. "Then-blank Enyo" (63), "post-swatly" (81), "cowl-maid" (100), "gold-haired hard-tasked hero" (73), "limped palace-ward" (118), "Ammonoracles" (118), "long-smashed Erytus" (122), "difficult dead once-darling" (125), "fear-chased figure" (123–24), "heart-deep reciprocity" (124), "shield-and-sworded" (121), and, on page 89 alone, "sea-god," "kid-sister," "sea-nymph," "sea-salt," "admiralty-god," "hair-things," "crew-cut," "third-persons," "neck-nape," and "blue-eyed"—such usages impel close verbal relationships between words which in turn mirror the fundamental, if not always apparent, relationships among the things words signify. At first blush the net effect of these verbal stratagems is, as Medusa charges, a style possibly "too mannered" (128). But considered within the thematic context of Barth's novella the style becomes functional and appropriate, medium merging with message. If the style at its most extreme jars our sensibilities, we should recall that *discordia concors* requires discord after all.

But despite their promise of unity, such verbal stratagems finally deliver a world irrevocably split. The neologisms are eccentric, peculiar to *this* work, not to language in general or to the world language serves. Similarly, alliteration depends on a series of *separate* words referring to separate things. "The essence of the pun," in Ellmann's words, "is not complete but incomplete juncture."[49] Even myths reflect but can never contain the immutable and eternal archetypes which inform them. For alliteration, puns, neologisms, compound words, and the language of myth in general remain verbal stratagems after all, and words belong to the realm of daily activity. Indeed, as I have argued earlier, Barth finds interesting the notion that words *constitute* daily activity, that language *is* "reality." Archetypal truth, everywhere and nowhere, remains nonreferential and thus lies outside the medium of language. A leap outside world and words is a leap into death—or mystical vision; but even mystics and heroes must return from the ineluctable void to a world where their vision cannot be communicated. Words, no matter how skillfully or originally combined, can go only so far in speaking the unspeakable. Be that as it may, truly mythopoeic language can evoke if it cannot designate archetypes. That is, the function of mythopoeic language is inspiration, not signification. We return to ancient texts, as does the genie (and Barth), to tap the springs of creativity from which myth flows, so that we may construct our own representations of preexistent traces.

But Bellerophon, hero *manqué* of the concluding novella in *Chimera*, returns to myths not for inspiration but as the objects of slavish imitation. He confuses mythic content with the truth it symbolizes—a truth that, underlying reason, cannot be rationally grasped. In his emulation of Perseus, Bellerophon reverses and thereby invalidates the proper relationship between archetypes and behavior. Archetypal truth is located not in the world of objective experience, which it shapes and where it is reflected, but within the individual. One can no more make contact with archetypal truth by mimicking the behavior of one who has than one can acquite literary genius by copying the works of Tolstoy. As Zeus tells Polyeidus, "By imitating perfectly the Pattern of mythic Heroism, your man Bellerophon has become a perfect imitation of a mythic hero" (297). In his attempt to live a life that points upward to the myths, Bellerophon has corrupted their transpersonal significance into the needs of his own personal ego. As Campbell explains, "The goal of myth is to dispel the need for such life ignorance by effecting a reconciliation of the individual consciousness with the universal will. And this is effected through a realization of the true relationship of the passing phenomena of time to the imperishable life that lives and dies in all."[50] Melanippe, embodiment of matriarchal consciousness, understands this perfectly. Uncomfortable with the phrase "human being, female" because it "puts her already into two categories from which her self feels more or less distinct; *herself* puts her into one," she tells Bellerophon of an identity "distinct from her 'Melanippe-self,' immortal because impersonal . . . a private, uncategorizable self impossible for her even to confuse with the name *Melanippe*—as Perseus, she believes, confused himself with the mythical persona *Perseus*, Bellerophon *Bellerophon*" (237–38). But Bellerophon, entangled in the male ego, dismisses Melanippe's point. "[My] identification with 'Bellerophon,'" he asserts, "is clear and systematic policy, not confusion" (238). Self-centered Bellerophon resists that self-annihilation prerequisite to rebirth which Zaman, the genie, and Perseus accept.

This resistance becomes explicit near the end of Section I when, interrupting his mimicry of "Anonymiad," Bellerophon writes: "Then it [his story] too must perish, with all things deciphered and undeciphered — no, no, scratch that: it *mustn't* perish, no indeed; it's going to live forever, sure, the voice of Bellerus, the immortal Bellerophon, that's the whole point" (291). The allusion to "Anonymiad" is both ironic and revealing, for the nameless minstrel of that tale joyfully accepts the realization Bellerophon defies: properly understood, immortality requires anonymity.

Near the end of Section II, Bellerophon struggles toward this understanding. "I couldn't speak to explain the difference between lies and myth, which I was but beginning to comprehend myself; how the latter could be so much realer and more important than particular man that perhaps I must cease to be the hero of my own, cease even to exist, cease somehow even to have existed" (295). Later, while falling to the marsh which will become his permanent home, Bellerophon moves even closer to the fundamental truth of myth: that his fame, "such as it was, is, and might have been, is as it were anonymous" (305). The melancholy tone of this pronouncement indicates resigned defeat, not joyful acceptance. Bellerophon still conceives of immortality in *personal* terms; "it's hardly to be imagined," he laments, "that those patterns we call 'Perseus,' 'Medusa,' 'Pegasus' . . . are aware of their existences, any more than are their lettered counterparts on the page" (305). Imprisoned in the masculine ego, Bellerophon remains oblivious to the transpersonal immortality androgynous vision promises. Had Bellerophon, like Giles before him, "let go" of his rationally conceived determination to emulate the Pattern, as Melanippe gently urges, he might have transcended ego boundaries. But because he will not trust the feminine voice within, he confuses Melanippe's lunar wisdom with Polyeidic sophistry. " 'Float with the tide,' I'm told. By whom? My mistress? Monstrous. I know who sticks in my throat" (157). Intellectually Bellerophon understands that creative achievement depends upon harmonious union of Logos and Eros, formative masculine and creative feminine powers. What he fails to grasp is that this union is inaccessible to the intellect. "The union of opposites," writes Jung, "is a transconscious process and, in principle, not amenable to scientific explanation. The marriage must remain the 'mystery of the queen,' the secret of the art."[51] Bellerophon must confront the blank before he fills it in. He does not.

The result is a botched life and a botched book — but that botched book is Bellerophon's, not Barth's. The "longeurs, lumps, lacunae" that Bellerophon complains of in his "beastly . . . , ill-proportioned" fiction (308) are as functional in their way as the verbal stratagems in "Perseid" are in theirs. Throughout *Chimera* Barth employs *"The Principle of Metaphoric Means"*: *"the investiture by the writer of as many of the elements and aspects of his fiction as possible with emblematic as well as dramatic value: not only the 'form' of the story, the narrative viewpoint, the tone, and such, but, where manageable, the particular genre, the mode and medium, the very process of narration — even the fact of the artifact itself"* (203). We have already seen how Barth's use of the logarithmic spiral as motif and structural principle in the first two novellas reinforces his theme of psychological transformation. As suggested earlier, this is replaced in "Bellerophoniad" by the circle, symbol of sterile repetition. Like Perseus, Bellerophon attempts to repeat his initial round of heroic adventures. But rather than killing Chimera "for real," as Melanippe advises, which means incorporating her feminine essence into his personality, thus transforming her from monster to guide as Perseus transformed, and was in turn transfigured by, Medusa, Bellerophon mounts Pegasus and heads straight for Olympian Zeus, patriarchal king of the gods. Bellerophon's continued identification with the Father reflects his circular course and signals his failure to achieve individuation. This failure is in turn reflected by Bellerophon's failure as an artist.

Failed art becomes a central metaphor in the novella. In employing that metaphor Barth has taken a considerable esthetic risk, for failed art as metaphor may be mistaken for *actual* failed art. Campbell Tatham, for example, after cogently analyzing Bellerophon's failure to integrate the anima into his psyche, then briefly discussing that failure's manifestation as failed art, holds Barth responsible for the artistic failure. Referring to the three endings of the story, Tatham writes, "It could be argued, I suppose, that the diversity of closings, the first two undermining each other while the third subverts the whole, suggests the final rejection of the Pattern and the verbal paradigm it embodies. But in favor of what?"[52] The answer lies not so much in "Bellerophoniad," though it is implicit even there, but in the first two novellas. Both works dramatize the propitious consequences, at the artistic and personal levels, of successful anima integration.

"Dunyazadiad," appearing first in *Chimera*, lies metaphorically nearer to the feminine springs of story and thus is relatively free of the self-conscious reflexivity which troubles "Perseid" and sabotages "Bellerophoniad." Indeed, its very accessibility is functional, serving as emblem of the narrative assurance which precedes exhausted possibilities. "Perseid," second in the series, is to a great extent the genie's retelling of "Dunyazadiad." Recast with fresh characters and a new setting but recognizably the same nonetheless, its less "transparent" prose style reflects the artist's need to find new ways to tell the old story. With each successive retelling the possible permutations of fictional elements and functions become further reduced; as Scheherazade notes, "the magic words in one story aren't magical in the next" (7). Virtuosity soon becomes necessary, self-consciousness unavoidable. In keeping with the Principle of Metaphoric Means, "Perseid" exhibits both, self-consciousness becoming as emblematic of Barth's concerns in that novella as is its relative absence in "Dunyazadiad." Significantly, the mannered style is more obtrusive in the earlier pages of the novella, when Perseus still struggles to unite Logos and Eros. In the final passages, however, style frees itself from self-conscious mannerisms and passion rescues virtuosity:

> My love, it's an epilogue, always ending, never ended, like . . . II–G, which winds through universal space and time. My fate is to be able only to imagine boundless beauty from my experience of boundless love — but I have a fair imagination to work with, and, to work from, one priceless piece of unimagined evidence: what I hold above *Beta Persei*, Medusa: not serpents, but lovely woman's hair. I'm content. So with this issue, our net estate: to have become, like the noted music of our tongue, these silent, visible signs; to *be* the tale I tell to those with eyes to see and understanding to interpret; to raise you up forever and know that our story will never be cut off, but nightly rehearsed as long as men and women read the stars. [133–34]

In that passage, which contains some of Barth's most effective and moving prose, masculine formative and feminine creative powers merge, forming a *conjunctio oppositorum* that mirrors the sacred marriage of Perseus and Medusa.

Because no such marriage occurs in "Bellerophoniad," the final passage of that novella's initial section winds down in hollow, truncated mimicry of its source: "So, well; their love, Bellerophon's and Melanippe's, winds through universal space and time and all; noted music of our tongue, silent visible signs, et cetera; Bellerophon's content; he really is; good night" (291). Narrative self-consciousness, sure sign of ego domination, reaches its apogee. Parody, that most rational of modes, becomes intensely reflexive, the novella mocking its processes at every turn. Such self-mockery, conspicuous by nature, is made even more conspicuous by Bellerophon's commentary: "if Polyeidus the Seer had realized that this final and trickiest effort in the literary-metamorphosis way would be freckled and soiled with as it were self-criticism, he'd've let Bellerophon smack into the muck and bubble there forever" (139). Indeed, the conspicuousness of the novella's alleged defects should be evidence enough that Barth intends them as functional.

Like its stylistic "flaws," the length of "Bellerophoniad" is functional. On the one hand, this length is determined by the general structural principle of the series. As Barth explains, "In the three *Chimera* novellas each novella happens to be about 1.6 times the size of the preceding novella, because that's the Fibonacci series, the golden ratio" which determines the relationship between whorls of a logarithmic spiral.[53] But the length of "Bellerophoniad" is functional in yet another sense. Barth has called *Giles Goat-Boy* a "gigantistic" novel, by which he means purposely inflated.[54] This inflation parodies the ways rational man tries to appropriate "reality" through his formulations of it, as though a large enough accumulation of facts about the world could somehow explain that world. But myth suggests that one can no more comprehend the cosmos by talking about it than one can become a mythic hero by imitating the Pattern. Thus prolixity underscores Bellerophon's dilemma. A talker, not a doer, as Anteia and others complain, he is bogged down in the very medium that he must transcend if he is to glimpse heroic truth—for the truth that mythopoeia communicates is the incommunicability of Truth. Within the tensions of that paradox myth is sustained. But even Bellerophon realizes that his language discloses disjunction, not counterpoise, "as though the pure Bellerophonic voice were tugged and co-opted now by Polyeidus this way, now Melanippe that; not to the end of dramatic harmony and tension, but discordantly, to stalemate and stagnation" (144). The excessive patter that accompanies his narrative, like his addiction to neat formulaic patterns (his diagram of Aristotle's classifications of ethical responsibility, of the genetic possibilities when gods and mortals mate, of the variations on Freitag's triangle, etc.), is emblematic of the fact that Bellerophon remains locked into masculine consciousness. If "Bellerophoniad" is, as Campbell Tatham maintains, "all too obviously *talk*,"[55] that very talkiness is itself functional. The medium of Bellerophon's message, a language of Logos unmediated by Eros, thus becomes invested with metaphoric value.

So do the media of that medium: writing and print. Even more than those *Funhouse* stories composed expressly for print, "Bellerophoniad" is self-consciously a *printed* artifact. Unlike those original mythic heroes who turned into the sounds of other people's voices relating the stories of their lives, Bellerophon turns into the *printed* version of his. Or, rather, Polyeidus turns into Bellerophon in "Bellerophoniad" form. For Polyeidus — "revision" of that proto-shape-shifter, Proteus, symbol of language in "Menelaiad" — symbolizes writing and print in "Bellerophonaid." In *Funhouse* Barth toys with the idea that language contains us; in *Chimera* he examines the notion that we are chirographically and typographically controlled. If writing, in replacing oral utterance, separated man from his external world and ultimately from himself, as Eric A. Havelock has argued,[56] then print, a copy of a copy, as it were, pushes him to still further removes. One reason for this, according to Marshall McLuhan, is that print, as an extension of sight, disturbed the harmonious interplay among the senses. Separation of the visual faculty from the interplay of the other senses made abstraction possible and led to our modern emphasis on explicitness, uniformity, and linear thought — the hallmarks of scientific writing. In a striking passage McLuhan writes, "It is easy to gauge the degree of acceptance of print culture in any time or country by its effect in eliminating pun . . . alliteration, and aphorism from literature."[57] In the light of McLuhan's statement, the relative absence in "Bellerophoniad" of those "feminine" verbal stratagems (pun, alliteration, etc.) characteristic of "Perseid" becomes significant.

Print intensifies our separation from that holistic state toward which myth inclines. Indeed, Walter Ong has recently speculated that writing (and particularly print, with its technological dependence) belongs to the realm of the father, unlike verbalized language, our "Mother tongue." "Writing and print," he writes, "despite their intrinsic value, have obscured the nature of the word and of thought itself, for they have sequestered the essentially participatory word—fruitfully enough, beyond a doubt—from its natural habitat, sound, and assimilated it to a mark on a surface, where a real word cannot exist at all."[58] Bellerophon, then, is not only trapped within a language leadened with Logos (he kills Chimera with a huge phallic pencil), but that language is itself contained within the closed system of print. Metaphorically, the replicative nature of print—the fact that it is not only a copy of a copy, but that every letter in a font of type replicates every other like it, and that every copy of a book reproduces exactly every other[59]—reinforces Bellerophon's own imitative stance. He is but a copy; he is several times removed from the truth he seeks to embody. When Bellerophon becomes the printed version of his life, the terms of the above metaphor merge, vehicle (print as a copy of written language) and tenor (Deliades as a copy of Bellerophon copying Perseus) springing together in an ironic union of opposites that parodies the *hieros gamos* forever lost to Bellerophon.

A final observation about the metaphoric value of the written and printed word: one of the many documents into which Polyeidus transforms himself is a letter from Jerome Bray detailing plans for a "revolutionary novel" entitled *NOTES*. Using five, a masculine number, as its "numerical base," and written entirely by a computer, *NOTES* effectively exemplifies a novel of pure virtuosity untempered by passion. The computer is a perfect if by now obvious symbol of excessive rationality and bears mythic associations in "Bellerophoniad" as well as in *Giles Goat-Boy* with the Father, from whom proceeds "the contradictions, good and evil, death and life, pain and pleasure, boons and deprivations"—in short, "all the pairs of opposites" which the Mother conjoins.[60] The computer is an extension of pure consciousness, which in Walter Ong's view accounts for its usefulness. "Relieving the mind of its onus of conscious but routine operations (such as computing, sorting, matching patterns, and so on)," Ong writes, "the computer . . . actually releases more energy for new kinds of exploratory operations by the human mind itself, in which the unconscious is deeply involved and which the computer, lacking an unconscious, cannot carry forward."[61] Among those operations deeply involving the unconscious is, of course, art. *NOTES*, then, is an artless artifact. The repetition of "reset," computer argot, throughout the final pages of "Bellerophoniad" suggests that it, too, may be computer produced. Thus Bellerophon has turned into his father, who has turned into an artifact printed by a computer. His identification with the masculine principle is complete.

Bellerophon learns of *NOTES* when, on Philonoë's advice, he seeks counsel from the Old Man of the Marsh (Polyeidus) on "how to open [his] life's closed circuit into an ascending spiral" (241). The four documents presented him provide that counsel — but conversely, serve as examples of how not to proceed.[62] The first document, a letter from Napoleon to King George III, promises a prospectus for the novel *NOTES*, described as *"the first genuinely scientific model of the genre,"* which *"will of necessity contain* nothing original whatever, *but be the quintessence, the absolute type, as it were the Platonic Form expressed"* (244). The second Polyeidic document, an epistle from Jerome B. Bray to Todd Andrews, contains that prospectus. *NOTES* will be accomplished by feeding various data, including "the corpus of existing fiction," into a computer, a kind of "mechanical Polyeidus" which will in turn analyze that data, "induce the perfect form from its 'natural' approximations . . . reduce that ideal to a mathematical model," then compose "its verbal embodiment" (250). Obviously Bray's plan to develop a pattern of the quintessential fiction so that he can produce one parallels Bellerophon's desire to acquire the Pattern of Mythic Heroism so that he can imitate it. Both attempts are based on the dualistic belief that essence ("the Platonic Form") is separate from its embodiment. But, as discussed earlier, archetypes (our modern version of pure Platonic forms) are not patterns but patterning forces; they may be revealed in art's various concrete forms, but they cannot be imitated. As part of his covert tactics Polyeidus emphasizes this point by including in the second letter references to pretense ("J.B. the Pretender"; Harrison Mack's insane pretense to be George III, mad, pretending to be Harrison Mack, sane), to plagiarism (Bray's charge that he, not Barth, is the authentic author of *Giles Goat-Boy;* his retributive plagiarism of Barth's earlier fictions), even to Barth's early statement that *Giles* and *The Sot-Weed Factor* are "novels which mimic the form of the novel, by an author who mimics the role of Author." But the epistles only confirm Bellerophon in his folly; he finds the first "obscurely touching" (245) and becomes as involved in the second as if, irony heaped on irony, "Bray's quest . . . had been [his] own" (252).

In his next metamorphosis Polyeidus tries another tack. He turns into the blank water-message that introduced a young Am-

brose into the mysteries of sex and art. That blank, as I have argued, represents that pre-linguistic state the separation from which
generates language. It symbolizes the pregnant, silent realm of the
archetypes, Heidegger's ground of Being. But whereas Ambrose's
spirit bears "new and subtle burdens" as a result of his confrontation with the blank,[63] Bellerophon is rendered heartsick. He flings
the water-message down, whereupon it turns into Perse, Ambrose's
ragamuffin companion, not Perseus, whom Polyeidus says he tried
to become. Coming as close to direct statement as his devious
trickster's nature will allow, Polyeidus advises Bellerophon that
getting Pegasus up again requires a balance of Logos, Athene's
magic bridle, and Eros, Aphrodite's sacred herb (a good metaphor
for "passionate virtuosity"). Instead of revisiting the locales of his
initial round of adventures à la "Perseid" he should "look up all the
women [he's] ever loved, in order; that's the sort of thing Aphrodite goes for" (260). Then Polyeidus turns into the long-promised
Pattern and Bellerophon's second round of heroic advantages is
underway.

That Polyeidus gives Bellerophon advice in the first place, that
his advice takes the form of written and printed manuscripts, and
that those manuscripts serve as negative examples are all appropriate to Polyeidus' role as a trickster figure. On the mythological
level the trickster is usually identified with Hermes, inventor of the
alphabet (thus Polyeidus' association with letters) and patron of
rebirth (this Polyeidus' guise as advisor). Herme's traditional identification with that symbol of androgyny, the caduceus, is echoed
in "Bellerophoniad" by Polyeidus' frequent association with
snakes[64] and by his advice concerning Pegasus and Aphrodite. On
the psychological level the trickster is a collective shadow figure,
which accounts for the inverted nature of Polyeidus' advice. In
Jungian terms, the shadow is constituted by repressed inferior
traits which the individual, through the process of projection, frequently views as directly opposed to his own character. Thus Polyeidus' various transfigurations into written documents reflect the
true nature of Bellerophon's copied persona. Bellerophon must
recognize who he really is, must come to terms with the shadow
side of his psyche before he can confront its feminine component.
For the shadow, as the figure closest to consciousness, "stands at
the very beginning of the way of individuation." And "the one
standing closest behind the shadow is the anima."[65] Thus Polyei-

dus, like Harold Bray before him, is only an apparent villain.[66] He represents the spirit of contraries which must be overcome if individuation is to be successfully undertaken. Typically, "Dum De De" misses the point.

Sympathetic readers of *Chimera* should not miss the point of "Bellerophoniad," however. That novella is to *Chimera* what *NOTES* is to it — a negative example, the intention of which is to clarify by contrast successful life and art in the first two novellas. But despite that pervasive concern with failure, its unhappy ending, like the happy endings of the first two novellas, is qualified. Bellerophon at last admits his real identity, thus coming to terms with his shadow if not with his anima. He also realizes that his story has failed, even though he remains ignorant as to why. Moreover, his story concludes not with another word, the last in a long series of words, but, significantly, with a blank. That blank, though never confronted by Bellerophon, stands as a mute testament to the pregnant silence out of which all myth proceeds and to which it beckons. It is that silence, the realm of the archetype, to which Barth's mythopoeic fictions pay tribute and at their best embody. Perhaps Barth's interest in the women's liberation movement, the issue with which this chapter began, derives at least in part from his hope that reflected in that movement may be seen the beginnings of the return of the Mother — not to the exclusion of the Father, for that would be to have come round full circle, and circles represent dead ends in Barth's fictions. What *Chimera* calls for, rather, is a harmonious blend of Logos and Eros, a *hieros gamos* of masculine and feminine opposites which, if seldom achieved in the "real" world, at moments flourish in the magic "as if" of Barth's mythopoeic fictions.

NOTES

1. Enck, "Interview," p. 28.
2. Gado, ed., *First Person*, p. 131.
3. Bellamy, *The New Fiction*, pp. 8–9. This statement is repeated with minor revisions in *Chimera* (New York: Random House, 1972), p. 199. Further references to this edition appear in parentheses in the text.
4. Frazer, *The Golden Bough*, VI, 211–12.
5. A circumstance referred to by Bellerophon: *Chimera*, p. 158.
6. Graves, "Introduction," *The Greek Myths: I*, p. 16.
7. Campbell, *The Masks of God: Occidental Mythology*, p. 155.

8. Graves, *The Greek Myths: I*, p. 17.

9. Morrell, *Barth*, p. 157.

10. Campbell, *The Masks of God: Primitive Mythology*, p. 160. In a portion later deleted from Barth's *Book Week* essay ("Muse, Spare Me") Barth writes that Scheherazade's fate "fits [the] fate of mythical heroes." The complete essay is located in the Library of Congress collection under the title "Publish or Perish" and is dated June 1965.

11. Campbell, *The Masks of God: Primitive Mythology*, p. 168.

12. Morrell, *Barth*, p. 149.

13. Bellamy, *The New Fiction*, p. 12.

14. Jung, *The Spirit in Man, Art, and Literature*, p. 96.

15. Ibid., p. 103.

16. Neumann, "On the Moon and Matriarchal Consciousness," p. 58.

17. On the reversible frame in *Chimera*, see Davis, "'The Key to the Treasure.'" In a later essay Davis argues that the role reversals implicit in Barth's metaphor are, indeed, sexist, as is the whole of *Chimera*. Her essay offers an interesting counter-argument to my reading. See Davis, "Heroes, Earth Mothers, and Muses."

18. Kennard, *Number and Nightmare*, p. 79. Kennard bases her argument on the grounds that the narrator calls Dunyazade "little sister," and thus must be Scheherazade. But the genie's last words to Scheherazade and Dunyazade are, "And I'll always love you, Scheherazade! Dunyazade, I'm your brother! Good night, sisters!" (33).

19. Quoted in Cirlot, *Dictionary of Symbols*, p. 360.

20. Neumann, *The Great Mother*, p. 106.

21. Ibid., p. 160.

22. Neumann, *Origins and History of Consciousness*, p. 210.

23. Ibid., p. 212.

24. Fordham, *Introduction to Jung's Psychology*, p. 53. See also Harding, *Woman's Mysteries*: "Love for a woman who carries the value of anima is not really love of the woman herself. It is almost entirely love of her as *anima*. An involvement of this character does not permit her to be herself but makes her a function of the man's own psyche and involves the demand that she shall conform to his ideal and fulfill his desire" (p. 196).

25. Thus Anteia's derision of "the male-supremist character of the great body of our classic myths . . . which she held to be the fabulated record of a bloody overthrow, by male pig patriarchs in ages past, of the original and natural matriarchy of the world" (277) is not solely feminist rhetoric.

26. Campbell, *The Masks of God: Occidental Mythology*, p. 78.

27. Ibid., p. 54.

28. Campbell, *The Masks of God: Primitive Mythology*, p. 28.

29. Morrell, *Barth*, p. 162.

30. As Morrell points out, "Perseid" means literally a shower of golden meteors that flash from the constellation Perseus every August (ibid., p. 147).

31. McKenzie, ed., "Pole-Vaulting in Top Hats."

32. Ibid., p. 138. Cf. Morrell, *Barth*, pp. 141–42.

33. Neumann, "On the Moon and Matriarchal Consciousness," p. 46.

34. Paradoxically, the recognition of another's separateness is prerequisite to the mythic realization that there is no separateness. To free oneself from ego-bondage, one must recognize that the world one encounters is to a large extent a world one has *projected*. Since the effect of projection is the isolation of the subject from his environment, meaningful relationships with that environment become impossible. In Jung's words, unconscious projections "lead to an autoerotic or autistic condition in which one dreams a world whose reality remains forever unattainable." By differentiating and then integrating into consciousness those unconscious aspects of the psyche (the shadow, the anima, the animus) from which projections emanate, one is able to overcome projections and become *present* to the world. Realization of the essence of oneself makes possible the realization of the essence of the world and leads ultimately to the realization that both essences are one; such a realization constitutes love in the mythic sense. See Jung, *Psyche and Symbol*, p. 8.

35. Campbell, *Hero with a Thousand Faces*, p. 280.

36. Neumann, "On the Moon and Matriarchal Consciousness," p. 57.

37. Campbell, *The Masks of God: Occidental Mythology*, p. 157.

38. See ibid., p. 24: "For whether we think of the victories of Zeus and Apollo, Theseus, Perseus, Jason, and the rest, over the dragons of the Golden Age, or turn to that of Yahweh over Leviathan, the lesson is equally of a self-moving power greater than the force of any earthbound serpent [i.e., feminine] destiny. All stand (to use Miss [Jane] Harrison's phrase) 'first and foremost as a protest against the worship of Earth and the daimones of the fertility of Earth.'"

39. Neumann, *Origins and History of Consciousness*, p. 216.

40. Ibid., p. 217.

41. Campbell, *The Masks of God: Occidental Mythology*, p. 171.

42. Ibid.

43. Ibid., p. 164.

44. Once again the metaphor is pertinent, for Medusa's veil, besides concealing her possibly still gorgonized features, suggests mythically the illumination Perseus eventually enjoys. The symbol of veiling, Neumann writes, represents "the regenerating power of the unconscious that in nocturnal darkness or by the light of the moon performs its task, *a*

mysterium in a *mysterium*, working from out of itself, out of nature, with no aid from the head ego" ("On the Moon and Matriarchal Consciousness," pp. 50–51).

45. Campbell, *The Masks of God: Occidental Mythology*, p. 171.

46. Campbell, ed., *Portable Jung*, p. 39.

47. "Approaching the Unconscious," in Jung, ed., *Man and His Symbols*, p. 67.

48. Ellmann, "The Politics of Joyce," pp. 45–46.

49. Ibid., p. 46.

50. Campbell, *Hero with a Thousand Faces*, p. 238.

51. Jung, *Mysterium Conjunctionis*, pp. 380–81.

52. Despite Tatham's conclusions, which are diametrically opposed to mine, I am indebted to "Anima Rising" for its perceptive insights into the nature of the anima. I have occasionally cited passages from Jung and Campbell that Tatham also quotes.

53. McKenzie, ed., "Pole-Vaulting in Top Hats," p. 157.

54. Gado, ed., *First Person*, p. 124. Cf. McLuhan's analysis of Rabelais's similar use of giganticism in *Gargantua*, in *The Gutenberg Galaxy*, pp. 179–82.

55. Tatham, "Anima Rising," p. 8.

56. Havelock, *Preface to Plato*.

57. McLuhan, *The Gutenberg Galaxy*, pp. 179–82.

58. Ong, *Interfaces of the Word*, p. 21.

59. Ibid., p. 305.

60. Campbell, *Hero with a Thousand Faces*, p. 145.

61. Ong, *Interfaces of the Word*, p. 47.

62. Morrell, *Barth*, p. 154.

63. Barth, *Lost in the Funhouse*, p. 56.

64. Warrick, "Circuitous Journey of Consciousness," p. 82. Warrick comments on Polyeidus' association with snakes but sees snakes as symbolic of self-consciousness, citing Harold Bloom's *The Visionary Company* in support of her contention. But Neumann and others see the snake — and particularly joined snakes, the uroboros — as a primordial symbol of the union of opposites the Mother contains; see, e.g., Neumann, *Origins and History of Consciousness*, pp. 1–11.

65. Jung, *Four Archetypes*, pp. 150, 151.

66. In the "Posttape" Giles says of Bray: "I had not called him flunkèd, I declared: his nature and origin were extraordinary and mysterious as my own; all that could be said was that he was my adversary, as necessary to me as Failure is to Passage. I.e., not only contrary and interdependent, but finally undifferentiable."

8
LETTERS
and the Literature of Replenishment:
A Kind of Conclusion

LETTERS was published in October 1979, not quite half a year after Barth's forty-ninth birthday. Almost as long as the first edition of *The Sot-Weed Factor*, Barth's most massive novel to date, and admittedly "beastly difficult" to write, *LETTERS* absorbed "seven years of [Barth's] mortal writing time."[1] Yet the effort seems to have rejuvenated rather than sapped his creative energies. "I find I'm just bubbling with other projects," he told Sarah Crichton shortly after the novel's publication. "As you approach fifty, you feel that even if you're going to lead a writerly life as long as Thomas Mann's or Nabokov's — and I think I will — it still only adds up to about eighty years. That only leaves three decades, and there's so much that one wants to do."[2] Indeed, 1982 saw the publication of Barth's eighth novel, *Sabbatical.*

Clearly, now is not the time for conclusions.

Nonetheless, any commentary genuinely responsive to Barth's seventh novel must necessarily function as a kind of conclusion, for *LETTERS* is at once a recapitulation and summa. As sequel, it re-orchestrates and extends the characters and concerns of Barth's previous six books; as epistolary novel, it recalls the origins and history of the genre in which Barth works. But *LETTERS* is also prolegomenon, adumbrating as it embodies the new directions Barth feels the novel must take if it is to remain a vital and consequential form.

In January 1980, only a few months after the publication of
LETTERS, Barth described those directions in an essay entitled
"The Literature of Replenishment." Published in the *Atlantic
Monthly*, the same journal in which "The Literature of Exhaustion"
first appeared, it has not achieved the éclat of that celebrated earlier essay, but it casts valuable light on the still-developing Barthian esthetic. Barth's topic is postmodernism, the esthetic category
into which he and writers like him are so frequently placed but
which remains inadequately defined. Most definitions, Barth complains, view "postmodernist" fiction as "faintly epigonic," merely
carrying "to its logical and questionable extremes the anti-rationa-
list, anti-realist, anti-bourgeois program of modernism" through
an emphasis on " 'performing' self-consciousness and self-reflexiveness." Were postmodernist fiction nothing more than an extension
of modernism or an intensification of certain of its aspects, or even
a repudiation of it as well as its predecessor, " 'traditional' bourgeois
realism" — were postmodernism nothing more than these, Barth concludes, then he would agree with detractors such as Gerald Graff
that it "is indeed a kind of pallid, last-ditch decadence, of no more
than minor symptomatic interest."

But in the hands of its most accomplished practitioners, postmodernist fiction becomes far more. Writers such as the Italian
fabulist Italo Calvino and the expatriate Columbian Gabriel
García Márquez achieve in their fictions what Barth terms a "postmodern synthesis" that transcends the antitheses of premodernist
and modernist modes of writing. They write with the twentieth-
century under their belts but not on the backs, neither repudiating
nor imitating modernism or premodernism. Thus in *Cosmicomics*
(1965) "Calvino keeps one foot always in the narrative past — characteristically the Italian narrative past of Boccaccio, Marco Polo,
or Italian fairy tales — and one foot in, one might say, the Parisian
structuralist present." And García Márquez sustains throughout
One Hundred Years of Solitude (1967) a "synthesis of straightfor-
wardness and artifice, realism and magic and myth, political passion and nonpolitical artistry, characterization and caricature,
humor and terror." Moreover, the "democratic . . . appeal" of
these works stands in sharp contrast to the "famous relative difficulty of access" inherent in much fiction of the high modernist
mode. Like good jazz or classical music, postmodernist fiction
bears repeated examination, but "the first time through should be

so ravishing — and not just to specialists — that one delights in the replay."

The success of these exemplary postmodernists demonstrates that the synthesis Barth describes is not an unattainable ideal. It demonstrates as well that the modernist "program" is essentially completed, and that postmodernist fiction, "not . . . the next-best thing after modernism, but . . . the *best next* thing," is well into the process of development. Indeed, Barth realizes retrospectively, "'The Literature of Exhaustion' was really about . . . the effective 'exhaustion' not of language or of literature but the aesthetic of high modernism." Significantly, from the corpus of his own work Barth cites *LETTERS* as an example of postmodernism, which suggests that "The Literature of Replenishment" will prove as indispensable a guide through the intricacies of this novel as "The Literature of Exhaustion" has for *Lost in the Funhouse.*

As we might expect, then, in *LETTERS* Barth has one foot in the past — America's historical past, the past of his own fictions, and the narrative past, particularly that of the English novel — and one in the post-structuralist present. As an "oldtime" epistolary novel, *LETTERS* evokes its premodernist models; as a parody and Heideggerean *Destruktion* of these models, it evokes the high modernist mode; as a synthesis and transcension of both, *LETTERS* exemplifies the postmodernist program. Accordingly, the "ground theme" of *LETTERS* is "the notion of First and Second Revolutions."[3] Not until near the novel's end, however, does the Author, Barth's overt persona in *LETTERS*, realize the true parameter of his theme. Learning by going where he has to go, the Author at first suspects that his theme may be simple revolution, rebellion against a presiding state of affairs. Later he decides that his theme is not rebellion but reenactment, "the attractions, hazards, rewards, and penalties of a '2nd cycle' isomorphic with the '1st'" (656). Ultimately he learns in a letter from Ambrose Mensch, his "alter ego and aesthetic conscience" (653), that the theme of *LETTERS* is neither rebellion nor reenactment, neither repudiation nor emulation of the past, but synthesis and transcension. "Cycle II must not reenact its predecessor," advises Ambrose — "echo, yes; repeat, no" (767). As we learned in *Chimera*, circles deplete; spirals replenish and extend.

One of Barth's major concerns in *LETTERS* may be seen as the forms of historical progression. Two forms he considers and then discards (repudiation and emulation of the past) because both represent ultimate denials of history. The former apprehends history as linear and causal, locating its utopian dream at the end of History. Advocated in *LETTERS* by Drew Mack, Hank Burlingame, and the various Cooks, among others, and prefigured by notions of schism, division, and alienation, it attempts to displace, violently if necessary, attendant states of affairs so that man may move closer to his ultimate victory, redemption from what Marx calls "the panorama of sin and suffering" that constitutes human history.[4] Emulation of the past, on the other hand, represented at various times in *LETTERS* by Jake Horner, Joe Morgan, Todd Andrews, Jerome Bray, and Ambrose Mensch, takes its place within the context of the archetype of the Eternal Return. As Eliade points out, "the myth of eternal repetition . . . has the meaning of a supreme attempt toward the 'staticization' of becoming, toward annulling the irreversibility of time. If all moments and all situations of the cosmos are repeated *ad infinitum*, their evanescence is, in the last analysis, patent; *sub specie infinitatis*, all moments and all situations remain stationary and thus acquire the ontological order of the archetype."[5] History is apprehended as cyclic, notions of mechanistic causality are rejected, and the utopian dream is located *in illo tempore*, before History began.

In contrast to these views, Barth validates the existence of what the Author calls "capital-H history" (431) by self-consciously situating himself and his novel in a historical context. Implicit in his comments about modernism in "The Literature of Replenishment" is the recognition that narrative innovation, no matter how "experimental," moves within the horizon opened up by tradition. One "more or less understands," Barth has said, "why the history of art, including the art of fiction has led it through certain kinds of stages and phases to where we are now, and one does ill to deny that history or pretend that it hasn't happened."[6] This is not to say that the writer is doomed to repeat the forms and figures of his tradition, forms the novel permutations of which approach the point of exhaustion. That is Bellerophon's error. Rather, any meaningful deviation from tradition must acknowledge its ineludible linkage with that tradition. As the genie in "Dunyazadiad," explains, "My project . . . is to learn where I am by reviewing where I've been — where we've *all* been."[7] One recycles the materials of the usable past in order to move beyond — to assimilate while transcending — that past. Revolution, the "true subject" of *LETTERS*, must therefore be understood in *both* its main senses: as orbital rotation (i.e., replication) and as momentous change.

In keeping with what he has termed the Principle of Metaphoric Means, Barth invests as many of "the elements and aspects" of *LETTERS* as he can with "emblematic as well as dramatic value" suggestive of revolution in both senses.[8] The War of 1812 is used not because Barth has any particular interest in that era, but because the war was popularly known as the "Second American Revolution." Recurrences abound: "repetitions, echoes, reverberations, second cycles of human lives."[9] As a sequel, *LETTERS* recycles characters and events from Barth's previous six works. Moreover, its own events and characters are themselves linked within a network of intriguing correspondences, "Portentous Coincidences" that may be nothing more than "Arresting But Meaningless Patterns" (384) or that could reflect synchronistically the "order complex unto madness" that Bellerophon suspects.[10]

Such correspondences extend as well to the novel's form and the circumstances of its publication. Seven years in the writing and published seven years after the publication of *Chimera*, *LETTERS*, which has seven letters in its title, is Barth's seventh book. Its eighty-eight epistles, exchanged by seven correspondents over a seven-month period, are "divided unequally into seven sections" (49), each section deriving its distinctiveness from the month— March through September 1969—in which the letters in that section are written. Each letter is assigned a letter of the alphabet from the novel's 88-letter subtitle: *An Old Time Epistolary Novel By Seven Fictitious Drolls & Dreamers, Each of Which Imagines Himself Actual.* When these alphabetical letters are arranged on a calendar according to the dates of composition of their corresponding epistolary letters, they not only spell out the novel's subtitle but form in capital letters its seven-letter title. Thus Barth's novel spells itself as it "tells" itself, its title simultaneously conveying each of the three major senses of the word *letters*: epistolary letters, alphabetical letters, and *belles lettres*, the latter of which Barth's *LETTERS* exemplifies, parodies, and replenishes. Typography thus becomes typology, the novel's title page itself serving as metaphor for the process of unfolding that *LETTERS* describes.

Indeed, *LETTERS* functions, in Steven Kellman's formulation, as a "self-begetting novel," a novel the central action of which is the process of its own composition.[11] Its ground situtation is this: a novelist named John Barth has decided to write a novel whose main characters (save one) or their proxies shall be drawn from his previous fictions. He writes to "actual" people who bear "coincidental" resemblances to his previous fictional characters, asking permission to include them in his novel-in-progress. Regular correspondence ensues, the letters eventually forming LETTERS. Among the matters discussed in this epistolary exchange is the Author's "Ongoing Latest" (192), the "projected" novel LETTERS, with Barth as Author asking for and receiving advice about its composition, some of which he rejects, some of which he incorporates into his "current project." From Todd Andrews, for example, the Author borrows the idea of making LETTERS a sequel to his previous works (191) and the Tragic View of History (431); from Lady Amherst, the conception of an epistolary novel (406); from Jake Horner, "certain alphabetical preoccupations" (431), the Anniversary View of History, and the notion of *Die Wiedertraum* (532); from A. B. Cook VI, information about the historical Cookes and Burlingames (431); from Jerome Bray, the concept of a "navel-tale" six-sevenths of the way through the novel (534), a concept he later abandons at Ambrose Mensch's suggestion (652); and from Ambrose, the ultimate form and theme of LETTERS (765–69). As readers, we witness narrative strategies as they are conceived, esthetic choices as they are being made. LETTERS thus recounts its own creation.

LETTERS projects the illusion of art in the process of becoming, an illusion replicated within the novel by other works in progress. Disclosed *in medio* are Reg Prinz's asymptotic film FRAMES and Jerome Bray's "revolutionary" work as it undergoes its various transformations from NOVEL to NOTES to NUMBERS, the first example of "Numerature." References are made to Ambrose Mensch's several half-finished, abandoned, and embryonic narratives; A. B. Cook VI, an inspired cross between Proteus and Pygmalion, attempts to convert History into his Galatea. Each of these artists and artists *manqués* struggles, like the Author of LETTERS, to complete his artwork. Significantly, none – including, as we shall see, the Author of LETTERS – achieves closure.

Neither do any of these works *begin* in an originary sense. Rather, they are presented as variations upon and extensions of predecessor texts. FRAMES, for instance, is an adaptation (albeit a very loose one) of the Author's various fictions. The computer-produced *NOTES* as projected by Bray will contain "nothing original whatever" (32). Even Cook's "Action Historiography" is nothing more than a reaction formation, an inversion replication of his father's prior actions which were in their turn an exact reversal of Cook's grandfather's actions, and so on through the receding chain of Cookes and Burlingames back to Henry Burlingame III. Within the context of *LETTERS* Barth's previous fictions are similarly denied originary status. *The End of the Road*, we learn, was derived from Jake Horner's discarded manuscript "What to Do Until the Doctor Comes" (339–41);[12] *The Floating Opera* sprang from a conversation a young Barth had with Todd Andrews at a New Year's Eve party in 1954 (83); parts of *Lost in the Funhouse* are from Ambrose Mensch's abandoned novel *The Amateur* (150); the plan for "Perseid" came from Ambrose (648–51), for "Bellerophoniad" from Bray (527–28); and, according to the disputed claims of Cook and Bray, *The Sot-Weed Factor* was borrowed from the former, *Giles Goat-Boy* from the latter. Reinforcing these fictive "inscriptions" is a system of bona fide echoes and allusions that self-consciously proclaims Barth's actual sources and influences. Without originary beginning or conclusive end, *LETTERS* seems to insist upon its status as a *mise en abyme*, a Derridean plexus of intertextual traces. But Barth is not quite ready to cast literary tradition into the ahistorical abyss of the deconstructionists.[13] The absence of beginning or of closure allows *LETTERS* to function, rather, as an effective metaphor for process. In emphasizing the processional, which is to say the *temporal*, Barth acknowledges the inevitability of history. (Perhaps in identifying himself as Author in *LETTERS* Barth acknowledges the derivation of author from the Latin *auctor*, "an increaser," a causer of continuance.)

Like that crustacean that recurs in his writings and that grows by excreting a spiral in reverse, Barth's esthetic demands that he locate possibility, which is by its nature future-directed, in the past. But the stance he takes *vis-à-vis* the past is not passive; to the contrary, it is intentional, projective. (The Barthian snail deliberately "directs its path toward the kinds of material shells are best made of."[14]) Describing his strategy for *LETTERS*, Barth said, "I decided to return to the eighteenth century — it wasn't my first visit — to examine the beginnings of the novel in English."[15] His "first visit," of course, produced *The Sot-Weed Factor*, the "im-

pulse" for which, Barth has noted, was "to sort of go to the roots of
the novel and see whether I could bring back something new."[16] His
design for *LETTERS* is similar: "my hope was to discover something [in the origins of the English novel] I could orchestrate to my
purpose."[17] In other words, Barth's reappropriation of the traditional novel is simultaneously a reinterpretation of that tradition
in terms of his own perspective. In Heideggerean terms, *LETTERS*
functions as a *repetition*, a resolute return to past tradition in order
to recover the possibilities that generated the tradition but that have
since become sedimented within it and thereby forgotten.

The affinity of Heideggerean thought to what may be construed
as Barth's theory of language has been remarked on throughout
this study. Similarly, Heidegger's stance regarding the philosophical
past bears suggestive analogies to Barth's own relationship to the
novelistic tradition. Before moving on to examine the particular
ways in which the conventions of the modernist and premodernist
novel have been expropriated for *LETTERS*, a brief consideration of
this stance should therefore prove advantageous. *LETTERS* may
be seen as Heideggerean repetition that is by nature hermeneutical, since the "force" it seeks to recover lies not "in what has already
been thought," but "in something that has not been thought and
from which what has been thought receives its essential space."[18]
In conducting his own hermeneutical de(con)struction (i.e., repetition)[19] of Western philosophy, Heidegger determined that this
"something that has not been thought" is the sheer presence of Being as the ground of being, of things-as-they-are. At the beginning
of Western thought, presence was conceived as *alethia*, "the rise of
the hidden [Being] into unhiddenness." But Plato redefined
presence as *eidos* (appearance, view), promoting a shift in the conception of truth from *alethia* (unconcealment) to *veritas*, "the
agreement of the mental concept (or representation) with the
thing."[20] From Plato and Greek science through Descartes and
seventeenth-century science to modern technology which, in having secured virtual domination by man over nature, reflects the
Nietzschean will to power, Western thought has continued to
sponsor an epistemological mode "which involves the perception
of things-as-they-are *(Physis) meta-ta-physika:* from after or
beyond or above the process of being."[21] Representational thinking, hallmark of the metaphysical, forces the existent, the thing-as-
it-is, to assume the "position of object"; more significantly, "only

what thus becomes an object *is*, is recognized as existent." This "objectification of Being" reaches its culmination in modern times, when world becomes *view*, spatialized surface or map.[22] Indeed, time itself becomes spatialized, the metaphysical severance of beings from Being engendering "a conceptual freezing of experience" through an insistence on permanency and objectivity.[23] Being, on the other hand, as its "gerundive and therefore verbal (and active) form" suggests, is not a "hypostatic essence" but a "primordial and active force" the unconcealment of which must occur *in time.*[24] This unconcealment is achieved through poetic language. The world exists within the word — not, as the structuralists insist, because man is trapped in a prisonhouse of language, but because, in Heidegger's elegant formula, language is the house of Being. Being is itself pre-linguistic and therefore ineffable, like the Jungian archetype, but poetic language *presences* Being within words and world. "Ontologically stated," Richard Palmer explains, "what a thing *is*, it is through the openness of language. Being is inseparable from the operation by which language causes earth to shine forth. . . . Language is therefore the 'house of being': it is there that being will be found; being resides in language; being, as the process by which language brings things into the open, is linguistic in nature."[25] As a bridge between the individual *(Dasein)* and the world of things *(Seienden)*, language transcends traditional subject-object dichotomies without repudiating subject or object, just as Heidegger's effort to "overcome metaphysics" involves "neither a destruction nor even a denial of metaphysics."[26] In summary, by recollecting "the truth of Being"[27] Heidegger's deconstructive repetition of the Western metaphysical tradition results in an overcoming of the "persistent confusion of beings and Being" that has characterized metaphysics during its long history. Moreover, in definining Being as a pre-linguistic force whose presencing occurs when words call forth a world, Heidegger validates the necessity of standing in open relationship to time and world, and the importance of the "language of experience."

Keeping the foregoing generalizations in mind, I turn now to specific elements of the premodernist and modernist novel that fall subject to Barth's deconstruction in *LETTERS*. The English novel, with its representational quiddity, grew out of the seventeenth-century paradigmatic shift whose chief features were Cartesean philosophy and the "new science." Though implicit in Western thought since Plato, it was "in the metaphysics of Descartes," according to Heidegger, that "the existent *was defined for the first time* as objectivity of representation, and truth as certainty of representation."[28] It is therefore not surprising that, in its repetition of the premodernist novel, *LETTERS* simulates the conventions of mimetic representation fundamental to the early genre. For the first time Barth relies upon the reader's knowledge of the contemporary world in a "realistic" fashion. *The Floating Opera* and *The End of the Road* are only nominally set in the "here and now," with little in either novel suggesting an antecedent reality. The intervening four works, though putatively set in the historical and mythic past or the Utopian future, actually occupy the realm of the "fabulous irreal" (52). So, finally, does *LETTERS.* But Barth's seventh novel also abounds with references to current events and personages ranging from Ted Kennedy and Chappaquiddick to Richard Nixon and Watergate, from Jimmy Carter's standing in the polls to the "latest" Dow Jones averages, from the Mars photos transmitted by Mariner-6 to Pier Angeli's birthday. As Brian Stonehill remarks, "We may learn from *LETTERS*, if we choose to, a prodigious amount about the world outside books: not only about American history, but also how to sail a skipjack, how to crack a code, what it's like to love at seventy, how it feels to lose a brother to cancer."[29] Moreover, the "absence or attenuation of environment" cited by critics as a persistent deficiency in Barth's previous fiction is replaced in *LETTERS* by a generosity of topographical description. Indeed, Barth's evocative portrait of the Chesapeake Bay area during Todd's farewell cruise aboard the *Osborn Jones* realizes a sense of place unsurpassed in the best of our regional novels. And if ultimately Barth insists that the characters in *LETTERS* are nothing more than alphabetical characters, letters on a page, *in the reading* they seem far more than the nonreferential "word-beings" Raymond Federman reminds us that all literary characters in fact are.[30] Lady Amherst, Barth's favorite character, is a particular triumph, yet another demonstration that in the hands of a writer of genius the printed word may indeed become flesh.

In addition to its contemporaneity and objective representation of "true-to-life" people and events, *LETTERS*, as a self-proclaimed "detente with the realistic tradition" (56), affectionately parodies the forms and devices of that tradition. We encounter such familiar motifs as the found manuscript, disguises, mistaken identities, and fateful coincidence. Blended with the epistolary form are elements of other narrative forms greatly favored in the eighteenth century: the picaresque novel and the travel book in the prenatal and posthumous letters of A. B. Cook IV, the historical novel in the letters of A. B. Cook VI, the journal in Jake Horner's letters, the autobiography in Lady Amherst's. Jerome Bray's mysterious powers and Dracula-like attire echo that element of the miraculous associated with the Gothic novel. By far Barth's most sustained homage to formal realism is the unfinished novel-within-a-novel, *The Amateur* by Arthur Morton King (a.k.a. Ambrose Mensch), in which Barth skillfully mimics the conventions of the domestic novel while exhibiting complete mastery over the unobtrusive "middle style" typical of the low-mimetic mode.

But if *LETTERS* were only a virtuoso exercise in the conventions of an outworn tradition, a blend of burlesque and devoir, it would stand as little more than an empty tour de force, a mere flamboyance. Even it if represented a serious attempt to revivify the mimetic tradition, as the sheer affectiveness of the novel's more memorable "realistic" episodes may seem to suggest, at this point in the development of the novel and of Barth's own canon *LETTERS* would be, at best, a regression. Of course, *LETTERS* is neither "regressive parody"[31] nor regressive realism but, as I have been insisting, a Heideggerean repetition. Barth rehearses the forms and figures of the traditional novel in order to locate the "something that has not been thought" in that tradition. What Barth finds concealed or forgotten in the history of his genre is *history* itself (as opposed to historiography, a distinction A. B. Cook VI also makes) — that is, the temporality of being. The traditional novel participates in the spatializing "revenge against time" inherent in the metaphysical tradition and reflects the corollary Will to Power over existence implicit in representational thinking. For his purposes in *LETTERS* Barth finds the metaphysical evasion of time and world most clearly embedded in the traditional novel's epistolary form, in its teleological structure, and in its status as preeminently a *printed* artifact.

The familiar letter, which presupposes a private and personal as opposed to a social relationship, was as much a product of the seventeenth-century paradigmatic shift as was the novel.[32] In adopting the familiar letter as a model for the formal bases of their novels, early writers such as Richardson were able to incorporate into their narratives the subjective inwardness that the recent rise of individualism had made relevant. Thus the "turn inward" usually associated with modernism actually begins much earlier in the history of the novel. Indeed, the intensification of what Heidegger calls "the monstrosity of subjectivism in the sense of individualism"[33] accelerates so rapidly in the thirty years between the publication of *Pamela* in 1741 and Smollett's *Expedition of Humphry Clinker* in 1771 that a significant shift in the technique of the epistolary novel ensues. Enmeshed in the Providential Christianity of his day, Richardson sought in the letter form a means to capture the introspective spiritual life of his characters. As Wolfgang Iser has demonstrated, Richardson's presentation of external reality "served mainly to portray the moral attitudes of his heroines," thereby faintly echoing Puritan typology. Smollett, on the other hand, not only rejects empirical reality as "a guide to preconceived truth" but also fragments reality in his novel "among the varying viewpoints of the characters." According to Iser, "Character and reality [in *Humphry Clinker*] are presented as complementary, each taking shape through the other, and *neither meant to propagate any set principle.*"[34] The development of the English novel mirrors that progressive internalization elemental to the Age of Metaphysics. Latent in Smollett's perspectivism, itself the corollary of Cartesean dualism, is the idealism that will dominate nineteenth-century literature and thought, and in that idealism resides the solipsism and linguistic determinism pervasive in the literature and thought of our own epoch. The genre that begins, in James M. Mellard's summary, "with man's trying to know a self through the emblems of a world that might lead him to God" progresses rapidly to a state that "the world and God (if posited at all)" are seen as contained "in the operations of the human mind."[35] In Heideggerean terms, the "objectification of Being" effects gradually but ineluctably the *subjectification* of being. [36]

Time, too, is subjected to objectification in the traditional novel. As Frank Kermode argues, realistic fiction attempts to project an illusion of *chronos*, "passing" time or "waiting" time, as opposed to *kairios*, "a point in time filled with significance" and therefore arrested, static. "Yet," he continues, "in every plot there is an escape from chronicity, and so, in some measure, a deviation from this norm of 'reality.'" This deviation is particularly acute in "the Richardsonian method of novels by epistolary correspondences," which "made sure that in the midst of voluminous detail intended to ensure realism, everything became *kairios* by virtue of the way in which letters coincided with critical moments." More significant for our purposes, *kairios* transcends chronicity by charging these critical moments "with a meaning derived from [their] relations *to the end*" of the novel. "All . . . plotting presupposes and requires that an end will bestow upon the whole duration and meaning."[37] The *telos* to which Kermode refers is most apparent in the classic novel, whose familiar "plots of action" conclude with a marked change in the protagonist's situation. In the eighteenth-century novel these situational changes usually involve marriage or death, conventions of narrative closure that, in their time, evoked public truths which themselves suggested conclusion.[38] But even in more recent "plots of character," in which the protagonist's consciousness rather than his situation is altered, the same Aristotelian sense of wholeness and completeness obtains at the novel's end.[39] According to William V. Spanos, this teleological structure may be seen as an outgrowth of the metaphysical worldview. The "Aristotelian literary work," he argues,

> is defined by a beginning that generates discords, a middle in which the discords intensify into crisis, and an *end* which not only resolves the discords but, like an *epiphany* (i.e., a simultaneous perception of the *unified totality*), reveals that the discords are, in fact, appearance, the result of partial or immediate experience. That is, like Aristotle's metaphysical universe, the Aristotelian literary work is grounded in a *telos*, an unmoved mover, a *logos* as presence, that determines and gives significance to the action — the events, the history, as it were — of the text from the end, *meta-ta-physika*. Since the Being (or Form) of the work is ontologically prior to its being (the temporal medium and the process it articulates) the essential formal imperative of the Aristotelian mimetic theory is thus the "spatialization of time."[40]

Like the "turn inward," temporal spatialization is not a peculiarity of the modern novel, although it emerges as a conscious device only relatively late in the novel's development. Rather, as Kermode and Spanos make evident, the spatialization of time inheres in the concept of objective representation out of which the novel grew, and it stands as a cardinal element in the genre from the beginning.[41]

But if the advent of the novel, with its intrinsic denial of temporality and its focus on individualism (and the separation of man from nature that individualism implies), may be seen as symptomatic of that stage in the development of the Metaphysical Age when the existent begins to be defined solely in terms of objectivity of representation, that stage could not have been reached without the emergence of print, the medium to which the novel alone is "essentially connected."[42] Print helped complete the distancing of man from his environment that began when writing began. Writing made possible the separation of observer from observed: "Plato wanted cleavage," writes Walter Ong, "and cleavage was what writing and, later and more effectively, print could furnish. Writing and print distance the utterer of discourse from the hearer, and both from the word, which appears in writing and print *as an object or thing.*"[43] Plato shifted the meaning of truth from an aspect of Being to the correctness or precision with which the idea in a subject's mind correlates with the *donnée* belonging to the object.[44] Can it be merely coincidental that Plato's word for representational truth, *eidos*, has its root in the Greek verb for seeing, and that print, as McLuhan and others have demonstrated, is an extension of sight, not only a visual but a *visualizing* medium? The emergence of typography, Ong explains, "effectively reduced sound to surface, hearing to vision. . . . [The] store of knowledge accumulated in print was no longer managed by repetitive, oral techniques, but by visual means, through print, tables of contents, and indices. Knowledge was tied not to spoken words but to texts. This separated knowledge from the lived world."[45] No wonder our first novelists, in their attempt to achieve verisimilitude, turned away from the "lived world" and toward texts for their models.[46] Textual management of knowledge also emphasized the spatializing tendency endemic to the novel and to the metaphysical view that the novel reflects.[47] Moreover, the characteristic inwardness of the early novel could not have been achieved without print. As Ian Watt observes, "the intimate and private effect" of the epistolary novel would be lost "on the stage, or through oral narration . . . print is the only medium for this type of literary effect."[48] Thus, in a very literal sense (with all the etymological implications of *literal* intended), the early novel's medium *is* its message.

If these observations are valid, certain widely held assumptions about the traditional novel require modification. For example, the notion that novels are "bibliocosms," "fictive models of the temporal world," is true only to a point.[49] For despite the accoutrements of time — linear narrative, and the "dimension of depth" in character and setting[50] — the traditional novel implicitly embodies that objectifying denial of temporal process that Heidegger identifies with the metaphysical view. Similarly, it is true only to a point that the novel is preeminently a mimetic form whose traditional orientation "has been not toward the author, the work, or the audience, but toward the universe that exists beyond author, work, audience."[51] Not only has inwardness been a salient characteristic of the novel from the start, but objective representation, the famed mimetic mode, is at base subjective, a denial of the integrity of the phenomenological world and an exercise of power over it.

Once conventional notions of the premodernist novel are thus modified, it becomes apparent that the relationship between the premodernist novel and the modernist novel is more continuous than generally supposed. Modernism's deemphasis of character and plot, for example, may be viewed as a logical extension of the inwardness of the early novel. Propelling this progressive movement inward, from Smollett's latent perspectivism through the psychological novels of the later James through the stream-of-consciousness novels of Woolf and Faulkner to the autotelic fictions of the high-modernist mode (*Pale Fire* or *Molloy* or Flann O'Brien's *At Swim Two-Birds*), is an increasingly militant insistence upon the primacy of human consciousness over an inessential external world. In Hulme's famous distinction, modern art moves from the "vital," with its empathic connection to nature, to the "geometrical," with its "tendency to abstraction" and its "feeling of separation in the face of outside nature." Similarly, form in the modern novel tends towards the geometrical, the abstract, the static. Such estheticism makes manifest the metaphysical desire to arrest time and objectify nature, a desire that is latent in the linear, metonymic forms of the classical novel. Finally, the classical novelists' awareness that their words are printed artifacts is elevated in modern fiction to a self-conscious device. In recent examples of the high-modernist mode such as B. S. Johnson's *The Unfortunates* (1969) or Raymond Federman's *Double or Nothing* (1971), print and even the page itself become intrinsic elements in the work's esthetic, just as paint becomes its own subject in abstract expressionistic art. In short, if the rise of the novel may be properly understood as a manifestation of the Metaphysical Age, then the modern novel is less a reaction against premodernism (as its practitioners and critics frequently insist) than a fulfillment of the metaphysical possibilities inherent in the genre.

Indeed, in its more radical forms, modernism extends these possibilities to the point of exhaustion. As Barth suggests in "The Literature of Replenishment," some of our more celebrated "postmodern" works are not postmodern at all, but examples of modernism *in extremis*. The novels of such self-proclaimed avant-gardistes as Raymond Federman and Ronald Sukenick, for example, are not formal breakthroughs so much as extensions of the modernist principles of esthetic autonomy and self-reflexiveness to near-autistic extremes. Despite much revolutionary posturing, even their critical statements echo in tone and substance the various manifestoes and artistic credos that flourished in the early decades of this century. In "Surfiction: A Position," Federman announces that the "new" fiction "will no longer be regarded as mirror of life, as a pseudo-realistic document, nor judged on the basis of its social, moral, psychological, metaphysical, commercial value, or whatever, but for what it is and what it does as an art form in its own right."[52] In so doing, he offers little more than a grandiloquent restatement of that famous modernist dictum, "A poem should not mean but be." Similarly, Jerome Klinkowitz, among established critics perhaps the most enthusiastic champion of writers like Federman, draws analogies to the symbolist poetry of Mallarmé and the modernist art of Jackson Pollock in describing the "post-contemporary" fiction he extolls. The unintended implication of Klinkowitz's analogy is that the "new aesthetic" informing "fiction's greatest renaissance" is not new at all, but an adaptation and intensification of the same principles that inform much modernist poetry and art.[53]

This is not to say that the actual fiction of Federman, Sukenick, and others is somehow less successful because of the exaggerated claims of its authors and supporters. The significance of an individual novel does not necessarily depend upon the degree to which that novel advances the state of the genre. It is appropriate, after all, to look with equal approbation upon the respective achievements of Saul Bellow, John Hawkes, and Italo Calvino, although Bellow is a premodernist, Hawkes a late-modernist, and Calvino a postmodernist. In short, fiction may be estimable without being momentous. To neglect so obvious a fact is to risk fomenting the kind of controversy currently raging among critics. One result of such imbroglios, as Gerald Graff observes, is "a body of 'criticism' that raises no *critical* questions whatsoever about the literature it deals with and is content to make technical observations or else develop an ideology that will help promote the field."[54] Unfortunately, Graff is not above ideological warfare himself. As chief spokesperson of the conservative-to-reactionary camp in our latter-day Battle of the Books, Graff deplores the recent shift away from a literature rich in "referential values." He argues, "One of the most useful functions that literature and the humanities could serve right now would be to shore up the sense of reality, to preserve the distinction between the real and the fictive, and to help us resist those influences, both material and intellectual, that would turn lying into a universal principle."[55] At the opposite extreme stands Klinkowitz, proponent of the Make-It-New contingent in contemporary American letters, who contends that literature referential to anything outside its own processes is itself a form of lying.[56] Ironically, Barth is cited as a negative example by both Graff and Klinkowitz. For Graff, Barth's fiction is overly "mannered," too anti-realistic, and its use of myth a confession that "modernity cannot be made intelligible as part of a continuous evolutionary process."[57] For Klinkowitz, Barth's fiction is hopelessly "Aristotelian," regressively mimetic, and, like Joyce's work, "safely substructured in myth," which is to say, moored to some external reference point and therefore insufficiently autonomous.[58] Both critics also find fault with Barth's university ties, Graff because he believes academe provides Barth with a ready-made audience for his wildly innovative, "willfully incomprehensible books,"[59] Klinkowitz because he thinks the academy's commitment to the "literary and philosophical tradition complemented by the experience of teaching these verities" discourages Barth from being innovative enough.[60] Apart from all this ideological pushing and hauling sits Barth's text, unengaged.

Because it assumes a middle ground, "The Literature of Replenishment" provides a necessary conjunctive to the competing views of Graff and Klinkowitz. Whereas Graff resists change and Klinkowitz promotes it, Barth seems to recognize that while change in the arts is seldom so radical as apologists for the avant-garde believe, change is constant nonetheless, and inevitable:

If the modernists, carrying the torch of romanticism, taught us that linearity, rationality, consciousness, cause and effect, naive illusionism, transparent language, innocent anecdote, and middle-class moral conventions are not the whole story, then from the perspective of these closing decades of our century we may appreciate that the contraries of things are not the whole story either. Disjunction, simultaneity, irrationalism, anti-illusionism, self-reflexiveness, medium-as-message, political Olympianism, and a moral pluralism approaching moral entropy — these are not the whole story either.

The fiction he proposes "will somehow rise above the quarrel between realism and irrealism, formalism and 'contentism,' pure and committed literature, coterie fiction and junk fiction." *LETTERS* strives to achieve this transcension by incorporating into its fictional process esthetic principles from both modernism and premodernism without repudiating or unself-consciously imitating these principles. Moreover, by concerning itself with its own process-of-becoming, *LETTERS* acknowledges the processional nature of all artistic creation as well as the temporal horizon within which literature must move.

Barth's contrapuntal manipulation of modernist techniques and the premodernist devices already examined risks but ultimately avoids discord. Indeed, modernist effects in *LETTERS* are frequently achieved through traditional means. Self-reflexiveness, for example, is almost completely absorbed into the novel's narrative flow. In previous works, particularly the more experimental *Funhouse* stories, Barth had countered "fiction's congenital defect of the illusion becoming real"[61] by self-consciously calling attention to the work's artificiality, thereby disturbing the suspension of disbelief that readers willingly grant to conventional narrative. But by making the process of composing *LETTERS* a central element in the novel's plot, references to that process, which in another context would constitute foregrounding, become in *LETTERS* wholly appropriate to the novel's "realistic" base. Illusionism and anti-illusionism, realism and irrealism, coalesce. Similarly, style in *LETTERS* is a fugue-like interplay of seven distinct rhetorical registers ranging from the "old-fashioned" transparent prose of *The Amateur* through the singular but readily intelligible prose of Lady Amherst to the virtually opaque prose of Jerome Bray. The latter's correspondence is particularly impervious, moving one reviewer to dismiss it as "noncommunications in computer jargon."[62] Yet, unlike those heavily foregrounded passages in *The Sot-Weed Factor* that approach hermetic purity, language in *LETTERS*, even at its most idiosyncratic, stops short of what Mas'ud Zavarzadeh describes as "low-message value at the zero-degree of interpretation."[63] A case in point is the opening paragraph of Bray's final letter:

> O see, kin, "G. III's" bottled dumps — oily shite! — which he squalidly hauled from his toilet's last gleanings. 5 broads stripped and, bride-starred, screwed their pearly ass right on our ram-part! You watched? Heard our growls and their screamings? Now Bea Golden ("G's" heir)'s Honey-Dusted 4 square: grave food for the bright hatch of maggots next year! Our females are all seeded; our enemies are not alive; so, dear Granama, take *me* to the hum of your hive! [755]

Similar to the seven messages in "Glossolalia," each of which corresponds metrically to the Lord's Prayer, this passage duplicates the metrical arrangement and approximates the rhyme scheme of the first stanza of our national anthem. In "Glossolalia," however, the metrical model seems to have been chosen randomly. It is the *fact* of an identical pattern in each of the messages, not the *source* of the pattern, which is significant. Barth's parodic rendition of "The Star-Spangled Banner," on the other hand, is not arbitrary, since the anthem evokes the novel's theme of second revolutions and specifically calls to mind the War of 1812, which figures prominently in *LETTERS*.

Language also functions differently in each work. With the exception of one or two sentences, "Glossolalia" is virtually without relevant referential value. One message, written entirely in nonsense syllables, actually achieves "zero degree of interpretation." Clearly, the significance of "Glossolalia" lies not in its "content"; rather, its *medium* constitutes the story's message (which concerns the tendency of language to arrange itself in seemingly meaningful patterns). In *LETTERS*, on the other hand, Bray's eccentric prose, while hardly devoid of virtuosity, contains much information crucial to an adequate understanding of Barth's complicated plot. For instance, in Bray's last letter, amidst the copious and diversionary lists of things that come in groups of seven, we learn the following pertinent facts: (1) that Jeannine Mack, pregnant, helplessly stoned on Honey Dust, her life in danger ("grave food for her bright hatch of maggots next year"), is Bray's prisoner at Comalot, and has somehow been "ingested" by LILYVAC; (2) that Bray has impregnated five women (Jeannine, Marsha Blank, Lady Amherst, Merope Bernstein, and Angie Mensch); (3) that Bray claims credits for the murders of Rodriguez, Thelma, Irving, Reg Prinz, and M. Casteene, and that he seems to know the whereabouts of the *Baratarian's* missing crew and cargo; (4) that the cargo consists of Honey Dust, the seventh ingredient of which is Harrison Mack's freeze-dried feces; (5) that he plans to arrange two more deaths, probably Ambrose's and Todd's in the Tower of Truth explosion; (6) that he will himself die in that explosion in compliance with the instructions he believes he has received from Granama via LILYVAC (but which were probably programmed into the computer by A. B. Cook VI); and (7) that the LEAFY ANAGRAM, properly deciphered, is Granama A. Flye, a.k.a. Kyuhaha Bray, Jerome's grandmother, to whom he will "ascend" on American Indian Day.

In the Bray passages language mediates between opacity and transparency, abstract formalism and "contentism," self-consciously directing attention to itself while still managing to *signify*. Yet by assimilating into a heavily foregrounded style the kind of information usually reserved for a more perspicuous use of language, Barth is not validating realistic theories of language. To the contrary, the presence of Bray's baroque prose style implicates the more conventional style of, say, the Todd Andrews letters, suggesting that language, whether foregrounded or not, is always irreal. Bemused by Ambrose's attempt to script an unfilmable sequence, Lady Amherst observes, "The words *It is raining* are as essentially different from motion pictures of falling rain as are either from the actual experience of precipitation" (393). Language is by nature a fabrication whose relationship to an antecedent reality is contingent and arbitrary if not illusory. Our "concepts, categories, and classifications are ours, not the World's," muses Ambrose, "and are as finally arbitrary as they are provisionally useful. Including, to be sure, the distinction between *ours* and *the World's*" (648). This point, although hard won, is firmly established. It is no longer necessary to insist upon the irrealistic nature of literature through a radically intransitive use of language. Rather, it is time to move on to a literature whose implicit theory of language transcends naive mimetic conceptions on the one hand and structuralist and post-structuralist theories of a "groundless" language on the other; a literature that acknowledges as unexceptionable the non-referential nature of language without wallowing self-consciously in its own intertextuality; a literature whose language, like the language of *LETTERS*, relinquishes any hope of signifying an external world while affirming the possibility that language, properly employed, may be revelatory of Being. Such an affirmation contains implications that are ethical as well as esthetic.

The use of language and style in *LETTERS* is intended to acknowledge premodernist and modernist models even as it transcends them. The novel's form strives for a similar synthesis. Premodernism is acknowledged in the work's metonymic dimension, particularly its Daedelean plot, which in ingenuity and intricacy rivals that of *The Sot-Weed Factor*. Modernist precepts, on the other hand, influence the novel's encompassing formal pattern. Considered separately from the work's metonymic dimension, this pattern veers sharply toward the realm of abstraction and idea. Like a blueprint for one of Ambrose's concrete narratives, the pattern is produced diagrammatically on the novel's title page and at one point is even presented in the form of a mathematical equation: "alphabetics = calendrics + serial scansion through seven several correspondents" (767). Although the letters, and thus the novel's events, are ordered in time (though not chronologically), within the context of the novel's formal configuration the relationship among the eighty-eight letters is entirely *lateral*, which suggests an inherent tendency toward temporal spatialization. Their sequence has been predetermined by Barth's conceptual design rather than by the natural momentum of the narrative. *LETTERS* does not disintegrate into a sterile formal exercise, however, because of the virtually seamless conjunction of its metaphorical and metonymic dimensions. Its formal pattern, though always apparent, is never intrusive, and the narrative development, its artificiality notwithstanding, in the reading flows naturally and apparently unimpeded by architectonic considerations. Indeed, as Ambrose points out, the narrative rhythm resulting from Barth's "geometrical" formal arrangement has homologs in the external world. Narrative in *LETTERS*, "like an icebreaker, like spawning salmon, incoming tide, or wandering hero, springs forward, falls back, gathers strength, springs farther forward, falls less far back, and at

length arrives—but does not remain at—its high-water mark"
(767). Not only does this incremental progression evoke the natural world, but it also helps counter the novel's formal tendency
toward temporal spatialization. To a degree, this tendency is
already moderated by the simple presence in *LETTERS* of a plot,
which one of Stanley Elkin's characters defines as "the language of
time."

The temporal ebb and flow of a plot whose development is incremental also builds suspense, which is of course a temporal state.
Significantly, this suspense is never wholly relieved. While Barth's
plot moves faithfully through the first four stages of Freytag's familiar triangle—Exposition, Conflict, Complication, Climax—it is defi-
cient in Denouement, that conventional narrative coda reserved for
the tying up of loose ends. Several important strands of Barth's prodigious plot are left dangling. Indeed, while the narrative in *LET-
TERS* ends, it does not achieve a sense of closure. The open-ended
plot certainly contributes to this sense of unresolved narrative tension. That ending, the reader will recall, finds Todd Andrews, Ambrose Mensch, and Jerome Bray in the Tower of Truth, around the
base of which Drew Mack has planted dynamite charges set to ex-
plode at 6:54 A.M., the precise instant of sunrise. The novel's narrative concludes at 6:53. But because the open ending has been for
some time one of the stock conventions of literature and film, its examples ranging from Frank Stockton's "The Lady or the Tiger" to
Roman Polanski's *Knife in the Water*, Barth's use of it in *LETTERS*
does not confute expectations so much as provide another link with
the narrative tradition. More pertinent to my point is the degree of
uncertainty surrounding the final role played by A. B. Cook VI in
determining the novel's events. Unlike the open ending, this uncertainty is not a function of the novel's plot so much as a betrayal of
the readers' expectations which have been deliberately generated by
that plot. At its narrative level, *LETTERS* functions very much like
a detective story. All the novel's clues and leads seem clearly to implicate Cook as the "Prime Mover" (475) behind the narrative's complex events, most of which have been arranged by Cook as part of
his Seven-Year Plan intended to launch a "Second American Revolution." He is responsible for moving the Remobilization Farm from
Pennsylvania to Fort Erie and for bringing Joe Morgan to the Farm.
He is also responsible for bringing Lady Amherst to Marshyhope U
as well as for her firing and eventual rehiring. He has gained control

of Reg Prinz's film, a "project" he plans to turn to his "own purposes" (583), and Bray's production of Honey Dust, which he plans to use in financing his Seven-Year Plan. Moreover, it is claimed or intimated that he has arranged the deaths of, among others, the Doctor, Joe Morgan, Reg Prinz, and his father, Henry Burlingame VI; the projected deaths of Ambrose, Todd Andrews, Bray, and possibly his own son; and the presumably fake deaths of M. Casteen and A. B. Cook VI, which is to say, of himself. These apparent facts are scattered, in true detective story fashion, throughout the lengthy narrative.

Suddenly, only twenty pages and five letters from the novel's end, a brief postscript attached to Cook's final letter and signed "Henry Burlingame VII" belies the facts as we have painstakingly constructed them and totally disrupts the anticipated narrative resolution. A. B. Cook VI, we learn, is not the father of Henry Burlingame VII but an imposter; the *lettres posthumes* of A. B. Cook VI are forgeries; Cook VI's copious accounts of "discovered and deciphered letters" and a "Pattern of generational rebellion and reciprocal cancellation," which in the aggregate cover over two hundred pages, are "disingenuous," an "elaborate charade." A. B. Cook VI, we further learn is *really* dead and his body has been destroyed by Burlingame VII. Moreover, the "'Second Revolution' shall be accomplished on schedule" (754), although not in the manner that A. B. Cook envisioned. The exact nature of that Revolution, beyond the facts that it will not be achieved by "overt rebellion" (754) and that it will transcend politics (635), remains obscure, as do the specifics of the Seven-Year Plan. We are left with questions, rather than with a neatly resolved plot. Is Cook VI dead or alive? Is Burlingame VII, a shadowy and peripheral figure until his last-second appearance, who he says he is? Have all the clues been red herrings? It is as though a reader, after having persisted through an 800-page whodunit, discovers at the narrative's end that the butler, whom all the evidence had seemed to implicate, is innocent, and that the real culprit will remain forever undisclosed.

Of course, Barth has not written a detective story at all. Rather, *LETTERS* functions as an anti-detective story, which William V. Spanos calls "the paradigmatic archetype of the postmodern literary imagination."[64] The "formal purpose" of the anti-detective story is "to evoke the impulse to 'detect' . . . in order to violently frustrate it by refusing to solve the crime,"[65] thereby calling into

question certain metaphysical assumptions about the universe that
are implicit in Aristotelian literature, which the classic detective
story epitomizes.

> As the form of the detective story has its source in the com-
> forting certainty that an acute "eye," private or otherwise, can
> solve the crime with resounding finality by inferring causal re-
> lationships between clues which point to it (they are "leads,"
> suggesting the primacy of rigid linear narrative sequence), so
> the "form" of the well-made positivistic universe is grounded
> in the equally comforting certainty that the scientist and/or
> psychoanalyst can solve the immediate problem by the induc-
> tive method, a process involving the inference of relationships
> between discontinuous "facts" that point to or lead straight to
> an explanation of the "mystery," the "crime" of contingent
> existence.[66]

Moreover, just as the reader of a detective story knows that the
narrative complications, no matter how tangled, will be resolved
at the novel's end, so Western thought tends to view the world
meta-ta-physika, logocentrically, imposing a teleological pattern
upon reality from the other side of time, as it were. By writing a
novel whose plot has a beginning and a middle but no end, Barth
contravenes the spatializing tendency in the traditional novel and
subverts what Paul de Man calls "the intent at totality of the inter-
pretative process." "The idea of totality," de Man explains, "suggests closed forms that strive for ordered and consistent systems
and have an almost irresistible tendency to transform themselves
into objective structures. Yet the temporal factor, so persistently
forgotten, should remind us that the form is never anything but a
process on the way to its completion."[67] Barth's avoidance of narrative closure results in a metaphor of process that works against
the sense of stasis inherent in his novel's formal pattern, thereby
preserving the idea of temporal progression crucial to the novel's
meaning.

It is in the interplay between the novel's metonymic and metaphorical dimensions that the "meaning" of *LETTERS* resides. By
skillfully combining the premodernists' tendency to imitate (or
think they are imitating) an order they found in "reality," and the
modernists' tendency to withdraw from external reality into the
self-contained confines of the artwork, Barth achieves a "postmodernist synthesis" of both extremes. In order to better understand

the nature of this synthesis, a final comment about the Modernist relationship to "reality" seems necessary. In a brilliant discussion Alan Wilde argues that modernist estheticism is less an abandonment of the world than a futile insistence that the world conform to the idea of order contained in art:

> Order indeed is nothing less than the age's talisman, its heroic response to "the incertitude of the void" and . . . to the inadequacies of human relationships and the frustrations of human hopes. But for what they will into being — those heterocosms of the imagination in which fragmentation is overcome, discontinuity transcended — the modernists demonstrably pay a price, namely, the need to suffer the distance and detachment that are the inevitable corollary of an overly exigent sense of control and the special stigmata of modernist irony, or, to put it differently, to endure unwillingly the estrangement of the self from the world it seeks too urgently to shape and endow with meaning. [68]

Unfortunately, Wilde is less convincing when he turns to postmodernism. Whereas the modernist artist insisted on having order *and* the world, thus remaining locked in an unresolved and unresolvable paradox — "desire [for the world] straining against the constraining form it has itself devised as the only possible response to its impossible hope for fulfillment"[69] — the postmodernist writer, according to Wilde, relinquishes the formal imperatives of his art and chooses the world in all its messiness and contingency. But these responses, offered by Wilde as alternatives, differ only in degree. The terms of the dilemma besetting modernist and postmodernist writers are identical: order or messiness, art or the world. In Wilde's schema, modernist writers opt for art, postmodernists for the world, but in both instances the essential opposition between art and reality is sustained. Moreover, while the postmodernists affirm the *necessity* of a world whose randomness and uncertainty they are willing to tolerate, it is not clear that they affirm its *worth.* Describing one of Donald Barthelme's "most attractive and attractively rendered figures," Wilde writes: "Neither a rebel nor an accomplice, he accepts what he must and assents to what he can: a totally ingratiating model of *Dasein,* the contingency of being-in-the-world."[70] Such acceptance evidences more resignation than conviction, resembling the projective philosophy of Heidegger less than the stance counseled by, say, Reinhold Niebuhr, whose famous prayer of acquiescence Vonnegut borrowed for *Slaughterhouse Five:* "God grant me the serenity to accept the things I cannot change, courage to change the things I can, and wisdom always to tell the difference."

Despite the allusion to Heidegger, the postmodernist response as Wilde describes it is not consistent with my understanding of either Heidegger or postmodernism. The antinomy between art and the world exists in our conceptions of both. To view external reality as "absurd" or "uncertain" or "random" is to indict the world for its failure to correspond to our preconceived standards of "order." All perception, Heidegger believes, is interpretive, since the progress of perceiving is directed by a "prior conceptuality," a notion which Kuhn's theory of paradigms closely resembles. But two kinds of interpretation exist: "that which arises out of a direct, prereflective, immediate, and yet interpretive intercourse with the world and that which merely points to something through constructing a proposition. The latter steps out of the original full and complex relationship into another kind of relationship which merely points."[71] The second kind of interpretation, which Heidegger calls the "apophantic as," is intrinsic to all metaphysical and representational relationships to the external world since it divides the epistemological field into the interpreter (the subject) and the object interpreted. Truth is then viewed as a correlation between the idea in the subject's mind and a *donnée* belonging to the object. But when the objects perceived cease to correspond to the prior interpretation in which perception is grounded (that is, when the traditional "instruments" of interpretation begin to break down, which Heidegger believes is now happening as the possibilities of the Metaphysical Age begin to reach their exhaustion point), a "rupture of the referential surface" occurs, and the something *as* something, which we have "forgotten" as a result of familiarity, "begins to achieve explicitness."[72] Anxiety follows, as the world-of-things simultaneously withdraws and, in its new inscrutability, "turns towards us . . . crowds round us in dread . . . oppresses us. There is nothing to hold on to."[73] In response to this phenomenon, the breakdown of the instrumentalized world, artists have either retreated into the artificially ordered world of art or, making a virtue of necessity, have embraced a world apparently beyond ordering.

The Heideggerean — and, I believe Barthian — response to this dilemma is quite different. Rather than resisting or embracing chaos, the terms of the dilemma are simply *transcended*. Thus in his concept of *Dasein* Heidegger draws together past, present, and future, *res extensa* and *res cogitans*, into a reciprocal totality.[74] Less metaphysically, Barth attempts a similar transcension of competing categories in *LETTERS*. Putting by the "apophantic as," which merely represents and explains, Barth adopts an artistic stance *vis-à-vis* the world and the literary tradition "that responds and recalls,"[75] that neither retreats from world and time nor imposes a willful order upon them. He proposes a language that *discloses* rather than represents the world, yet which acknowledges that the world has no existence apart from our poetic "saying" of it. He chooses a form that mediates between premodernist realism and modernist formalism, thereby acknowledging the world's ontological "thereness" while insisting that the intelligibility of the world depends upon our ordering perceptions of it.

Put in different terms, Barth achieves in *LETTERS* a balance between form and flux. On the one hand, the novel's spatial/geometrical design, its anagrammatic games, its various puns and allusions suggest a Nabokovian presence who has fashioned from the messiness of history and experience an ordered permanence; on the other hand, its open ending counters the idea of fixed stability contained in the novel's form. But if Barth evokes the reader's impulse to detect order only to subvert that impulse, we must keep in mind that it is an impulse in which Barth himself delights — indeed, the very impulse that has motivated his novel's elaborately crafted formal design. Although flux and form strain for superiority in *LETTERS*, the result is an esthetic standoff, an equipoise of destruction and design. Barth transcends the dichotomy between form and chaos by affirming their interdependence. Man's rage for order issues from an awareness of raging disorder. If the order art erects in the face of chaos is life generating, the life of art is itself generated by the disorder which surrounds it and into which it must periodically collapse if words and world are to continue.[76] This constant interplay between order and chaos, Apollonian form and Dionysian energy, insures that regenerative process which constitutes authentic historicality.

The metaphysical view is ahistorical in its desire to convert temporal process into a spatialized map or world picture. According to Heidegger, the modern age is now entering "the definitive and probably the most persistent segment of its history": the battle of worldviews:

> The basic process of modern times is the conquest of the world as picture. . . . [Man] fights for the position in which he can be that existent which sets the standard for all existence and forms the directive for it. Because this position is secure and itself organized and expressed as world view, the modern relation to the existent in its decisive development becomes a debate between world views. . . . For this battle of world views, and in accord with the significance of this battle, man brings into play the unlimited power of calculation, planning, and cultivation of all things.[77]

The prognosis is mass destruction, the most obvious symbol of which is the explosion. Yet metaphysical, calculative thinking "already had annihilated things as things long before the atom bomb exploded. The bomb's explosion is only the grossest of all gross confirmations of the long-since accomplished annihilation of the thing: the confirmation that the thing as a thing remains nil."[78]

In *LETTERS* the various explosions (in which at least ten characters die) may also be seen to symbolize the annihilation of the thing implicit in calculative, objective, technological thinking. The battle of competing perspectives is evident in the novel's several wars and revolutions, in the foreign and domestic intrigue practiced by the various Cooks and Burlingames, even in the esthetic skirmishes between Prinz and Ambrose over the relative superiority of filmic or written literature. Other manifestations in *LETTERS* of the metaphysical will to power include the technological manipulation of nature (e.g., the recurring references to insecticides) and a general tendency toward giganticism, evident in references to the arms race (e.g., p. 713) and in the unrestrained growth of Marshyhope State University.[79] As usual, however, Barth's primary thematic concern is neither sociological nor political but interpersonal. In a word, his concern is love. That which goes on between men and women remains for Barth "not only the most interesting but the most important thing in the bloody murderous world."[80] Just as the metaphysical mind reduces things to an objective state, thereby stripping them of their ontological integrity, their depth and suggestiveness, so are certain love relationships in Barth's fiction based on a similar will to power, as the loved one is coerced into an identity corresponding to an idea in his or her lover's mind.[81] Expressed so baldly, such a statement may resemble a recipe for romance from *The Art of Loving*. By now, however, it should be apparent that love in Barth's fiction is considered never in isolation, but always in the larger context of epistemological and esthetic concerns. Love, epistemology, and esthetics have functioned, at least since *The Sot-Weed Factor*, as a mutually enforcing, interdependent complex.

While it is implicit throughout *LETTERS*, the epistemology-esthetics-love nexus emerges most clearly in Barth's treatment of the Lady Amherst–Ambrose Mensch affair. The first five stages of that affair are dominated by Ambrose's obsession with pattern, as he forces the relationship into rigid consonance with "the sequence of his major prior connexions with women" (386). The esthetic correlations are readily apparent. On the one hand, Ambrose, a self-proclaimed "last-ditch provincial Modernist" (767), is an arch-formalist whose determination to impose a pattern on his life is replicated in his dedication to pure form in art. On the other hand, Lady Amherst embodies for him the Great Tradition of Western Literature whom he wishes "to get . . . one final time with child" (767). Just as the early stages of his affair with Lady Amherst lack the reciprocity necessary to a meaningful relationship, so does his stance *vis-à-vis* the literary tradition lack the regenerative reciprocity of the Heideggerean repetition. On the contrary, his stance is combative, coercive, "a running warfare against the province of Literature" (333). Just as he puts Germaine "through sundry more or less degrading trials" (767), so does he test the traditional elements of fiction, moving from realism through a series of formal experiments that culminates in the most rarefied formalism: the preservation and possible publication of his graphs and charts in lieu of writing, to which he bids farewell.[82] Implicit in Ambrose's attitude toward art and Lady Amherst is an epistemology. In true metaphysical fashion, he has divided the epistemological field into subject and object, then forced the thing itself to correspond to his idea of that thing. More a spy upon than a participant in the world, he enjoys observing life through the large *camera obscura* into which his family has converted the Menschhaus tower, thereby displaying the heavy visual bias of the metaphysical view. For Lady Amherst, who insists upon a fundamental involvement with the world, microscopes and telescopes never work (298). But until the climactic, penultimate stage of his affair with Germaine, Ambrose prefers to keep at arm's length a world with which his relationship remains decidedly representational. [83]

On the seventh stroke of the sixth lovemaking of Ambrose and Germaine's wedding night, which occurs on the sixth day of the sixth week of the sixth stage of their affair, Ambrose experiences a vision of plenum and loss. Plenum because he sees "in an instant" all the sevens and sevenths that include and will follow their climactic lovemaking; loss because he likewise sees that a seventh love affair of which the "7th stage with G is surely the foreshadow" is "surely to come" (768). What he doesn't see is that the seventh "affair" will not involve another woman, whom he "shall love to distraction and in vain" (768), but death. Four days after writing his last letter, Ambrose is presumably killed in the Tower of Truth explosion, a fate to which he unknowingly alludes when he describes that seventh affair as "terminal" and associates it with the itching, possibly cancerous, bee-mark on his temple (768). Though she remains unaware of the exact nature of the loss, Germaine, who shares Amby's vision of unity, also anticipates its collapse. But her premonition produces no anxiety. "That vision," she writes, "I cannot say whether it is the cause of my serenity or whether it was a vision of serenity. Doubtless both. Should Ambrose one day cease to love me; should he go to other women, I to other men . . . should my dear friend come even to deny (God forfend!) that he *ever* loved me, even that he ever *knew* me . . . I should still (so I envision) remain serene, serene" (691). It is not that Ambrose and Germaine's vision of fulfillment makes bearable its inevitable loss, but that plenum implies loss as surely as form chaos. For Heidegger, authentic selfhood becomes possible only when the certainty of death is fully and freely accepted. *"Authentic Being-towards-death — that is to say, the finitude of temporality — is the hidden basis of Dasein's historicality."* [84] As we have seen, in *The Sot-Weed Factor* Henry Burlingame III and in *Chimera* Shah Zaman each learn versions of this important lesson. Similarly, Ambrose can move into time only when the finitude of his own temporality is embraced; he can achieve authentic historicality only when the inevitable end of his personal history is accepted.

As a result of his vision of plenum and loss, Ambrose is able to enter into a relational involvement with the temporal world, signified in part by his farewell to formalism (768). More important, he is now able unreservedly to love Lady Amherst, whom he describes in one of his last references as "the self-existent" (768). That phrase, with its suggestive echoes of Heidegger's terms for the "phenomenon" viewed ontologically rather than ontically (e.g., "self-blossoming emergence," "self-manifestation, self-representation, standing there, presence"),[85] means not that his relationship with Lady Amherst has finally been divested of his own perspective, but that their involvement has at last become reciprocal, unitary, dialogic. Ambrose achieves his vision while locked in conjugal embrace with Lady Amherst. The significance of this scene extends beyond its obvious echo of George's visionary embrace with Anastasia and Barth's conscious use of the mythic symbolism of the sex act as *conjunctio oppositorum*. It suggests as well the visceral nature of all authentic being-in-the-world. Physicality in Barth's fiction is frequently perceived through the intellect, which explains the farcical nature of many of his sex scenes. But at least since *The Sot-Weed Factor* the body usually wins in Barth's books. From the beginning, flesh and death have been linked in Barth's canon, with an acceptance of the former implying acceptance of the latter. Ambrose's entrance into the physical and temporal world is consecrated by an act of physical love. At last he makes love to *Lady Amherst*, not to a fancied embodiment of some past lover or to "Literature Incarnate." In embracing her as she is — in the flesh, as it were — he embraces as well the death that flesh implies. Whereas in *Giles Goat-Boy* George attains immortality by moving outside clocktime, in *LETTERS*, as in *Chimera*, death is transcended through the paradoxical acceptance of an ineluctable finitude. Whereas *Giles Goat-Boy* encourages the letting go of the world of perceptual categories, and *Funhouse* the holding on to the temporal world of words and men, *LETTERS*, in another paradox, suggests that we hold onto the physical and temporal world *only* by letting go, only by letting be the things-that-are.[86]

The vehicle of Ambrose's newly acquired capacity to "care" is language.[87] Of course, Amby has always been a wordsmith, but his relationship toward his medium, like his attitude toward the literary tradition and the world, was typically combative, "a lover's quarrel" with language (313). In true formalist fashion, what he had striven to do was to rid words of their referentiality, to "say the unseeable" (333), to construct a text "whose language is preponderantly nonvisual, even nonsensory in its reference" (398). By the end of *LETTERS*, however, post-vision Ambrose embraces

a language that, if not referring to the world, at least reveals it.
Ambrose writes,

> If one imagines an artist less enamored of the world than of
> the language we signify it with, yet less enamored of the lan-
> guage than of the signifying narration, and yet less enamored
> of the narration than of its formal arrangement, one need *not*
> necessarily imagine that artist therefore forsaking the world
> for language, language for the processes of narration, and
> those processes for the abstract possibilities of form. . . .
> *Might he/she not as readily, at least as possibly, be imagined*
> *as thereby (if only thereby) enabled to love the narrative*
> *through the form, the language through the narrative, even*
> *the world through the language?* . . . And, thus imagined,
> might not such an artist . . . aspire at least to . . . an honor-
> ary degree of humanity? . . . And if . . . this artist contrived
> somehow to attain that degree, might he not then find himself
> liberated to be (as he has after all always been, but is enabled
> now more truly, freely, efficaciously to be) in the world?
> [650–51].

That extended quotation serves admirably as a definition of what I
have called throughout this study the "language of reality."

Most of the remaining major characters in *LETTERS* are incapable of completing a "step-back from representational thinking." A. B. Cook VI's relationship to the past is as combative and
coercive as Amby's was toward the literary tradition before his vision. A practitioner of " 'action historiography': the *making* of
history as if it were an avant-garde species of narrative" (73), Cook
ruthlessly uses and, when necessary, destroys anything or anyone
who might divert history from the course he would impose on it.
Similarly, Jerome Bray attempts to overpower life by forcing upon
it a preordained pattern. Like Bellerophon, Bray aspires to herohood; also like his mythic counterpart, he attempts to attain it
through a perfect imitation of the mythic pattern. Bray's desire to
ascend to Granama parallels Bellerophon's equally futile desire to
ascend to Olympus: "Echo, yes; repeat, no," advises Ambrose in
his final letter. But Bray is caught up in a hermetic circle of pure
mimesis, as automatic and mechanical as his computer. Indeed,
the computer-argot "RESET" punctuating Bray's correspondence is
itself a parody of the fruitless repetition in which Bray is trapped.
Similarly seized by a compulsion to repeat, Jacob Horner treats the

past as a storehouse from which he obsessively draws lifeless facts to sort by date, as one might sort a box of buttons according to color. His literal withdrawal from the world to live under the Doctor's care at the Remobilization Farm parallels as it grossly confirms the similar withdrawal from the ontological world implicit in Bray and Cook's ontic relationship to reality.

Todd Andrews also fails to achieve a relational involvement with the world, although his opportunity for success is far greater than that of the three characters just mentioned. At first glance, the Todd Andrews of *LETTERS* seems far more humane and far saner than the Andrews of *The Floating Opera*. The earlier Todd displayed both a compulsive need to be in rational control of a world he feared and a pathological tendency to manipulate situations and people, even to the point of contemplating mass murder. The Andrews of *LETTERS*, on the other hand, seems genuinely to care about other people; on at least two occasions he actually saves Drew Mack's life. Moreover, his loving descriptions of the Chesapeake Bay area seem to reveal an intimate familiarity with the physical world, and his Tragic View suggests an ability to live in that world while at the same time accepting its incertitude and contingencies. As the novel progresses, however, we come to realize that the differences separating the early and late Todd Andrews are finally superficial. The Tragic View, despite the initial appeal of its apparent good sense and balance, provides Todd with a rationale for his inability to care deeply for the world. In accordance with this view, Todd "has no final faith that all the problems he addresses admit of political solutions—in some cases, of any solution whatever—any more than the problems of evil and death; yet he sets about them as if they did" (88). He is surprised when anything works, and merely disappointed when it fails. Todd's stance—which, as a matter of fact, resembles the acquiescence counseled in Niebuhr's prayer—is little more than a rhetorical pose; it lacks the relational context that Ambrose gains through his vision.

Todd approaches a similar vision. Shortly after saving Drew at the Choptank Bridge, he begins to tremble "toward a vast new insight" virtually opposite from the one reached at the end of *The Floating Opera*. "There I premised that 'nothing has intrinsic value'; here I began to feel . . . that Nothing *has* intrinsic value . . . which is as much as to say: *Everything* has intrinsic value!"

(96). Todd comes "perilously close to something 'beyond' the Tragic View," to a realization of the interdependency of plenum and loss, Everything and Nothing. But he retreats from "The Mystic Vision" that alone would have delivered him to the onto-logical, temporal world, returning safely to his "home waters: ra-tionalist-skeptical BLTVHism" (96).

As in *The Floating Opera*, Todd avoids intimations of ultimate unity as surely as he avoids meaningful involvements with the physical world and with women. This is nowhere more clear than in his affair with Jeannine Mack aboard the skipjack *Osborn Jones*. The good and possibly incestuous sex they enjoy, so obviously therapeutic for Jeannine, will, the reader anticipates, also relieve Todd of his despair (he has determined once again to kill himself) and possibly catapult him *à la* the Ambrose/Germaine, Giles/ Anastasia couplings into "Mystic Vision." The opposite transpires. On the day when Jeannine is to leave the yacht, Todd desires her one more time. "I desired her specifically *a tergo*, puppy-dog style, the way I'd first seen myself in the act of coition, in the mirror of my bedroom in your [his father's] house, with Betty June Gunter, on March 2, 1917, the day that young woman relieved me of my virginity" (707). The allusion could not be more revealing. For in that earlier coupling with Betty June, Todd's pathological hatred and fear of the flesh and his concomitant retreat into rationality emerged most forcefully.[88] Four decades later Todd once again treats a human being as an object, sending a distraught Jeannine, who looks "recently raped" (707), back into madness at the Re-mobilization Farm and, eventually, to her death at the hands of Je-rome Bray. When apprised that Jeannine is missing from the Farm, Todd admits that his regret, while "real," is "mild," and that his "concern for the woman [is] equally real, but on balance no greater than before she'd come to see me" (711). This is the Tragic View with a vengeance, revealing Todd's lack of authentic care for and involvement in a world he ultimately fears.

That fear receives explicit treatment on the last evening of Todd's "farewell cruise." Awakened by the "shocking noise" of a predator destroying its victim, Todd stands on deck "trembling in [his] sweat." "Nature bloody in fang and claw!" he exclaims. "Under me, over me, 'round about me, everything killing every-thing! . . . Horrific nature; horrific world: out, out!" Todd's subse-quent suicide does not signify his willingness to accept death in the manner of Ambrose and Lady Amherst. Rather, it represents his final retreat from the physical world, whose finitude he finds threatening to the point of unacceptability. Todd's rhetorical stance remains intact — "No, nothing wrong; everything is right, and full to overflowing with intrinsic value" — but it is undermined by his rejection of any involvement with the world — "except that I remain alive" (730).

In his relationship with the temporal world and with other people, Todd fails to achieve *mutuality*, the term with which Germaine and Ambrose christen their sixth stage together. That term, with its suggestion of oppositions overcome, serves as an apt description of Barth's own epistemological-ethical-esthetic stance in *LETTERS*. Whereas premodernism overemphasizes the world of objective reality, thereby blinding itself to that subjectivism underlying all representational theories of reality, and whereas modernism overemphasizes the essentially subjective ordering properties of the human mind, thereby blinding itself to the ontological "thereness" of the world of physical fact, *LETTERS* strives for a middle ground between these apparent oppositions, thereby achieving a postmodernist synthesis of both. "In other words," as Lady Amherst explains, "the relation between fact and fiction, life and art, is not imitation of either by the other, but a sort of reciprocity, an *ongoing* collaboration or reverberation" (233). I have italicized *ongoing* because it suggests the temporal, dynamic nature of this collaboration, without which historical progression would be impossible. Moreover, *LETTERS* further makes clear that this ongoing interchange between perceiver and perceived, subject and object, provides a source of unity the idea of which (one is tempted to write, "the search for which") has remained a persistent concern throughout the Barthian canon.

While *LETTERS* lacks narrative closure, it does not lack a sense of resolution. This resolution, however, has little to do with the linear trail of clues which entices only to subvert efforts at solution, which mimics only to mock clotural narration. Near the end of *LETTERS* Ambrose hints at the true nature of the novel's resolution: "*Dénouement:* not the issue of G's appointment with Dr. Rosen tomorrow, or of her pregnancy, or of the dawn's early light 9/20/69, or of the puzzle of Barataria and *Baratarian:* all those locks, and whatever lies beyond them, may be diversions: the real treasure (and our story's resolution) may be the key itself: illumination, not solution, of the Scheme of Things" (768). *LETTERS* illuminates that which is hidden, incipient, in Barth's first two novels and which emerges gradually through the next four books: the true source and nature of the unity Barth has sought from the beginning. This unity is not located beyond the categories of subject and object, in the mystic realm to which George ascends or in the mythic past of *Funhouse* and *Chimera*, but in the reciprocal, dialogic interchange between self and other. The poetic act of saying delivers the world to man and man to the world. While approached in the previous books, this point receives unambiguous emphasis in *LETTERS*. Thus the novel functions as a kind of conclusion. Of course, Barth has written and will continue to write subsequent books; doubtless his esthetic will continue to evolve. But in *LETTERS* the reader senses the end of a stage in Barth's developing esthetic. The world, Barth has come to realize, does not exist *in* so much as *through* the word. This notion informs as it explains the passionate virtuosity of John Barth.

NOTES

1. "PW Interviews: John Barth," p. 6.

2. Ibid., p. 8.

3. Barth, *LETTERS* (New York: Putnam's, 1979), p. 533. Subsequent references to this edition appear in parentheses in the text.

4. Quoted in White, *Metahistory*, p. 281. White's study has influenced my thinking about the role of history in *LETTERS* throughout this chapter.

5. Eliade, *Myth of the Eternal Return*, p. 123.

6. Bellamy, *The New Fiction*, pp. 4–5. On the relationship of *LETTERS* to the novelistic tradition, see Schulz, "Barth, *LETTERS*, and the Great Tradition."

7. Barth, *Chimera*, p. 10.

8. Ibid., p. 203.

9. Reilly, "Interview," p. 10.

10. Barth, *Chimera*, p. 147.

11. Kellman, *The Self-Begetting Novel*.

12. Which was actually the first (later discarded) title of *The End of the Road*. See Morrell, *Barth*, p. 15.

13. In the Derridean paradigm, there are no texts, only textuality, for the "various individuated examples" of textuality that we identify as texts "are not really individuated, or closed, since in them we can trace count-

less inscriptions of other texts in the retentions and protentions of the sign" (Lentricchia, *After the New Criticism,* p. 181).

14. Gado, ed., *First Person,* p. 129.

15. Reilly, "Interview," p. 3.

16. Bellamy, *The New Fiction,* p. 6.

17. Reilly, "Interview," p. 3.

18. Heidegger, *Identity and Difference,* p. 48.

19. Heidegger's term is of course *destruction, deconstruction* having become the "property" of Jacques Derrida and his followers. As a hermeneutical method, Derridean deconstruction attempts to expose the "decenteredness" of all discourse and, by extension, the ultimate "undecidability" of any text. While he makes it absolutely clear that Being transcends signification, Heidegger nonetheless acknowledges a center of sorts, although Being, as *vis primitiva activa,* remains a moving center. Because *destruction* possesses connotations which work against the notion of "recollection forward" that it actually denotes, I have chosen to use the term *deconstruction* — but in a Heideggerean, rather than a Derridean, sense.

20. Martin Heidegger, "Plato's Doctrine of Truth," in Barrett and Aiken, eds., *Philosophy in the Twentieth Century,* III, 267, 257.

21. Spanos, "De-struction and the Question of Postmodern Literature," p. 108.

22. Heidegger, "The Age of the World View," pp. 348–49.

23. Martin Heidegger, "The Way Back into the Ground of Metaphysics," in Kaufman, ed., *Existentialism from Dostoevsky to Sartre,* p. 219. See also Heidegger, "The Age of the World View," e.g., "In the historical disciplines just as in the natural sciences the procedure aims at representing the permanent and making history an object" (p. 346).

24. Magliola, *Phenomenology and Literature,* p. 66. See also "The Way Back into the Ground of Metaphysics," where Heidegger, writing about *Dasein* ("Being Present" or "Being There"), explains: "The True being of this being present . . . is deeply concealed in the earliest names of Being. But . . . in being present there moves, unrecognized and concealed, present time and duration — in one word, time. Being as such is thus unconcealed owing to time. Thus time points to unconcealedness, i.e., the truth of being" (Kaufman, ed., *Existentialism from Dostoevsky to Sartre,* p. 216).

25. Palmer, "The Postmodernity of Heidegger," p. 423.

26. Heidegger, *On the Way to Language,* p. 20.

27. "The Way Back into the Ground of Metaphysics," in Kaufman, ed., *Existentialism from Dostoevsky to Sartre,* p. 211.

28. Heidegger, "The Age of the World View," p. 349.

29. Stonehill, "A Trestle of *LETTERS,*" p. 265.

30. Federman, ed., *Surfiction*, p. 13.

31. "Regressive parody" is Jerome Klinkowitz's term for the novels of Barth and Pynchon. See his *Literary Disruptions*.

32. Watt, *The Rise of the Novel*, p. 176.

33. Heidegger, "The Age of the World View," p. 352.

34. Iser, *The Implied Reader*, pp. 71, 76.

35. Mellard, *The Exploded Form*, p. 34.

36. The "more completely and thoroughly the conquered world stands at our disposal," Heidegger writes in "The Age of the World View," "the more objective an object seems to be, the more subjectively — that is, the more prominently — does the *subjectum* rise up, and the more inevitably do contemplation and explanation of the world and doctrine about the world turn into a doctrine of man, into anthropology. It is no wonder that humanism arises only when the world becomes a view" (pp. 352–53). *Humanism*, in Heidegger's lexicon, signifies "that philosophical interpretation of man which explains and evaluates the existent as a whole from the viewpoint of and in relation to man" (p. 353). In the context of humanism thus defined, Heidegger concludes, "all objectivity is as such also subjectivity" ("The Way Back into the Ground of Metaphysics," p. 214).

37. Kermode, *The Sense of an Ending*, pp. 50, 51, 47, 46.

38. Public truth, argues David Daiches, provided the early novelist with "a storehouse of symbols with guaranteed responses" (*The Novel and the Modern World*, p. 5). "For a love story to end in marriage was a 'happy' ending, since the convention was to accept marriage as the final reward of virtuous love — as a conclusion rather than as a beginning" (p. 4).

39. As David H. Richter has convincingly argued in *Fable's End*. Also relevant is Friedman, *The Turn of the Novel*. Crane defines "plots of action" and "plots of character" in "The Concept of Plot and the Plot of *Tom Jones*," in his *Critics and Criticism*.

40. Spanos, "Breaking the Circle," p. 436.

41. Kermode, uncomfortable with the "critical fiction" of spatial form, prefers to see books (bibliocosms) as "fictive models of the temporal world," not time-defeating but time-redeeming (*The Sense of an Ending*, pp. 54, 52). The seminal commentary on spatial form in the modern novel is Frank's "Spatial Form in Modern Literature," in *The Widening Gyre*.

42. Watt, *The Rise of the Novel*, p. 196.

43. Ong, *Interfaces of the Word*, p. 283.

44. See Magliola, *Phenomenology and Literature*, p. 65.

45. Ong, *Interfaces of the Word*, p. 297.

46. "Rereading the early English novelists," the Author writes to Lady Amherst, "I was impressed with their characteristic awareness that

they're *writing* — that their fictions exist in the form, not of sounds in the ear, but of signs on the page, imitative not of life 'directly,' but of its documents" (52–53).

47. Print, writes Ong, "intensifies the commitment of sound to space which writing, and most intensively alphabetic writing, initiates. Typography makes words out of preexisting objects (types) as one makes houses out of bricks: it hooks up the words in machines and stamps out on hundreds of thousands of surfaces exactly the same spatial arrangement of words — constituting the first assembly line; and it facilitates indexing to locate physical places where specified knowledge can be retrieved through the eyes" (*Interfaces of the Word*, p. 281).

48. Watt, *The Rise of the Novel*, p. 196.

49. Kermode, *The Sense of an Ending*, p. 54.

50. "Depth, the projection of three-dimensional space, gives objects a time-value because it places them in the real world in which events occur. Now time is the very condition of that flux and change from which . . . man wishes to escape when he is in a relation of disequilibrium with the cosmos; hence non-naturalistic styles shun the dimension of depth and prefer the plane" (Frank, *Widening Gyre*, p. 56).

51. Mellard, *The Exploded Form*, p. 29.

52. Federman, ed., *Surfiction*, p. 8.

53. Klinkowitz, *Literary Disruptions*, p. 32. Federman explicitly connects the innovations of "surfiction" with modern painting in Federman and Sukenick, "The New Innovative Fiction," p. 141.

54. Graff, "Some Doubts about 'Postmodernism,'" p. 102.

55. Graff, *Literature against Itself*, pp. 13, 12.

56. Klinkowitz, "The Effacement," p. 388.

57. Graff, *Literature against Itself*, pp. 57, 208. Graff is specifically addressing modernist fiction in this passage, but in a more recent essay he explicitly relates Barth's *LETTERS* to Joyce's use of myth. What "makes Barth's narrative hang together, even more than in Joyce," he argues, "is not the vision of historical change but a structure of repeating motifs. For a novel with so much history in it, *LETTERS* is oddly unhistorical" ("Under Our Belt"). Obviously, Graff's argument is diametrically opposed to my own.

58. Klinkowitz, "The Effacement," p. 383.

59. Graff is applying Gene Lyons's definition of "classroom-oriented writers" to novelists like Barth ("Some Doubts about 'Postmodernism,'" p. 105).

60. Klinkowitz, "Barth," p. 408. This essay contains Klinkowitz's only extended analysis of Barth's fiction.

61. Klinkowitz, *Literary Disruptions*, p. 156.

62. Towers, "Return to Sender," p. 30.

63. Zavarzadeh, *The Mythopoeic Reality.*

64. Spanos, "The Detective and the Boundary," p. 154.

65. Ibid.

66. Ibid., p. 150.

67. de Man, *Blindness and Insight,* pp. 31–32.

68. Wilde, *Horizons of Assent,* p. 128.

69. Ibid., p. 37.

70. Ibid., p. 184.

71. Palmer, "Postmodernity of Heidegger," p. 417.

72. Heidegger, *Being and Time,* pp. 104–7.

73. Heidegger, "What Is Metaphysics?," p. 366.

74. On this point see Langan, *The Meaning of Heidegger:* "*Dasein* gathers up from the past the light that other generations have brought to bear on the *Seienden* and then, extending the range of previous insight, prolongs the tradition toward the future, which it thus builds out existentially. So it is that *das Sein Kommt nach Hause*" (p. 118). See also Lentricchia: "*Dasein* is a constitutive structure of world, and its being-in *(insein)* refers to its fundamental involvement, its intentionality; but world is, in turn, the basic constitutive structure of *Dasein.* The circular, unitary, reciprocal involvement of subject and object in Heidegger's thought is . . . evidence of . . . a conviction that *Dasein* and world as ontological, not ontic, are never to be interpreted with categories drawn from the ontic spheres of *res extensa,* never to be reduced to the subject-object model that tends to dominate the history of Western thought. . . . As instrumental totality, as field of human activity, world is not only the context or ontological ground which permits entities to come forward and be seen, but also the context of the discoverer of entities. World is the 'there' of *Dasein,* and *Sein* is the being of the world. Human being is both center and circumference" *(After the New Criticism,* p. 86).

75. Heidegger, "The Thing," in *Poetry, Language, Thought,* p. 181.

76. See my discussion of the return to origins in Barth's fiction, in Ch. 6. I should point out once again that this disorder is really a *sense* of disorder — a perceived disorder which occurs when the paradigms we use to arrange flux begin to break down. In the mythic view, this perceived disorder is really cosmic unity incomprehensible outside of mystical vision. In the Heideggerean paradigm, it is Being, the ground out of which being is called.

77. Heidegger, "The Age of the World View," p. 353–54.

78. Heidegger, "The Thing," in *Poetry, Language, and Thought,* p. 170.

79. "The gigantic," writes Heidegger, "is . . . that through which the quantitative becomes a peculiar quality and thus a distinctive type of greatness" ("The Age of the World View," p. 354).

80. Barth, *Lost in the Funhouse*, p. 113.

81. See Ch. 7.

82. "The *plan*, he acknowledges, is dandy," writes Lady Amherst; "he has preserved his graphs and charts, may attempt to publish them as is. But he will not after all, at this hour of the world, *write*" (436).

83. At one point Ambrose confesses to "having . . . long since turned [his back] on reality" (151).

84. Heidegger, *Being and Time*, p. 437.

85. Heidegger, *An Introduction to Metaphysics*, pp. 14, 100.

86. Cf. Heidegger's reference to the "step back from the thinking that merely represents — that is, explains — to the thinking that responds and recalls," in "The Thing," in *Poetry, Language, and Thought*, pp. 181–82.

87. "Care" *(Sorge)* is a central concept in Heidegger's thought. "The *Dasein* who manages . . . to *care* realizes his responsibility as the unique source of meaning in the world and realizes, in the same instant, his own nothingness as a finite being" (Langan, *The Meaning of Heidegger*, p. 28).

88. See Ch. 2.

Bibliography

Barrett, William. *Irrational Man: A Study in Existential Philosophy*. Garden City, N.Y.: Doubleday, 1962.

_____, and Henry D. Aiken, eds.` *Philosphy in the Twentieth Century*. Vol. 3. New York: Random House, 1962.

Barth, John. "Muse, Spare Me." *Book Week*, 26 Sept. 1965, pp. 28–29.

_____. "The Literature of Exhaustion." *Atlantic Monthly*, Aug. 1967, pp. 29–34.

_____. *The End of the Road*. Rev. ed. Garden City, N.Y.: Doubleday, 1967.

_____. *The Floating Opera*. Rev. ed. Garden City, N.Y.: Doubleday, 1967.

_____. *The Floating Opera*. New York: Appleton-Century-Crofts, 1956.

_____. *The Sot-Weed Factor*. Rev. ed. Garden City, N.Y.: Doubleday, 1967.

_____. *Giles Goat-Boy*. Garden City, N.Y.: Doubleday, 1966.

_____. *Lost in the Funhouse*. Garden City, N.Y.: Doubleday, 1968.

_____. "Seven Additional Author's Notes." In *Lost in the Funhouse*. New York: Bantam, 1969.

_____. *Chimera*. New York: Random House, 1972.

_____. *LETTERS*. New York: Putnam's, 1979.

_____. "The Literature of Replenishment." *Atlantic Monthly*, January 1980, pp. 65–71.

_____. "Tales within Tales within Tales." *Antaeus* 43 (Autumn 1981): 45–63.

_____. "Some Reasons Why I Tell the Stories I Tell the Way I Tell Them Rather Than Some Other Sort of Stories Some Other

Way." *New York Times Book Review*, 9 May 1982, pp. 6, 29–31, 33.

Bate, Walter Jackson, ed. *Criticism: The Major Texts.* New York: Harcourt, Brace, and World, 1952.

Battestin, Martin C., ed. *Twentieth-Century Interpretations of "Tom Jones."* Englewood Cliffs, N.J.: Prentice-Hall, 1968.

Beckett, Samuel. *How It Is.* New York: Grove Press, 1964.

————. *Stories and Texts for Nothing.* New York: Grove Press, 1967.

Bellamy, Joe David. "'Algebra and Fire': An Interview with John Barth." *Falcon* 4 (1972): 5–15.

————, ed. *The New Fiction: Interviews with Innovative American Writers.* Urbana: University of Illinois Press, 1974.

Bloom, Harold. *The Visionary Company.* Ithaca: Cornell University Press, 1971.

Bluestone, George. "John Wain and John Barth: The Angry and the Accurate." *Massachusetts Review* 1: 3 (1960): 528–89.

Bly, Robert. "Looking for Dragon Smoke." In *Naked Poetry: Recent American Poetry in Open Forms*, ed. Stephen Berg and Robert Mezey. Indianapolis: Bobbs-Merrill, 1969.

Borges, Jorge. *Labyrinths: Selected Stories and Other Writings.* Ed. Donald A. Yates and James E. Irby. New York: New Directions, 1964.

Brown, Norman O. *Life against Death: The Psychoanalytical Meaning of History.* New York: Vintage, 1959.

Bruns, Gerald L. *Modern Poetry and the Idea of Language: A Critical and Historical Study.* New Haven: Yale University Press, 1974.

Burke, Kenneth. *Language as Symbolic Action.* Berkeley and Los Angeles: University of California Press, 1966.

Campbell, Joseph. *The Hero with a Thousand Faces.* Cleveland: Meridian, 1956.

————. *The Masks of God: Primitive Mythology.* New York: Viking, 1959.

————. *The Masks of God: Occidental Mythology.* New York: Viking, 1972.

————, ed. *The Portable Jung.* New York: Viking, 1971.

Cirlot, J. E. *A Dictionary of Symbols.* New York: Philosophical Library, 1962.

Crane, R. S., ed. *Critics and Criticism: Ancient and Modern.* Chicago: University of Chicago Press, 1952.

Daiches, David. *The Novel and the Modern World.* Chicago: University of Chicago Press, 1939.

Davis, Cynthia. "'The Key to the Treasure': Narrative Movements and Effects in *Chimera*." *Journal of Narrative Technique* 5: 2 (1975): 105–15.

―――. "Heroes, Earth Mothers, and Muses: Gender Identity in Barth's Fiction." *Centennial Review* 24: 3 (1980): 309–21.

DeGeorge, Richard and Fernande, eds. *The Structuralists from Marx to Levi-Strauss*. Garden City, N.Y.: Doubleday Anchor, 1972.

de Man, Paul. *Blindness and Insight: Essays in the Rhetoric of Contemporary Fiction*. New York: Oxford University Press, 1971.

Dembo, L. S., and Cyrena N. Pondrom, eds. *The Contemporary Writer: Interviews with Sixteen Novelists and Poets*. Madison: University of Wisconsin Press, 1972.

Diser, Philip E. "The Historical Ebenezer Cooke." *Critique* 10: 3 (1968): 48–59.

Dryden, Edgar. *Melville's Thematics of Form: The Great Art of Telling the Truth*. Baltimore: Johns Hopkins University Press, 1968.

Dufrenne, Mikel. *Language and Philosophy*. Trans. Henry B. Veatch. Bloomington: Indiana University Press, 1963.

Eliade, Mircea. *Myth and Reality*. New York: Harper, 1968.

―――. *The Myth of the Eternal Return: Or, Cosmos and History*. Princeton: Princeton University Press, 1974; Bollingen Series XLVI.

―――. *Myths, Dreams, and Mysteries*. New York: Harper, 1975.

Ellison, Ralph. "Society, Morality, and the Novel." In *The Living Novel: A Symposium*, ed. Granville Hicks. New York: Macmillan, 1957.

Ellmann, Richard. "The Politics of Joyce." *New York Review of Books*, 9 June 1977.

Enck, John. "John Barth: An Interview." In L. S. Dembo and Cyrena M. Podrom, eds., *The Contemporary Writer*. Madison: University of Wisconsin Press, 1972.

Ewell, Barbara C. "John Barth: The Artist of History." *Southern Literary Journal* 5: 2 (1973): 32–46.

Farwell, Harold. "John Barth's Tenuous Affirmation: 'The Absurd, Unending Possibility of Love.'" *Georgia Review* 28 (Summer 1974): 290–306.

Federman, Raymond, ed. *Surfiction: Fiction Now and Tomorrow*. Chicago: Swallow Press, 1975.

――― and Ronald Sukenick. "The New Innovative Fiction." *Antaeus* 20 (Winter 1976): 138–49.

Fiedler, Leslie. *Love and Death in the American Novel.* New York: Criterion Books, 1960.

Fish, Stanley. *Self-Consuming Artifacts: The Experience of Seventeenth Century Literature.* Berkeley and Los Angeles: University of California Press, 1972.

Fordham, Frieda. *An Introduction to Jung's Psychology.* Middlesex, England: Penguin, 1975.

Frank, Joseph. *The Widening Gyre: Crisis and Mastery in Modern Literature.* Bloomington: Indiana University Press, 1968.

Frazer, James. *The Golden Bough.* 3d ed. Vol. 6. London: Macmillan, 1923.

Freud, Sigmund. *Collected Papers.* Vol. 3. Trans. Alix and James Strachey; ed. Ernest Jones. New York: Basic Books, 1959.

Friedman, Alan. *The Turn of the Novel: The Transition to Modern Fiction.* New York: Oxford University Press, 1966.

Frost, Robert. *Complete Poems of Robert Frost.* New York: Holt, Rinehart, and Winston, 1964.

Frye, Northrop. "Literature and Myth." Pp. 27–56 in J. Thorpe, ed., *Relations of Literary Study: Essays on Interdisciplinary Contributions.* New York: Modern Language Association, 1967.

Gado, Frank, ed. *First Person: Conversations on Writers and Writing.* Schenectady, N.Y.: Union College Press, 1973.

Gardner, John. *On Moral Fiction.* New York: Basic Books, 1978.

Garis, Robert. "What Happened to John Barth?" *Commentary,* October 1966, pp. 89–90, 92, 94–95.

Garvin, Paul L., ed. and trans. *A Prague School Reader on Esthetics, Literary Structure and Style.* Washington: Washington Linguistics Club, 1955.

Gass, William H. *Fiction and the Figures of Life.* New York: Alfred A. Knopf, 1970.

Glasheen, Adaline. *A Third Census of Finnegans Wake.* Berkeley and Los Angeles: University of California Press, 1977.

Goffman, Erving. *Frame Analysis: An Essay on the Organization of Experience.* New York: Harper, 1974.

Graff, Gerald. *Literature against Itself: Literary Ideas in Modern Society.* Chicago: University of Chicago Press, 1979.

———. "Some Doubts about 'Postmodernism.'" *Par Rapport* 2: 2 (1979): 101–6.

———. "Under Our Belt and Off Our Back: Barth's *LETTERS* and Postmodern Fiction." *TriQuarterly* 52 (Fall 1981): 150–64.

Gras, Vernon W., ed. *European Literary Theory and Practice: From Existential Phenomenology to Structuralism.* New York: Delta, 1973.

Graves, Robert. *The Greek Myths.* Vols. 1 and 2. Rev. ed. Middlesex, England: Penguin, 1972.

Harding, M. Esther. *Woman's Mysteries: Ancient and Modern.* New York: Putnam's, 1971.

Harris, Charles B. *Contemporary American Novelists of the Absurd.* New Haven: College and University Press, 1971.

Harris, Victoria A. "Criticism and the Incorporative Consciousness." *Centennial Review* 25: 4 (1981): 417–34.

Hart, Clive. *Structure and Motif in Finnegans Wake.* Evanston: Northwestern University Press, 1962.

Hartrack, Justin. *Wittgenstein and Modern Philosophy.* New York: New York University Press, 1965.

Havelock, Eric A. *Preface to Plato.* Cambridge: Harvard University Press, 1963.

Hawkes, John. "*The Floating Opera* and *Second Skin.*" *Mosaic* 8: 1 (1974): 17–28.

Heidegger, Martin. *Existence and Being.* Trans. R. F. C. Hull and Alan Crick. Chicago: Henry Regnery, 1949.

_____. *An Introduction to Metaphysics.* Trans. Ralph Manheim. New Haven: Yale University Press, 1959.

_____. *Being and Time.* Trans. John Macquanie and Edward Robinson. New York: Harper and Row, 1962.

_____. *Identity and Difference.* Trans. Joan Stambaugh. New York: Harper and Row, 1969.

_____. *Poetry, Language, Thought.* Trans. Albert Hofstadter. New York: Harper, 1971.

_____. *On the Way to Language.* Trans. Peter D. Hertz. New York: Harper and Row, 1971.

_____. "The Age of the World View." Trans. Marjorie Grene. *Boundary 2* 4: 2 (1976): 341–55.

Hofstadter, Albert. *Truth and Art.* New York: Columbia University Press, 1965.

Holder, Alan. "'What Marvelous Plot Was Afoot?' History in Barth's *The Sot-Weed Factor.*" *American Quarterly* 20 (1968): 576–604.

Hume, David. *A Treatise of Human Nature.* Ed. L. A. Selby-Bigge. London: Oxford University Press, 1967.

Iser, Wolfgang. *The Implied Reader: Patterns of Communication in Prose Fiction from Bunyan to Beckett.* Baltimore: Johns Hopkins University Press, 1974.

Jakobson, Roman, and M. Halle. *Fundamentals of Language.* The Hague: Mouton, 1956.

Jameson, Fredric. *The Prison-House of Language: A Critical Account of Structuralism and Russian Formalism.* Princeton: Princeton University Press, 1972.

Joseph, Gerhard. *John Barth.* Minnesota Pamphlets on American Writers No. 91. Minneapolis: University of Minnesota Press, 1970.

Jung, C. G. *Psyche and Symbol.* Ed. Violet S. deLaszlo. Garden City, N.Y.: Doubleday Anchor, 1958.

_____. *Mysterium Coniunctionis.* Trans. R. F. C. Hull. Princeton: Princeton University Press, 1970; Bollingen Series XX.

_____. *The Spirit in Man, Art, and Literature.* Trans. R. F. C. Hull. Princeton: Princeton University Press, 1972; Bollingen Series XX.

_____. *Four Archetypes: Mother/Rebirth/Spirit/Trickster.* Trans. R. F. C. Hull. Princeton: Princeton University Press, 1973; Bollingen Series XX.

_____, ed. *Man and His Symbols.* Garden City, N.Y.: Doubleday, 1964.

Kaplan, Harold. *The Passive Voice: An Approach to Modern Fiction.* Athens: Ohio University Press, 1966.

Kaufmann, Walter, ed. *Existentialism from Dostoevsky to Sartre.* New York: Meridian Books, 1956.

_____. *The Portable Nietzsche.* New York: Viking, 1968.

Kellman, Steven. *The Self-Begetting Novel.* New York: Columbia University Press, 1980.

Kennard, Jean E. *Number and Nightmare: Forms of Fantasy in Contemporary Fiction.* Hamden, Conn.: Archon, 1975.

Kermode, Frank. *The Sense of an Ending: Studies in the Theory of Fiction.* New York: Oxford University Press, 1968.

Kierman, Robert F. "John Barth's Artist in the Fun House." *Studies in Short Fiction* 10: 4 (1973): 373–80.

Klein, James Robert. "The Tower and the Maze: A Study of the Novels of John Barth." Ph.D. dissertation, University of Illinois at Urbana-Champaign, 1971.

Klinkowitz, Jerome. *Literary Disruptions: The Making of a Post-Contemporary American Fiction.* Urbana: University of Illinois Press, 1975.

_____. "The Effacement of Contemporary American Literature." *College English* 42: 4 (1980): 382–89.

_____. "John Barth Reconsidered." *Partisan Review* 49: 3 (1982): 407–11.

Koestler, Arthur. *The Roots of Coincidence: An Excursion into Parapsychology.* New York: Vintage, 1972.

Korkowski, Eugene. "The Excremental Vision of Barth's Todd Andrews." *Critique* 18: 2 (1976): 51–58.

Kuhn, Thomas S. *The Structure of Scientific Revolutions.* 2d ed., enlarged. Chicago: University of Chicago Press, 1970.

Lacan, Jacques. *The Language of the Self.* Trans. and ed. Anthony Wilden. New York: Delta, 1975.

Laing, R. D. *The Divided Self.* Baltimore: Penguin, 1965.

———. *The Politics of Experience.* New York: Ballantine, 1968.

Langan, Thomas. *The Meaning of Heidegger: A Critical Study of an Existential Phenomenology.* New York: Columbia University Press, 1959.

LeClair, Thomas. "John Barth's *The Floating Opera:* Death and the Craft of Fiction." *University of Texas Studies in Language and Literature* 14 (Winter 1973): 711–30.

———. "Death and Black Humor." *Critique* 17: 1 (1975): 17–18.

Lehan, Richard. *A Dangerous Crossing: French Literary Existentialism and the Modern American Novel.* Carbondale: Southern Illinois University Press, 1973.

Lentricchia, Frank. *After the New Criticism.* Chicago: University of Chicago Press, 1980.

Locke, John. *An Essay Concerning Human Understanding.* Ed. Peter H. Nidditch. London: Oxford University Press, 1975.

McConnell, Frank D. *Four Postwar American Novelists.* Chicago: University of Chicago Press, 1977.

McKenzie, James, ed. "Pole-Vaulting in Top Hats: A Public Conversation with John Barth, William Gass, and Ishmael Reed." *Modern Fiction Studies* 22: 2 (1976): 131–51.

McLuhan, Marshall. *The Gutenberg Galaxy: The Making of Typographic Man.* New York: Signet, 1969.

Magliola, Robert R. *Phenomenology and Literature.* West Lafayette: Purdue University Press, 1977.

Majdiak, Daniel. "Barth and the Representation of Life." *Criticism* 12 (1970): 51–67.

Martin, Dennis M. "Desire and Disease: The Psychological Pattern of *The Floating Opera.*" *Critique* 18: 2 (1976): 17–33.

Mellard, James M. *The Exploded Form: The Modernist Novel in America.* Urbana: University of Illinois Press, 1980.

Melville, Herman. *Moby-Dick.* Ed. Harrison Hayford and Hershel Parker. New York: Norton, 1967.

Mercer, Peter. "The Rhetoric of *Giles Goat-Boy.*" *Novel* 4: 2 (1971): 147–58.

Merivale, Patricia. *Pan the Goat-God: His Myth in Modern Times.* Cambridge: Harvard University Press, 1969.

Morrell, David. *John Barth: An Introduction.* University Park: Pennsylvania State University Press, 1976.

Morris, Christopher D. "Barth and Lacan: The World of the Moebius Strip." *Critique* 17: 1 (1975): 69–77.

Murdoch, Iris. *Sartre, Romantic Rationalist.* New Haven: Yale University Press, 1959.

Murphy, Richard W. "In Print: John Barth." *Horizon,* Jan. 1963, pp. 36–37.

Nahal, Chaman. *The Narrative Pattern in Ernest Hemingway's Fiction.* Rutherford, N.J.: Farleigh Dickinson University Press, 1971.

Neumann, Erich. *The Origins and History of Consciousness.* Princeton: Princeton University Press, 1954; Bollingen Series XLII.

_____. "On the Moon and Matriarchal Consciousness." In Patricia Berry, ed., *Father and Mother: Five Papers on the Archetypal Background of Family Psychology.* Zurich: Spring, 1973.

_____. *The Great Mother: An Analysis of an Archetype.* 2d ed. Princeton: Princeton University Press, 1974; Bollingen Series XLVII.

Nicholson, Marjorie Hope. *The Breaking of the Circle: Studies in the Effect of the "New Science" upon Seventeenth-Century Poetry.* Rev. ed. New York: Columbia University Press, 1960.

Nolland, Richard W. "John Barth and the Novel of Comic Nihilism." *Wisconsin Studies in Contemporary Literature* 7: 3 (1966): 239–57.

Olderman, Raymond M. *Beyond the Waste Land: A Study of the American Novel in the Nineteen-Sixties.* New Haven: Yale University Press, 1972.

Ong, Walter J. *Interfaces of the Word: Studies in the Evolution of Consciousness and Culture.* Ithaca: Cornell University Press, 1977.

Ortega y Gasset, José. *The Dehumanization of Art and Other Essays on Art, Culture, and Literature.* Princeton: Princeton University Press, 1968.

Palmer, Richard. "The Postmodernity of Heidegger." *Boundary 2* 4: 2 (1976): 411–32.

Peckham, Morse. *Man's Rage for Chaos: Biology, Behavior, and the Arts.* New York: Schocken, 1967.

Pfeffer, Rose. *Nietzsche: Disciple of Dionysus.* Lewisburg, Pa.: Bucknell University Press, 1972.

Prince, Alan. "An Interview with John Barth." *Prism*, Spring 1968, pp. 42–62.

"PW Interviews: John Barth." *Publishers Weekly*, 22 Oct. 1979, pp. 6–8.

Reilly, Charlie. "An Interview with John Barth." *Contemporary Literature* 22: 1 (1981): 1–23.

Richter, David H. *Fable's End: Completeness and Closure in Rhetorical Fiction*. Chicago: University of Chicago Press, 1974.

Rogers, Robert. *A Psychoanalytical Study of the Double in Literature*. Detroit: Wayne State University Press, 1970.

Rovit, Earl. "The Novel as Parody: John Barth." *Critique* 6: 2 (1963): 77–85.

Ryle, Gilbert. *The Concept of Mind*. London: Hutchinson's University Library, 1949.

Saussure, Ferdinand de. *Cours de linguistique générale*. Paris: Presses Universitaires de France, 1965.

Schickel, Richard. "*The Floating Opera*." *Critique* 6: 2 (1963): 53–67.

Scholes, Robert. *The Fabulators*. New York: Oxford University Press, 1967.

Schulz, Max F. *Black Humor Fiction of the Sixties: A Pluralistic Definition of Man and His World*. Athens: Ohio University Press, 1973.

———. "Characters (Contra Characterization) in the Contemporary Novel." Pp. 141–54 in John Halperin, ed., *The Theory of The Novel: New Essays*. New York: Oxford University Press, 1974.

———. "Barth, *LETTERS*, and the Great Tradition." *Genre* 14: 1 (1981): 95–115.

Sears, Sallie, and Georgiana W. Lord, eds. *The Discontinuous Universe: Selected Writings in Contemporary Consciousness*. New York: Basic Books, 1972.

Slethaug, Gordon E. "Barth's Refutation of the Idea of Progress." *Critique* 12: 3 (1972): 11–29.

Smith, Herbert F. "Barth's Endless Road." *Critique* 6: 2 (1963): 68–76.

Spanos, William V. "The Detective and the Boundary: Some Notes on the Postmodern Literary Imagination." *Boundary 2* 1: 1 (1972): 147–68.

———. "Breaking the Circle: Hermeneutics as Dis-closure." *Boundary 2* 5: 2 (1977): 44–57.

———. "De-struction and the Question of Postmodern Literature: Towards a Definition." *Par Rapport* 2: 2 (1979): 117–22.

Spencer, Sharon. *Space, Time and Structure in the Modern Novel.* New York: New York University Press, 1971.

Stark, John. *The Literature of Exhaustion: Borges, Nabokov and Barth.* Durham: Duke University Press, 1974.

Steiner, George. *After Babel: Aspects of Language and Translation.* New York: Oxford University Press, 1975.

Stonehill, Brian. "A Trestle of *LETTERS.*" *fiction international* 12 (1980): 259–68.

Stubbs, John C. "John Barth as a Novelist of Ideas: The Themes of Value and Identity." *Critique* 8: 2 (1965–66): 101–16.

Tanner, Tony. *City of Words: American Fiction, 1950–1970.* New York: Harper and Row, 1971.

Tatham, Campbell. "The Gilesean Monomyth: Some Remarks on the Structure of *Giles Goat-Boy.*" *Genre* 3 (December 1970): 364–75.

———. "John Barth and the Aesthetics of Artifice." *Contemporary Literature* 12: 1 (1971): 60–73.

———. "Message [Concerning the *Felt* Ultimacies of One John Barth]." *Boundary 2* 3: 2 (1975): 259–87.

———. "Anima Rising: Notes toward a Mediating Fiction." Unpublished essay read at Modern Language Association annual meeting, New York, December 1976.

Tharpe, Jac. *John Barth: The Comic Sublimity of Paradox.* Carbondale: Southern Illinois University Press, 1974.

Tilton, John. *Cosmic Satire in the Contemporary Novel.* Lewisburg, Pa.: Bucknell University Press, 1977.

Towers, Robert. "Return to Sender." *New York Review of Books,* 20 December 1979, pp. 30–33.

Turbayne, Colin Murray. *The Myth of Metaphor.* Rev. ed. Columbia: University of South Carolina Press, 1970.

Vernon, John. *The Garden and the Map: Schizophrenia in Twentieth-Century Literature and Culture.* Urbana: University of Illinois Press, 1973.

Vieth, David. "Toward an Anti-Aristotelian Poetic: Rochester's *Satyr Against Mankind* and *Artemisia to Chloe,* with Notes on Swift's *Tale of a Tub* and *Gulliver's Travels.*" *Language and Style* 5 (1972): 123–45.

Vintanza, Victor J. "The Novelist as Topologist: John Barth's *Lost in the Funhouse.*" *Texas Studies in Language and Literature* 19: 1 (1977): 83–97.

Vonnegut, Kurt, Jr. *Cat's Cradle.* New York: Dell, 1970.

Warnke, Frank J. *Versions of the Baroque: European Literature in the Seventeenth Century.* New Haven: Yale University Press, 1972.

Warrick, Patricia. "The Circuitous Journey of Consciousness in Barth's *Chimera.*" *Critique* 18: 2 (1976): 73–85.

Watt, Ian. *The Rise of the Novel.* Berkeley and Los Angeles: University of California Press, 1957.

Weixlmann, Joseph. "The Use and Abuse of Smith's *General Historie* in John Barth's *The Sot-Weed Factor.*" *Studies in American Humor* 2: 2 (1975): 105–15.

_____. *John Barth: A Bibliography.* New York: Garland, 1976.

Wheelock, Carter. *The Mythmaker: A Study of Motif and Symbol in the Short Stories of Jorge Luis Borges.* Austin: University of Texas Press, 1969.

White, Hayden. *Metahistory: The Historical Imagination in Nineteenth Century Europe.* Baltimore: Johns Hopkins University Press, 1973.

Wilde, Alan. *Horizons of Assent: Modernism, Postmodernism, and the Ironic Imagination.* Baltimore: Johns Hopkins University Press, 1981.

Wittgenstein, Ludwig. *Tractatus Logico-philosophicus.* Trans. D. F. Pears and B. F. McGuinness. London: Routledge and Kegan Paul, 1961.

Young, Philip. *Three Bags Full: Essays in American Fiction.* New York: Harcourt Brace Jovanovich, 1972.

Zavarzadeh, Mas'ud. *The Mythopoeic Reality: The Postwar American Nonfiction Novel.* Urbana: University of Illinois Press, 1976.

Index

A Note on the Author

Charles B. Harris, a native of LaGrange, Texas, is the chairman of the English department at Illinois State University. He is the author of *Contemporary American Novelists of the Absurd* and of numerous articles on John Barth and American fiction in journals such as *Studies in the Novel, Critique, Centennial Review, Psychocultural Review,* and *Mississippi Quarterly.*